SCHOLASTIC

ACTIVE™ Grammar for Classes 6 to 8

Anne Seaton Y H Mew

Name ______________________________

Class ______________________________

Previously published as English Grammar for Students and English Grammar for Students Workbook by Learners Publishing Pte Ltd, a division of Scholastic Inc.

This edition 2012
Reprinted 2012, 2013 (twice), 2014 (fifth time), 2015 (thrice), 2016 (twice), 2017, 2018, 2020, 2023, 2025, 2026

ISBN 978-81-8477-744-4

Preface

The study of formal grammar in schools has always been a controversial issue. In Britain, for example, there was little formal teaching of grammar for many years, and it is thought that the standard of written English has declined as a result. This has caused much concern among educators, and has prompted a determination to re-introduce the teaching of grammar into the curriculum.

Scholastic ACTIVE™ Grammar for Classes 6 to 8 has been specially written in the light of this development. It aims at giving students systematic guidance in their study of English grammar. The definitions or explanations of each grammatical concept or topic are given in clear and concise language, and are easy to understand. The numerous examples put each topic in context. The additional notes, such as **Grammar Help** and **Did you know?**, elaborate or further clarify the less straightforward grammatical points.

Much attention has been given to presentation and layout so as to make the book learner-friendly. It is hoped that this book will give students a clear idea of grammatical structure and help lay a strong foundation for good English.

 ISBN 978-81-8477-744-4

What you'll find in this book

 ISBN 978-81-8477-744-4

5 Verbs 92 — 151

6 Adverbs 152 — 162

7 Prepositions 163 — 180

8 Conjunctions 181 — 189

9 Interjections 190 — 192

 ISBN 978-81-8477-744-4

10 SENTENCES 193 — 196

11 PHRASES 197 — 167

12 CLAUSES 203 — 216

13 MORE ABOUT SENTENCES 217 — 226

14 DIRECT AND INDIRECT SPEECH 227 — 234

15 PUNCTUATION 235 — 243

 ISBN 978-81-8477-744-4

1 Nouns

Read the following passage. All the items in bold function, in one way or another, as nouns.

Big game

Conservationists are concerned about what is happening to **big game** in **Kenya**. Kenya, a **country in eastern Africa**, is the **home** of several large **species** of **wildlife**, including **lions** and **elephants**.

For many decades, the wildlife has attracted **crowds** of tourists to Kenya, wishing to go on **safari**. Until the 1970s, some of the tourists were big-game hunters. They went there not just to admire the **prides** of lions and the **herds** of elephants, but also to shoot them. **Safaris** for hunters were popularized by **Teddy Roosevelt, the US president,** who went on **a hunting trip to East Africa** in 1909, and, later, by **the novelist Ernest Hemingway**, who did likewise.

In the 1970s, there was a good deal of **anxiety** about dwindling stocks of wildlife in the **country**. Indeed, **people** in the world in general were beginning to worry about those animals which were in danger of becoming extinct. **Conservation** and **preservation** were beginning to become **issues of great importance** and, as a **consequence** of this, Kenya imposed a **ban** on big-game hunting in 1977.

Recently, however, the Kenyan **government** passed a **bill** allowing local **committees** to grant to ranch owners licences which would enable them to hunt. The sponsors of the new bill say that it is designed to improve the **management** of large wild animals, such as **lions** and **lionesses**. These, they claimed, were increasingly coming into conflict with human populations and causing **serious problems**. They add that **revenues from the hunting licences** and those obtained from the sale of animal products will be put into the conservation budget.

There have been calls of **outrage** from conservationists. They say that illegal hunting for the **procurement** of **bushmeat** and **ivory** is **a difficult enough situation**. Licensed hunting will exacerbate greatly **the existing problem**.

Common Nouns
Count Nouns
Uncount Nouns
Singular Nouns
Plural Nouns
Proper Nouns
Collective Nouns
Abstract Nouns
Masculine, Feminine and Neuter Nouns
Compound Nouns
Noun Phrases
Noun Phrases that Explain

 ISBN 978-81-8477-744-4

Nouns are divided into **common nouns** and **proper nouns.** In this book, you will find out about the different kinds of common nouns and proper nouns.

Common Nouns

Common nouns are words for people, or things, or animals, or ideas.

- **Here are some words for people.**

trainer	manager	barber
secretary	optician	plumber
coach	police officer	footballer
carpenter	boxer	sailor
wrestler	dressmaker	veterinarian
salesman	acrobat	cashier
magician	shepherd	juggler
driver	singer	farmer
artist	florist	photographer
dancer	doctor	teacher
burglar	nurse	
architect	politician	
engineer	lawyer	
dentist	accountant	
scientist	banker	

A **barber** is *also called a* ***hairdresser***.

The short form of ***veterinarian*** *is* ***vet***.

Spell Well

Words for people have different endings. You will find the common ones here.

- **Some words for people end in -er. You add -r or -er to a verb to make the word for the person. For example:**

baker	painter	writer	buyer	dancer
seller	driver	climber	miner	reporter
piper	photographer	composer	teacher	weaver

- **Some words for people end in -or. For example:**

actor	inspector	collector	instructor	conductor
inventor	director	sailor	editor	sculptor

- **Some words for people end in -ist. For example:**

artist	pianist	cartoonist	receptionist	cyclist
scientist	dentist	tourist	motorist	typist

- **Some words for people end in -ian. For example:**

comedian	musician	guardian	optician	historian
politician	librarian	veterinarian		

 ISBN 978-81-8477-744-4

The words for your relations are nouns.

grandfather	grandmother
father	mother
sons	daughters
brothers	sisters
uncles	aunts
nephews	nieces
cousins	

You can use ***grandpa*** or ***grandad*** for ***grandfather***. You can use ***grandma*** or ***granny*** for ***grandmother***. You can use ***dad*** or ***daddy*** for ***father***. You can use ***mum*** or ***mummy*** for ***mother***. In American English, you can use ***mom*** or ***mommy*** for ***mother***.

Did you know?

You can make a chart to show the relationships between members of a family. You call this chart a **family tree**.

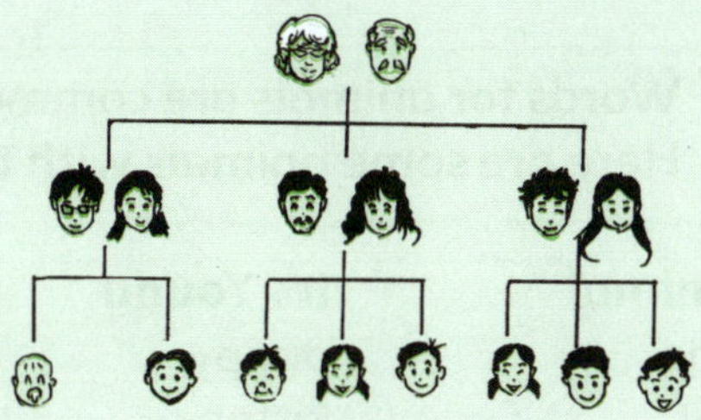

You will find lots of fruits and vegetables in the supermarket.

These common nouns are words for fruits.

apple	banana	raspberry
peach	orange	grape
pear	strawberry	plum
durian	honeydew	kiwi fruit
lychee	avocado	
longan	mango	
apricot	blueberry	
grapefruit	coconut	
watermelon	guava	
pineapple	papaya	
custard	apple	
cantaloup	cherry	
nectarine	date	
fig	lemon	
starfruit	orange	

*Another word for **kiwi fruit** is Chinese gooseberry.*

 ISBN 978-81-8477-744-4

These common nouns are words for vegetables.

potato
yam
tomato
cauliflower
broccoli
celery
asparagus
spinach
leek
cabbage

French bean
green pepper
pumpkin
sweet potato
cucumber
pea
eggplant

lettuce
onion
carrot
spring onion
sweet corn

*Another word for **eggplant** is **brinjal**.*

*In American English, **corn** and **maize** are other words for **sweet corn**.*

Words for animals are common nouns. Here are some animals with their young.

Animal	Its Young
dog	puppy
cat	kitten
bear	cub
fox	cub
leopard	cub
lion	cub
tiger	cub
wolf	cub
cow	calf
elephant	calf
whale	calf
horse	foal
sheep	lamb
deer	fawn
kangaroo	joey
frog	tadpole
goat	kid

*A **kid** also means a child or a **young person**.*

Have you seen these animals in the zoo?

panda
mongoose
moose
antelope
koala
anteater
camel

monkey
chimpanzee
reindeer
snake
rhino
zebra
giraffe

gorilla
crocodile
hippo

***Hippo** is the short form of **hippopotamus**. **Rhino** is the short form of **rhinoceros**.*

 ISBN 978-81-8477-744-4

Words for birds are common nouns too. Here are some birds with their young.

Bird	Its Young
bird	nestling
goose	gosling
duck	duckling
hen	chick
owl	owlet
eagle	eaglet
swan	cygnet
peacock	peachick

These common nouns are words for insects.

fly
ant
bee
wasp

cicada
beetle
cricket
locust
hornet
greenfly
moth
butterfly
termite
mosquito

grasshopper
praying mantis
daddy-long-legs
ladybird

> *In American English, a **ladybird** is called a **ladybug**.*

dragonfly
cockroach

These common nouns are words for fishes and other water creatures.

prawn
crab
whale
shark
lobster
squid
oyster
walrus
turtle

seahorse
goldfish
dolphin
swordfish
octopus
clam
mussel
seal

starfish
carp

 ISBN 978-81-8477-744-4

These common nouns are words for places.

bank
restaurant
cinema
farm
airport
hospital
museum
post office
factory
mosque
supermarket
synagogue
department store

bookshop
apartment
nursery
library
swimming pool
church
school
office
temple
gymnasium

hotel
park
theatre
zoo
police station
sports centre
railway station

*Another word for **railway station** is **train station**.*

*The short form of **gymnasium** is **gym**.*

These are common nouns for objects, tools and machines.

kite
bath
sofa
pencil
apron
clock
toaster
drill
pliers
lawnmower
television
fan
bicycle
ship
cement-mixer

gate
desk
keys
boots
computer
calculator
oven
hammer
axe
spade
radio
spectacles

aeroplane
refrigerator
truck
motorcycle
saw
vacuum cleaner
telephone
camera
racket

***Racket** can be spelt **racquet**.*

*Another word for **spectacles** is **glasses**.*

Spell Well

The short form of **television** is **TV**.
The short form of **telephone** is **phone**.
The short form of **refrigerator** is **fridge**.
The short form of **bicycle** is **bike**.
The short form of **motorcycle** is **motorbike**.
The short form of **aeroplane** is **plane**.

 ISBN 978-81-8477-744-4

Count Nouns

Most nouns are **countable nouns**, or **count nouns** for short. We call them countable nouns because they refer to people or things that you can count.

- When you are talking about only one person, animal, or place, or thing, you can put **a** or **an** before the noun.

a doctor
a tower
a child
a game
a spider
an owl
a park
an egg

a castle
a swimmer
a canoe
a panda
an emperor
a mountain
an ice cream
a statue

a lady
a ship
a squirrel
a problem
a python
an umbrella
a rainbow
an atlas

Grammar Help

- You usually put a or an before singular count nouns.
- You put **an** before words beginning with vowels:

a e i o u

But some words don't follow this rule. For example, you use **a** (not **an**) before these words that begin with u. The vowel u in these words sounds like the word **you**.

a uniform
a university
a utensil
a unicorn
a union
a unit
a useful tool
a user

- You usually put **a** before words beginning with the other letters of the alphabet called **consonants**:

b c d f g h j k l m
n p q r s t v w x y z

But some words don't follow this rule. For example, you put **an** (not **a**) before these words that begin with h. The h is not pronounced in these words:

an hour
an honest man
an honour
an heirloom
an heir
an honorary post
an heiress

- You put **the** before a count noun when there is only one.

the sun
the moon
the sky

the front door of our house
The television is brand new.
The baby is sleeping.

- You can use numbers or quantity words with count nouns.

one sumo wrestler
four corners
eight tentacles
one hundred dollars
a million people
some pizzas

two chopsticks
five fingers
ten bowling pins
a thousand years
lots of cushions
not many people

three kilometres
seven dwarfs
ten thousand insects
plenty of seats

 ISBN 978-81-8477-744-4

Uncount Nouns

Some nouns are called uncountable nouns, or uncount nouns for short. We call them uncountable because they are words for things you can't count.

electricity, furniture, toothpaste, hair cream, information, iron

food, cheese, butter, chalk, wind, scenery

paper, fog, dust, salt, ice, hair, cotton, metal, music, silver, glass, plastic, tea, silk

gas, water, cloth, heat, jam, milk, wood

grass, ink, coffee, sand, air, rice, wine

hay, powder, rain, glue

steel, bread, sugar, snow

*When the word **paper** means a newspaper or an exam paper, it is a count noun. The plural is **papers**.*

*When the word **iron** means an electric tool for pressing clothes, it is a count noun. The plural is **irons**.*

- *When the word **glass** means a drinking cup, it is a count noun. The plural is **glasses**.*
- *The word **glasses** also means **spectacles**.*

Grammar Help

- You can put words like a piece of before uncount nouns, and use them as count nouns.

a **loaf** of bread	a **piece** of bread	a **piece** of cheese
a **bar** of chocolate	a **jar** of jam	a **jar** of honey
a **drop** of blood	a **drop** of water	a **grain** of rice
a **lump** of sugar	a **pinch** of salt	a **strand** of hair
a **piece** of furniture	a **piece** of information	a **piece** of news
a **piece** of cloth	a **piece** of chalk	a **piece** of paper
a **sheet** of paper	a **bar** of soap	a **cake** of soap
a **speck** of dust	a **cloud** of dust	a **gust** of wind
a **fall** of snow	a **shower** of rain	a **pool** of water
a **blade** of grass	a **bale** of hay	a **pane** of glass

- You can then use numbers and quantities with these words to show the plural form. For example, you can say:

  five pieces of paper　　**three slices** of bread
  a few lumps of sugar　　**a few grains** of rice

- Fruit is usually an uncount noun. For example, you can say:

  a bowl of fruit

  You can use **a piece of fruit** to refer to a single apple, pear, banana, guava, and so on. For example:

  Do have a piece of fruit.

  But when you are talking about **different kinds of fruit**, you can use fruit as a count noun. For example:

  Is tomato a vegetable or **a fruit**?
  apples, pears and other **fruits**

 ISBN 978-81-8477-744-4

Singular Nouns

Count nouns can be singular or plural.
When you are talking about just one person, animal, place or thing, you use a singular count noun. We say that these nouns are singular, or that they are in the singular.

a nightingale
a bungalow
an engineer
an owl
a pram

a stadium
a windmill
a sparrow
a van

a bench
a taxi

a tent
a worker

a cook
a train

*Another word for **taxi** is **cab**. A **taxi-driver** is also called a **cabby**.*

Here are some more nouns that are in the singular.

a line
a triangle
a rectangle

*Another word for **rectangle** is **oblong**.*

a square
a parallelogram
a toothbrush
a computer
a keyboard
an envelope
a skateboard
a staircase

an oval
a star
a diamond
a brush
a cylinder
a pyramid
a ladder
a circle
a letter

a tie
a cube
a cone
a comb
a slide
a graph
a map
a globe
a stamp

a heart
a sphere
a handkerchief

*The short form of **handkerchief** is **hankie** or **hanky**.*

Plural Nouns

When you are talking about two or more people, animals, places or things, you have to make the count noun plural. We say these nouns are plural, or that they are in the plural.

Plural nouns usually end in -s.

Singular	Plural
a giant	giants
a lamp	lamps
an island	islands
an owl	owls
a clock	clocks
an egg	eggs
a camel	camels

Singular	Plural
a bat	bats
a mask	masks
a jar	jars
a mat	mats
a hawk	hawks
a photo	photos
a penguin	penguins

 ISBN 978-81-8477-744-4

Here are some more plural nouns that end in -s.

Singular	Plural	Singular	Plural
a game	games	a rope	ropes
a plate	plates	a ladle	ladles
a bone	bones	a face	faces
a slice	slices	a piece	pieces
a size	sizes	a case	cases

Spell Well

- If a singular noun ends in **-e**, like **bone** or **plate**, you just add **-s** to make the plural.
- If a singular noun ends in **-ce**, **-se** or **-ze**, like **face, niece, case, noose, size**, adding an **-s** makes another syllable. So, the plurals **faces, nieces, slices, cases, nooses, sizes** all have two syllables.

With some nouns, you add -es to make them plural.

Singular	Plural	Singular	Plural
an arch	arches	a bench	benches
a branch	branches	a ditch	ditches
a church	churches	a wish	wishes
a lunch	lunches	a match	matches
a peach	peaches	a sandwich	sandwiches
a torch	torches	a watch	watches
a witch	witches	a box	boxes
a fax	faxes	a fox	foxes
an address	addresses	an atlas	atlases
a bus	buses	a circus	circuses
a class	classes	a dress	dresses
a glass	glasses	a cross	crosses
a bush	bushes	a brush	brushes
a dish	dishes	a flash	flashes

Spell Well

- When the last letters of singular nouns are **ch**, **sh**, **s** or **x**, you usually add **-es** to form the plural.
- The words **stomach** and **monarch** end in **-ch** but you add **-s** (not **-es**) to form the plural. This is because the **-ch** in these words sounds like **k**.

 ISBN 978-81-8477-744-4

With some nouns that end in -o, you just add -s to form the plural.

Singular	Plural	Singular	Plural
an avocado	avocados	a cello	cellos
a cuckoo	cuckoos	a rhino	rhinos
a hippo	hippos	a video	videos
a kangaroo	kangaroos	a zoo	zoos
a kilo	kilos	a kimono	kimonos

But with some nouns that end in -o, you add -es to form the plural.

Singular	Plural	Singular	Plural
a tomato	tomatoes	a potato	potatoes
a flamingo	flamingoes	a hero	heroes
a tornado	tornadoes	a volcano	volcanoes
a dingo	dingoes		

With some nouns that end in -o, you can add -s or -es to form the plural.

Singular	Plural	Plural
a halo	haloes	halos
a mango	mangoes	mangos
a torpedo	torpedoes	torpedos
a mosquito	mosquitoes	mosquitos
a zero	zeroes	zeros
a buffalo	buffaloes	buffalos
a memento	mementoes	mementos

With some nouns that end in -y, you form the plural by changing the y to i, and adding -es.

Singular	Plural	Singular	Plural
a lady	ladies	a cherry	cherries
a family	families	a strawberry	strawberries
a fairy	fairies	a trophy	trophies
a diary	diaries	a jelly	jellies
a baby	babies	a factory	factories
a lily	lilies	a story	stories
a spy	spies	a library	libraries

 ISBN 978-81-8477-744-4

- **But if there is a vowel before the y, you just add -s to form the plural.**

Singular	Plural	Singular	Plural
a toy	toys	a key	keys
a monkey	monkeys	a tray	trays
a donkey	donkeys	a turkey	turkeys
a chimney	chimneys	a storey	storeys
a valley	valleys		
a bay	bays		
a buoy	buoys		
a trolley	trolleys		
a runway	runways		
a jersey	jerseys		

*In American English, **storey** is spelt **story**, and **storeys** is spelt **stories**.*

- **With some nouns that end in -f, the plural ending is -ves. You change the f to v, and add -es.**

Singular	Plural	Singular	Plural
a leaf	leaves	a thief	thieves
an elf	elves	a calf	calves
a wolf	wolves	a loaf	loaves
a bookshelf	bookshelves	a half	halves
a sheaf	sheaves		

- **But with some nouns ending in -f, you can either add -s or change the f to v, and add -es.**

Singular	Plural	Plural
a dwarf	dwarfs	dwarves
a scarf	scarfs	scarves
a hoof	hoofs	hooves

- **With some nouns that end in -f or -fe, you just add -s to form the plural.**

Singular	Plural	Singular	Plural
a chief	chiefs	a roof	roofs
a cliff	cliffs	a giraffe	giraffes

 ISBN 978-81-8477-744-4

■ **But with some nouns ending in -fe, you change f to v, and add -s.**

Singular	Plural
a knife	knives
a life	lives

Singular	Plural
a wife	wives

■ **The plural of some nouns is the same as the singular.**

Singular	Plural
an aircraft	aircraft
a deer	deer
a bison	bison
a shellfish	shellfish
a goldfish	goldfish
a reindeer	reindeer
a carp	carp
a salmon	salmon

Singular	Plural
a sheep	sheep
a fish	fish

*You can use **fishes** as the plural of fish when you are talking about **different kinds of fish**. For example, you can say: the various **fishes** of the Indian Ocean.*

■ **The plural form of some nouns is different from the singular form.**

Singular	Plural
a goose	geese
a foot	feet
an ox	oxen
a child	children
a mouse	mice

*The plural of the **mouse** that you use with your computer can be **mice** or **mouses**.*

Singular	Plural
a louse	lice
a tooth	teeth
a woman	women
a man	men

*The plural of **man** is **men**, but the plural of **human** is **humans**.*

Grammar Help

■ **You don't add -s to words like dozen (a dozen is twelve), hundred and thousand when you use a number before them. For example, you say:**

two dozen roses
four thousand soldiers
three hundred students
two million dollars

But you can say:

dozens of roses
thousands of people
hundreds of balloons
millions of insects

 ISBN 978-81-8477-744-4

Nouns
Pronouns
Adjectives
Determiners
Verbs
Adverbs
Prepositions
Conjunctions
Interjections
Sentences
Phrases
Clauses
More about Sentences
Direct and Indirect Speech
Punctuation

Some nouns are always plural.

pyjamas	trousers	jeans	shorts	pants
bermudas	briefs	goggles	tongs	pincers
binoculars	pliers	scissors	braces	tights
spectacles	sunglasses	shears		

*Another word for **spectacles** is **glasses**.*

*In American English, **suspenders** is the word for **braces**.*

Some nouns are usually used in the plural form.

shoes	sneakers	slippers	sandals	boots
chopsticks	socks	stockings	gloves	

You can put **a pair of** before plural nouns like **trousers**, **jeans** and **pants** to make them into singular nouns.

a pair of trousers	a pair of jeans	a pair of scissors
a pair of spectacles	a pair of pants	a pair of shorts
a pair of shoes	a pair of pliers	a pair of socks
a pair of chopsticks	a pair of tongs	a pair of slippers
a pair of binoculars	a pair of sandals	a pair of goggles
a pair of boots	a pair of gloves	a pair of stockings

You can use **pairs of** with a number or a quantity word when there is more than one pair.

two pairs of eyes	eight pairs of pliers
three pairs of scissors	ten pairs of chopsticks
four pairs of pyjamas	several pairs of boots
five pairs of spectacles	How many pairs of sandals?

Grammar Help

- **Some nouns have a plural form, but are really singular uncount nouns. For example:**

  maths **measles**
  news **mumps**

- **You use a singular verb with such nouns. For example, you say:**
  The news is good.

- **The short form for mathematics is maths, but the short form in American English is math.**

 ISBN 978-81-8477-744-4

Proper Nouns

So far, you have been looking at common nouns. Now we are going to look at proper nouns.

Proper nouns are special names given to people, places and things. They always begin with a capital letter.

People's names are proper nouns.

Charles Dickens
Snow White
Santa Claus
Robinson Crusoe
Florence Nightingale
Nelson Mandela
Michael Jackson
Abraham Lincoln
Albert Einstein
Mahatma Ghandi
Helen Keller
Frankenstein
Professor Black
Robin Hood
Harry Potter
Cinderella

David
Sharon
Kim
Diana
May Ling
Robert
Aladdin
Ivan
Dr Lee
Beethoven
Ali Baba

Hassan
Kumar
Mum
Dad
Mr Young
Miss Brown
Auntie
Uncle
Sumiko
Granny
Grandad

Did you know?

Your name and the names of your friends are also proper nouns.

The names of the months are proper nouns.

January

January is the first month of the year.

February
March
April
May

June
July
August
September

October
November
December

The names of the days of the week are proper nouns too.

Sunday
Monday
Tuesday
Wednesday
Thursday
Friday
Saturday

Did you know?

- **Sunday is the first day of the week.**
- **A table which shows the days, weeks and months of the year is called a calendar.**

 ISBN 978-81-8477-744-4

The names of festivals are proper nouns.

the Spring Festival
Dragon Boat Festival
Independence Day
the Lantern Festival
the Mooncake Festival

The **Mooncake Festival** is also known as the **Mid-Autumn Festival**.

Children's Day
Thanksgiving Day
Christmas
Easter
Yom Kippur
Mother's Day
Hari Raya Puasa
the Water Festival

Halloween
Vesak Day
Thaipusam
Deepavali

Deepavali is also known as the **Festival of Lights**.

The names of countries and their capital cities are proper nouns as well.

Country	Capital City
Great Britain	London
China	Beijing
India	New Delhi
Japan	Tokyo
Korea	Seoul
France	Paris
Belgium	Brussels
Italy	Rome
Pakistan	Islamabad
Egypt	Cairo
Spain	Madrid
Thailand	Bangkok
Germany	Berlin
United States of America	Washington DC

The names of famous places and buildings are proper nouns too. Here are some of them.

the Statue of Liberty
the Tower of London
the Great Wall of China
the Leaning Tower of Pisa
the Sphinx
Borobodur
The Vatican
the Taj Mahal
the Colosseum
Angkor Wat
the Eiffel Tower

the Little Mermaid
the Arc De Triomphe
the Grand Canyon
the Summer Palace
St Paul's Cathedral
the Millennium Dome
the Sydney Opera House

Did you know?

These places and buildings are **famous landmarks**. Do you know in which countries you can find these landmarks?

 ISBN 978-81-8477-744-4

- **The names of people who live in a country are also proper nouns.**

Country	People
Australia	Australians
Britain	the British
Canada	Canadians
China	the Chinese
Egypt	Egyptians
France	the French
Germany	Germans
India	Indians
Indonesia	Indonesians
Italy	Italians
Japan	the Japanese
Korea	Koreans
Malaysia	Malaysians
Pakistan	Pakistanis
the Philippines	Filipinos
Russia	Russians
Singapore	Singaporeans
South Africa	South Africans
Spain	Spaniards
Switzerland	the Swiss
Thailand	Thais
United States of America	Americans

- **The names of oceans, lakes, seas, rivers and mountains are proper nouns.**

the Pacific Ocean
the Mediterranean Sea
the Yangtze River
the West Lake
Niagara Falls

the Indian Ocean
the Thames
Lake Michigan
the Himalayas
the Rockies

the Dead Sea
the Alps
Mount Fuji
Mount Everest

Did you know?

- You often use **the** before names of oceans, seas, rivers and mountain ranges.
- **Mount** means **mountain.**
  It is often used as part of a proper noun. For example:
  Mount Everest   Mount Fuji
  Mount Sinai
- The short form of **Mount** is **Mt.**

 ISBN 978-81-8477-744-4

Nouns
Pronouns
Adjectives
Determiners
Verbs
Adverbs
Prepositions
Conjunctions
Interjections
Sentences
Phrases
Clauses
More about Sentences
Direct and Indirect Speech
Punctuation

Collective Nouns

Collective nouns are words for groups of people, animals or things.

- **Here are some words for groups of people. They are singular count nouns.**

a community	a family	a team	a choir
an orchestra	a company	a band	a firm
a corporation	an audience	a club	a crew
a committee	a group	a gang	the staff
the government	the army		

Grammar Help

Although these collective nouns are singular, they are sometimes used with a plural verb.

For example, you can say:

A gang of thieves has (or **have**) stolen the picture.
My family **was** (or **were**) pleased to see me.

- **Here are more collective nouns that you can use for groups of people.**

a **battalion** of soldiers	a **class** of children
a **troop** of soldiers	a **host** of angels
a **troupe** of dancers	a **board** of directors
a **troupe** of performers	a **panel** of doctors
a **troupe** of actors	a **panel** of judges
a **company** of actors	a **team** of players
a **crowd** of people	a **horde** of savages
a **multitude** of people	a **gang** of robbers
a **congregation** of worshippers	

Grammar Help

- **Some plural nouns don't end with -s, and they don't have a singular either. For example:**

  people　　cattle　　the police

  These are collective nouns too.

- **You use a plural verb with these collective nouns. For example, you say:**

  The police **have caught** the thief.
  The cattle **are grazing** in the fields.

 ISBN 978-81-8477-744-4

Groups of animals, birds and fishes sometimes have their own special collective nouns.

a **shoal** of fish
a **herd** of cattle
a **pack** of wolves
a **flock** of sheep
a **flock** of birds
a **watch** of nightingales
a **school** of whales
a **school** of dolphins
a **gaggle** of geese
a **swarm** of bees
a **pride** of lions
a **stud** of horses
a **drove** of ponies
a **brood** of chickens
a **litter** of kittens
a **litter** of puppies
a **litter** of cubs
a **herd** of elephants
a **herd** of cattle
a **nest** of rabbits
a **troop** of monkeys
an **army** or a **nest** of ants

Here are some collective nouns that you can use for groups of things.

a **bunch** of keys
a **bunch** of grapes

a **list** of names
a **range** of hills
a **set** of tools
a **set** of cutlery
a **set** of crockery
a **set** of stamps
a **pile** of plates
a **suite** of rooms

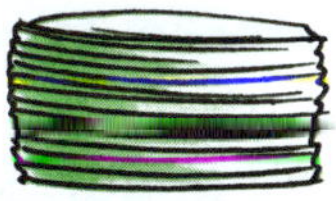

a **suite** of furniture
a **volley** of bullets
a **wad** of bank notes
a **flotilla** of yachts
a **series** of diagrams
a **nest** of tables
a **peal** of bells
a **set** of dishes
a **row** of lamp posts
a **row** of houses
a **range** of numbers
a **bouquet** of roses
a **comb** of bananas
a **heap** of stones
a **string** of beads
a **bunch** of flowers

a **clutch** of eggs
a **cluster** of trees
a **clump** of trees
a **chain** of events
a **collection** of books
a **constellation** of stars
a **fleet** of ships
a **flight** of steps
a **galaxy** of stars
a **series** of books
a **pack** of cards
a **pile** of newspapers

 ISBN 978-81-8477-744-4

Abstract Nouns

Words for ideas and feelings and other things that you cannot touch are called abstract nouns. Words for things that you can touch, such as chair, table, cat, dog, are called concrete nouns.

Words like beauty, truth, anger, danger, hatred and jealousy are abstract nouns. Many abstract nouns are uncountable, like the ones just mentioned. But some abstract nouns, such as a feeling, an idea, a thought, a lie, are countable.

Snow White's stepmother was admiring her own **appearance** in the mirror. The mirror could not tell her a **lie**, so it told her the **truth**: Snow White was more beautiful than she was. The stepmother was full of **anger**. She wanted to kill Snow White.

Snow White was in great **danger**. She ran away to escape her stepmother's **hatred** and **jealousy**, and joined the seven dwarfs in the woods.

One day, the stepmother came in **disguise** and gave Snow White a poisoned apple. She took a **bite** and fell down dead.

The **death** of Snow White filled the stepmother with **delight**. But the seven dwarfs were full of **grief** and **sadness**. In their **despair**, they laid Snow White in a glass coffin so that her **loveliness** should never be out of their **sight**.

One day, a handsome prince passed by and saw her lying there. He was struck with her **beauty** and fell in **love** with her.

 ISBN 978-81-8477-744-4

The prince gave her a **kiss**, and she came back to **life** again. And so, to everyone's **joy**, they married, and lived in great **happiness** for the rest of their **lives**.

But Snow White's stepmother was punished for her **wickedness** by **death**.

Some abstract nouns end in -ness. For most of these words, you just add -ness to the adjectives.

Adjective	Abstract Noun
kind	kindness
red	redness
thick	thickness
soft	softness
bold	boldness
great	greatness
harsh	harshness
round	roundness
useful	usefulness
sick	sickness
willing	willingness
mad	madness
friendly	friendliness
happy	happiness
lazy	laziness
ugly	ugliness
lonely	loneliness
dry	dryness
shy	shyness
sly	slyness

Adjective	Abstract Noun
sad	sadness
rich	richness
sweet	sweetness
loud	loudness
dark	darkness
weak	weakness
eager	eagerness
numb	numbness
forgetful	forgetfulness
ill	illness
dumb	dumbness

Spell Well

When an adjective ends in -y, you change the y to i and add -ness. But the adjectives dry, shy and sly do not follow this rule.

For these three adjectives, you just add -ness.

Did you know?

Abstract nouns ending in -ness are usually words for qualities.

 ISBN 978-81-8477-744-4

Some abstract nouns end in -ion.

action
addition
admission
ambition
confusion
co-operation
creation
decision
decoration
dictation
direction
division
education
exploration
excursion
fascination
formation
illusion
imitation
intention
invasion
omission
promotion
repetition
rejection
solution
subtraction
tradition
vacation
vision
attention
generation

Some abstract nouns end in -y, -ty or -ity.

ability
activity
beauty
courtesy
eternity
fantasy
ferocity
honesty
jealousy
liberty
loyalty
majesty
majority
maturity
modesty
minority
nobility
novelty
penalty
popularity
poverty
probability
quality
quantity
reliability
reality
responsibility
robbery
severity
timidity
totality
unity

Masculine, Feminine and Neuter Nouns

Masculine nouns are words for men and boys, and male animals and birds.

Feminine nouns are words for women and girls, and female animals and birds.

Male	Female	Male	Female
boy	girl	man	woman
grandfather	grandmother	father	mother
son	daughter	brother	sister
uncle	aunt	nephew	niece
bridegroom	bride	emperor	empress
king	queen	prince	princess
wizard	witch	gentleman	lady
actor	actress	waiter	waitress
host	hostess	steward	stewardess
policeman	policewoman	fiancé	fiancée
landlord	landlady	husband	wife

 ISBN 978-81-8477-744-4

- **Here are some masculine and feminine nouns for animals.**

Animal	Masculine	Feminine
chicken	cock	hen
cattle	bull	cow
deer (large)	stag	hind
deer (small)	buck	doe
leopard	leopard	leopardess
dog	dog	bitch
duck	drake	duck
fox	fox	vixen
goose	gander	goose
horse	stallion	mare
lion	lion	lioness
pig	boar	sow
sheep	ram	ewe
tiger	tiger	tigress
peacock	peacock	peahen

*Other words for **cock** are **rooster** and **cockerel**.*

Grammar Help

- You can use **he** to refer to male animals, and **she** to refer to female animals.
- But you can use **it** for both male and female animals.

- **But a lot of nouns are used for both males and females. We say these nouns belong to the common gender.**

babies
pupils
doctors
dentists
managers
presidents
reporters
singers
children
students
lawyers
architects
astronauts
prime ministers
editors
dancers
parents
teachers
engineers
accountants
scientists
officers
artists
acrobats

 ISBN 978-81-8477-744-4

- We know that a lot of nouns refer to **things**, such as places, objects, machines, tools rather than to **people** or **animals**. They are called **neuter nouns**.

  Here are some examples.

hospital
washing machine
penknife
gymnasium
computer
stool
cave
mobile phone

museum
table
book
stick
fire
floor
pen
drill

school
chair

broom
carpet

Grammar Help

You use **it** to refer to neuter nouns.

Compound Nouns

Compound nouns are nouns that consist of two words or more.

Many compound nouns are written as one word, and their plural is formed in the regular way.

classroom	classrooms	dishwasher	dishwashers
handphone	handphones	screwdriver	screwdrivers

When the compound noun is written as two words, or as two words joined by a hyphen, you add s to the second word.

book club	book clubs
fire engine	fire engines
shopping centre	shopping centres
word-processor	word-processors

With most compound nouns of three words or more, you add s to the first word, which is usually a noun.

son-in-law	sons-in-law
lady-in-waiting	ladies-in-waiting
commander-in-chief	commanders-in-chief
lily-of-the-valley	lilies-of-the-valley
cul-de-sac	culs-de-sac
passer-by	passers-by

But in some cases, the first word isn't a noun, and s comes at the end of the whole compound.

forget-me-not	forget-me-nots

Did you know?

A cul-de-sac is a street that is closed at the end. It's a French word, but in French it means 'the bottom of a bag'.

 ISBN 978-81-8477-744-4

Noun Phrases

So far, we have been looking mostly at nouns that are single words. Some nouns are made up of more than one word. They are called **noun phrases**.

Here are some noun phrases.

the girl in red	the night sky	the sly fox
the way home	the Eiffel Tower	a famous writer
a strange story	a difficult riddle	a television set
a lot of food	a swarm of bees	a bowl of soup
some children	the midday sun	school uniform
Benjamin's pencil	world population	dirty socks

Noun Phrases that Explain

- Sometimes, you use a noun phrase before somebody's name to explain who they are.

  Here are some examples.

my sister Jill	**my cousin** Jean
my brother David	**our teacher** Miss Lee
their dog Rex	**our friends** the Smiths
her husband Jack	**his sons** Dave and Jason
my best friend Kate	**the singer** Michael Jackson
the composer Bach	**the painter** Van Gogh

- Sometimes, you add a name as an extra piece of information after a noun phrase.

  Here are some examples.

the home of ballet, Russia

our new car, a Honda

his mother tongue, Malay

Did you know?

You need a **comma** before a name when you are adding it as an extra piece of information after a noun phrase.

 ISBN 978-81-8477-744-4

Nouns
Pronouns
Adjectives
Determiners
Verbs
Adverbs
Prepositions
Conjunctions
Interjections
Sentences
Phrases
Clauses
More about Sentences
Direct and Indirect Speech
Punctuation

- **Sometimes, you add a noun phrase as an explanation after a name.**
  Here are some examples.

Mr Lal, **our football coach**

Sue, **an American cousin of mine**

Mr Rahim, **Dad's golfing partner**

Gillian and Molly, **Mum's colleagues**

Michael Jackson, **the well-known singer**

We often practise conversation with Mrs Clement, **our English teacher.**

Katie, **my friend at school**, met with an accident yesterday.

Steve, **our leader**, is a good swimmer.

Robert, **our next-door neighbour**, has bought a new car.

Peter and Judith, **my two cousins**, are coming to stay with us.

Did you know?

When you add a noun phrase after somebody's name, you need a comma at the beginning of the noun phrase, and another comma at the end of it, if it comes in the middle of a sentence.

Exercise 1

In these sentences, choose some, any, a or an to fill in the gaps.

1. Help yourself to ____________ cheese and ____________ plate.
2. Isn't there ____________ ice cream left?
3. I need to buy ____________ bread and ____________ litre of milk.
4. Harry never does ____________ work.
5. We had ____________ lovely holiday with ____________ beautiful weather.

Some, Any, A/An

- You can use **some** with uncountable nouns.
- In sentences with a negative word such as **not** or **never**, you often use **any** instead of **some.**

 ISBN 978-81-8477-744-4

6. Don't you ever eat ____________ meat?

7. I've got ____________ interesting news to tell you.

8. I found ____________ money in ____________ old purse.

9. Sam has ____________ new apartment so he needs ____________ furniture.

10. I want to buy ____________ handphone, but I can't find ____________ information about them.

11. Remember to pack ____________ toothpaste and ____________ soap.

12. Have ____________ toast, or would you prefer ____________ egg and ____________ bacon?

Exercise 2

Choose a word from the box to fill in the gaps in the following sentences. One has been done for you.

advice	clothing	cutlery
equipment	fruit	furniture
information	news	stationery
work		

1. A spoon is a piece of ____cutlery____.

2. A pencil is a piece of ____________________.

3. An announcement is a piece of ____________________.

4. A guava is a piece of ____________________.

5. A chest of drawers is a piece of ____________________.

6. A fact is a piece of ____________________.

A Piece of What?

- You often use **a piece of** before uncountable nouns. For example, you refer to **a chair** as **a piece of furniture** and **an apple** as **a piece of fruit.**

 ISBN 978-81-8477-744-4

7. An exercise bike is a piece of ____________.

8. An assignment is a piece of ____________.

9. A suggestion is a piece of ____________.

10. A tee-shirt is a piece of ____________.

Exercise 3

Put capital letters in the right places in the names below, and add the at the beginning wherever you think it is needed.

1. eiffel tower ____________
2. mount fuji ____________
3. lake superior ____________
4. leaning tower of pisa ____________
5. united kingdom ____________
6. statue of liberty ____________
7. great britain ____________
8. grand canyon ____________
9. black sea ____________
10. new delhi ____________
11. tiananmen square ____________
12. brahmaputra ____________
13. tower of london ____________
14. merlion ____________

Famous Places and Things

- Famous objects as well as places have capital letters.
- A famous object or landmark often needs **the** before it: the Sphinx; the Taj Mahal.
- The names of seas, oceans, rivers and mountain ranges often have **the** before them: the Atlantic Ocean; the Himalayas.

 ISBN 978-81-8477-744-4

15. indian ocean ____________________

16. philippines ____________________

17. north pole ____________________

18. gulf of mexico ____________________

19. andes ____________________

20. arctic circle ____________________

 ISBN 978-81-8477-744-4

2 PRONOUNS

Read the following passage. The items in bold are all pronouns of one kind or another.

Blog

A great many workers occasionally complain about their boss. You may well have done so about **yours**. Most of the time, **we** may assure **ourselves** that we are quite happy with our working conditions, but then the boss does something to upset **us** and we grumble.

If **you** are sensible, you share your complaint only with people who are close to you. Groups of friends often use **each other** in this way. It would be indiscreet of you to voice your complaint in public in the office. **Who** might be listening? You should ask yourself if there is **anyone** listening who may wish you harm. **What** might **they** do with the information?

The listener may be **someone whom** you have previously offended. **They** may possibly tell your boss and your position in the firm may be affected in some way. It would depend on the boss, but **that** is quite a possibility.

Modern technology has made it far easier for people to communicate with **one another**, even with people **whom** they do not know. Some people still write their private thoughts in a diary, but others write **theirs** in a blog. A blog is short for weblog, a personal journal intended for public viewing on a website.

There is a major problem with electronic communication. People sending it tend to forget the huge extent of their potential readership. They often feel as though they are writing to intimate friends, but **this** is not the case.

In some countries, workers who have written complaining blogs about the boss have been given cause to blame **themselves**. Their blogs have been brought to the attention of their bosses and some of **them** have been sacked because of **them**.

That should be a warning to **everyone**. Be careful what you write on the Internet!

 ISBN 978-81-8477-744-4

A **pronoun** is a word that takes the place of a common noun or a proper noun.

Personal Pronouns

The words I, you, he, she, it, we and they are called personal pronouns. They take the place of words for people, animals, places or things.

My name is Lisa. **I** am ten.

Here is my mother. **She** works in a bank.

Here is my father. **He** is a baker.

Here is our cat. **It** likes fish.

Tommy, **you** are a greedy cat.

Peter is not at school today. **He** is ill.

Here are Michael and Susan.
They are my brother and sister.

Michael, Susan and I often go to the playground.
We play football there.

This is our school. **It** is the last building in the street.

These are the windows of my classroom. **They** look out on to the playground.

Good morning, children! **You** may sit down now.

Monica, Jim and Susan! Please, will **you** hand out the books?

Grammar Help

- In each of these examples, the personal pronoun is used as the **subject** of the sentences.
- The **subject** is the person, animal or thing that does the action shown by the verb. For example:
  Subject → **Tom** has gone to the shop.
  Subject → **He** has bought an ice cream.

- **The words me, you, him, her, it, us and them are also personal pronouns for people, animals, places or things.**

I'm in the kitchen. Mum is teaching **me** how to cook.

Oh, Lisa! What a mess! Mum told **you** to be careful.

Where is Michael? Everybody is looking for **him**.

Here is Mrs Li, my teacher. All the children like **her**.

The floor is dirty. Dad is mopping **it**.

 ISBN 978-81-8477-744-4

Nouns
Pronouns
Adjectives
Determiners
Verbs
Adverbs
Prepositions
Conjunctions
Interjections
Sentences
Phrases
Clauses
More about Sentences
Direct and Indirect Speech
Punctuation

Uncle Harry collected **Mary** and **me** and took **us** to the cinema.

Goodbye, **kids**! Mum will collect **you** at four o'clock.

Here are **your sandwiches**, kids. Put **them** in your schoolbags.

Fingers off **the chocolate cake**! Leave **it** alone!

A stranger stopped **Jane** and asked **her** the way to the swimming pool.

Phone **George** and ask **him** to come with **us** for a swim.

Where are **my clean trousers**? Oh, somebody has left **them** on the bed.

Grammar Help

- In each of these examples, the personal pronoun is used as the **object** of the verb.
- The **object** is the person, animal or thing that receives the action shown by the verb. For example:

  Tom has bought an ice cream. *(object)*
  He is enjoying it. *(object)*

Grammar Help

- I is the **first person singular.**

  You always spell it with a capital letter.

  You is the **second person singular**, and also the **second person plural.**

  He, she and **it** are the third **person singular.**

  You use **he** for men and boys, **she** for women and girls, and **it** for things.

  You can also use **it** for babies and animals when you don't know their sex.

  But when you do know their sex, you use **he** or **she**.

  We is the **first person plural.**

  They is the **third person plural.**

  You use **they** for people, animals and things.

- Here is a table to remind you about **personal pronouns.**

	Subject	Object
First person singular	I	me
Second person singular	you	you
Third person singular	he she it	him her it
First person plural	we	us
Second person plural	you	you
Third person plural	they	them

 ISBN 978-81-8477-744-4

Reflexive Pronouns

The words myself, yourself, himself, herself, itself, ourselves, yourselves and themselves are called reflexive pronouns.

They refer to the person or animal that is the subject of the verb.

I made this cake **myself**.

Be careful with the knife. You'll cut **yourself**.

Michael is looking at **himself** in the mirror.

Susan has hurt **herself**.

Our cat washes **itself** after each meal.

We organized the party all by **ourselves**.

Come in, children, and find **yourselves** a seat.

Baby birds are too young to look after **themselves**.

Grammar Help

- **Here is a table to remind you about reflexive pronouns.**

	Singular		Plural	
First person	(I, me)	**myself**	(we, us)	**ourselves**
Second person	(you)	**yourself**	(you)	**yourselves**
Third person	(he, him)	**himself**	(they, them)	**themselves**
	(she, her)	**herself**	(they, them)	**themselves**
	(it)	**itself**	(they, them)	**themselves**

- **There are several ways of using reflexive pronouns.**
  - as object of the verb:
    I hurt **myself**.
  - as object of preposition:
    She's all by **herself**.
  - as indirect object of a verb:
    He poured **himself** a drink.
  - as emphasizer of a noun or personal pronoun:
    I didn't see the accident **itself**, but I heard the crash.
    She had trained the horse **herself**.

 ISBN 978-81-8477-744-4

Possessive Pronouns

The words mine, yours, his, hers, ours and theirs are called possessive pronouns.

You use possessive pronouns to talk about things belonging to people.

This bat is **mine.**

Tom, where's **yours?**

This skateboard is **his.**

Helen has lost her kitten. Is this kitten **hers?**

This is our neighbour's car. But where's **ours?**

I've got my sandwiches, and here are **yours.**

Lisa has eaten her lunch, but Jane and Mary haven't had **theirs** yet.

Grammar Help

- **Possessive pronouns** (mine, yours, his, hers, ours and theirs) have the same meanings as **possessive determiners** (my, your, his, her, its, our and their). But they are used differently.
  - **Possessive determiners** come before nouns. For example, you say:
    This is **my** bat. That is **your** bat. This is **our** car.
  - **Possessive pronouns** can stand on their own. They are not used before nouns. For example, you say:
    This bat is **mine.** That bat is **yours.** This car is **ours.**
  - **Its** is not usually used as a **possessive pronoun;** you use **its** as a **possessive determiner** before a noun. For example, you say:
    The cat carried **its** kittens into the garden.
- Here is a table to remind you about **possessive pronouns** and **possessive determiners.**

	Singular		Plural	
	Possessive pronouns	Possessive determiners	Possessive pronouns	Possessive determiners
First person	mine	my	ours	our
Second person	yours	your	yours	your
Third person	his	his	theirs	their
	hers	her	theirs	their
	–	its	theirs	their

 ISBN 978-81-8477-744-4

Relative Pronouns

The words who, whom, whose, which and that are called relative pronouns.

You use relative pronouns to say something that describes the person or thing you are talking about, or shows which one you mean.

A lot of people **who** eat junk food get too fat.

Where is the waiter **who** served us?

They have found the man **whom** they want to interview.

The police have found the man **for whom** they were searching.

I have a friend **whose** mother drives a taxi.

Special arrangements are made for children **whose** parents work abroad.

Here is the shop **which** (or **that**) sells computer equipment.

Suitcases **which** (or **that**) you can wheel along are the best.

Grammar Help

- **The relative pronoun who, like the interrogative pronoun who, can be used as the object of a verb as well as the subject:**

  The police would like the woman **who** telephoned them last night to contact them again.

  Is there anyone here **who** you haven't met before?

- **Whom is only used as an object. For example, you can say:**

  They have found the man **who** they want to interview.

  They have found the man **whom** they want to interview.

- **You can use who and whom with prepositions. For example, you can use who and whom like this with the preposition for:**

  The police have found the man **who** (or **whom**) they were searching **for**.

  The police have found the man **for whom** they were searching.

- **You can use that instead of which. For example:**

  This is the bus **that** (or **which**) passes the zoo.

- **But after a preposition you use which, not that. For example:**

  The bus **for which** we were waiting never came.

Did you know?

- **Who and whom refer to people.**
- **Whose can refer to people or things. For example:**

  a tree **whose** branches touch my window

- **That can refer to things or people. For example:**

  the man **that** called

  the table **that** we reserved

 ISBN 978-81-8477-744-4

Interrogative Pronouns

The words who, whom, whose, what and which are called interrogative pronouns.

You use these pronouns to ask questions.

Who broke the window?

Who is he talking to?

Who are those people ?

Whom are you taking to the dance ?

Whom is he talking to?

Whose is this umbrella?

Whose are these gloves ?

Whose is the best drawing ?

What is your dog's name?

What are you yelling for ?

What is the time ?

What do you want to be when you grow up?

Which of these bags is yours?

Which do you prefer ?

Which of them is the tallest?

Grammar Help

- **Who can be used as the object of a verb as well as the subject. Whom is used only as the object. For example, you can say:**

  Who are you taking to the dance?

  or

  Whom are you taking to the dance?

- **You can use who or whom with prepositions. For example, you can use who and whom like this with the preposition to:**

  Who (or Whom) is he talking to?

  or

  To whom is he talking?

 ISBN 978-81-8477-744-4

Demonstrative Pronouns

The words this, these, that and those are called demonstrative pronouns. They are showing words.

This is my house. **That** is John's house.

This is a hill. **That** is a mountain.

These are sheep. **Those** are goats.

These are donkeys. **Those** are horses.

What is **this**? What are **those**?

Wait till you hear **this**.
I haven't heard **that** before.

Did you drop **this**?
No, **that's** not mine.

You'll have to work harder than **this**.

We can do better than **that**.

Who is **that** knocking at the door?

What is **this** crawling across the carpet?

You mean you won? **That's** amazing!

This is awful; the computer keeps crashing.

There's one thing you must all remember, and it's **this**.

Hello! Who is **that** speaking, please?
Hi, Jane! **This** is Michael!

Hello! Is **that** you, George?

Grammar Help

- You use **this** and **these** when you point to things **near** to you. You use **that** and **those** when you point to things **further away**.
- You also use **this** to refer to something you are about to say, or do. You use **that** to refer to something that has already been said, or that has happened. For example:

  This is how you do it.
  That was clever.
- **Demonstrative pronouns** can be singular or plural.
- When you answer the telephone, in British English you say 'Who is **that**?' to ask who is at the other end, but in American English you ask 'Who is **this**?'

 ISBN 978-81-8477-744-4

Indefinite Pronouns

The words **anyone, someone, everyone** and **no-one** are called **indefinite pronouns.** You use **indefinite pronouns** when you are not referring to any particular person.

You can also use the forms **anybody, somebody, everybody** and **nobody.**

Is **anyone** at home?
Has **anyone** seen my cat?
Doesn't **anyone** want to play?
I can't see **anybody** on the beach.

Someone is at the door.
Someone has dropped their passport.
There is **somebody** in the distance.

Where is **everyone**?
Everyone has got the right answer.
Are there enough seats for **everybody**?

No one knows the way out of the jungle.
No one can beat John at chess.
I tried to telephone you, but **nobody** answered.

Grammar Help

- You often use anyone or **anybody** instead of **someone** or **somebody** in questions. For example, you can say:

  Is anyone (or anybody) there?

- You use **anyone** or **anybody** instead of **someone** or somebody after not. For example, you say:

  I don't know **anyone** (or **anybody**) here.

- The indefinite pronouns are **singular**. You use them with a singular verb. But you can also use the plural pronouns **they, them** and **themselves**, and the plural possessive determiner **their**, to refer to the indefinite pronouns.

Somebody has left **their** coat behind.

When you get a present from **someone**, do you always remember to thank **them**?

I can hear **someone** crying; perhaps **they've** hurt **themselves**.

Everyone needs a friend, don't **they**?

Has **everyone** collected **their** free gift?

Nobody knows the answer, do **they**?

Grammar Help

- Some people prefer to use **he or she, him or her, himself or herself**, and his or her to refer to the indefinite pronouns. For example, you can say:

  Can **everyone** see **himself or herself** in the mirror?
  Noone likes having **his or her** teeth drilled.

- The interrogative pronoun **who** is like an indefinite pronoun in some ways, and you can use **they, them, their** and **themselves** to refer to it. For example, you can say:

  Who has forgotten **their** schoolbag?

 ISBN 978-81-8477-744-4

- The words **anything, something, everything** and **nothing** are indefinite pronouns too.

Do you need **anything** from the supermarket ?
Can you see **anything**?
No, I can't see **anything**.

Would you like **something** to drink?
I can feel **something** crawling up my back.
I have **something** important to tell you.

Grammar Help

- **You often use anything instead of something in questions. For example, you can say:**
  Have you had anything to eat?
- **You use anything instead of something after not. For example, you say:**
  I haven't had **anything** to eat.

Mum has bought **everything** she wants.

Everything is ready for the meal.

There's **nothing** left in the fridge.

Children get bored when they have **nothing** to do.

- **None is an indefinite pronoun too. It means not any. It is the negative form of some. You can use none to refer to uncountable nouns or plural nouns.**

Sue has some big posters but Kim has **none**.

None of this food is good for you.

None of those answers are correct.

None of these letters are yours.

I looked in the fridge for some ice cream, but there was **none** there.

We all play a musical instrument, but **none** of us play the piano.

Lots of snow fell yesterday, but **none** of it was left this morning.

Did you know?

When you say **there is none** or **there are none**, you mean the same as **there isn't any** or **there aren't any**.

Grammar Help

When none refers to a plural noun, you can have a plural verb with it, but some people prefer to use a singular verb. For example, you can say:

None of those answers **are** correct.
or
None of those answers **is** correct.

 ISBN 978-81-8477-744-4

One is often used as a pronoun as well as a number. You use it to refer to singular countable nouns.

Have an orange.
I've already got **one**, thanks.

Which is your desk?
The **one** by the door.

Our computer is worn out so we are buying another **one**.

This house is bigger than our old **one**.

One of my friends has a tortoise.

Sue has lost **one** of her books.

Hand your exam papers to **one** of the staff.

There are lots of Chinese students.
Which **one** do you mean?
That **one**, carrying a backpack.

Grammar Help

You can use ones as the plural of one. For example, you can say:

I've torn my new jeans, so I'm wearing my old **ones**.
I want to keep these big marbles, but you can have those small **ones**.

Reciprocal Pronouns

The pronouns each other and one another are called reciprocal pronouns.

Tom and Susan blamed **each other** for the mistake.
They made friends with **one another** on the first day they met.

Grammar Help

Reciprocal pronouns express the idea of something done by each member of a group or couple to each of the others. Notice the difference between **reciprocal** pronouns and **reflexive** pronouns:

His parents blamed **themselves** for his bad behaviour. (**reflexive**)

His parents blamed **each other** for his bad behaviour. (**reciprocal**)

Some people like to reserve **each other** for a situation where only two are involved, but most people use **each other** and **one another** interchangeably, however many are involved.

 ISBN 978-81-8477-744-4

Exercise 1

Say in which person the personal pronoun is in the sentences below. One has been done for you.

1. Where is David? **He**'s sitting on the wall.

   (______third person singular______)

2. Was the weather good? No, **it** rained all week.

   (________________________________)

3. Boys, don't forget to take your sandwiches with **you**.

   (________________________________)

4. Susan and Jane missed the bus, so **they** were late.

   (________________________________)

5. Hi, Sally! **You** look very smart today!

   (________________________________)

6. Mum says **she**'ll phone later.

   (________________________________)

7. Miss Lee thanked Harry for helping **her**.

   (________________________________)

8. Hello, Mum! **We**'re home!

   (________________________________)

9. Come and play with Jenny and **me**.

   (________________________________)

10. The message from George says please phone **him** this evening.

    (________________________________)

 ISBN 978-81-8477-744-4

11. Dad drove **us** to our dancing class.

    (______________________________)

12. Pick up your jeans and fold **them** neatly.

    (______________________________)

Exercise 2

Fill in the correct personal pronoun in the following sentences. One has been done for you.

1. Take this note and give ____ it ____ to your parents.
2. Joe said __________ couldn't come to the party.
3. Where are my glasses ? Oh, here __________ are, on the table.
4. Call Anna and tell __________ dinner is ready.
5. Hello, Sam! Are __________ going to the swimming pool?
6. If there's anything missing, just add __________ to the list.
7. Helen is staying at home today because __________ has a cold.
8. Good morning, Miss Lee! May __________ carry that

   bag for __________?
9. In the classroom, __________ each have our own pegs to hang our bags on.
10. My twin brother and __________ are very alike; people

    often mix __________ up.
11. Pick up your chairs quietly and put __________ on top of your desks.
12. Harry had a sore throat, so Mum took __________ to the doctor.

 ISBN 978-81-8477-744-4

Exercise 3

Fill in the correct reflexive pronouns in the following sentences. One has been done for you.

1. Did you hurt ___yourself___ when you fell over?
2. Mum baths the baby but I bath ____________.
3. All the guests helped ____________ to food and drink.
4. We are looking at ____________ in the mirror.
5. Can you all look after ____________ while I go out for a minute?
6. Susan is making ____________ a skirt.
7. Jim, did you build that model all by ____________?
8. A cat spends a lot of time licking ____________ all over.
9. I know the door is locked because I locked it ____________.
10. The castle ____________ isn't open to visitors, but the garden is.
11. Children may burn ____________ if they play with matches.
12. Ben has locked ____________ in his bedroom.

 ISBN 978-81-8477-744-4

3 Adjectives

Read the following passage. The items in bold are all adjectives or adjectival phrases.

A ban on smoking

Dear Anne

I am really enjoying my **three-week Irish** trip. The people are very **helpful** and **friendly** and all around there is **lovely**, **fertile**, **green** countryside. They say that the land is **green** because it is **wetter** than most other places, but there have been **cloudless** skies, so far.

I'm staying in a **beautiful little** town. It's just as **pretty** as my village at home, if not **prettier**. The area is **mountainous** and I feel so **energetic**! At home, as you know, I tend to be **inactive**. I have become a lot **healthier** because of the climbing.

In fact, I am in the **healthiest** state that I've been in for many years, partly because of the ban on **smoking in public places** in Ireland. As you know, I've taken a **part-time** job in a computer firm and I assumed that smoking would be **forbidden** in the office. However, it is also banned in bars and restaurants. When I heard this, I was so **happy**. It was a **marvellous** discovery for a dedicated non-smoker like myself! Indeed, I was so **thrilled** that I nearly decided to make Ireland my **permanent** home. As it is, I am going to get a **later** flight home.

At first, it seemed **inconceivable** to me that I could have a drink or a meal without inhaling someone's cigarette smoke. An evening out is so much **pleasanter** now. Both food and wine are much **better** and **tastier**. I presume the **heaviest** smokers now stay at home.

I'm encouraging my friend Pete to stop smoking, which is not **easy**. In fact, it is extremely **difficult**. However, he is finding the wearing of nicotine patches quite **successful** and I am **hopeful** that he'll soon be a non-smoker!

Love

Jim

 ISBN 978-81-8477-744-4

An **adjective** is a **describing word**. It describes people or things. Words for people and things are nouns, so adjectives describe nouns.

Adjectives often come **before** the noun they describe.

a **beautiful** princess
a **noisy** classroom
a **cruel** emperor
a **brave** soldier

a **sharp** knife
a **good** boss
a **big** balloon
a **large** house

a **polite** boy
a **dirty** floor
a **tiny** insect
a **close** friend

a **cold** day
a **sour** fruit
a **red** dress
a **kind** lady

Adjectives can come **after** the person or thing they describe, later in the sentence.

Honey is **sweet**.
This sum is **difficult**.
John's handwriting is **neat**.
The bus is very **crowded**.
Why are you so **impatient**?
Those flowers are **beautiful**.
The children are keeping **quiet**.
Everyone is **equal** before the law.
Pinocchio's nose grew **longer** and **longer**.

The sea is **rough** today.
The water is very **hot**.
The lady was **kind** to us.

Adjectives have lots of endings.

Some adjectives end in **-ful**.

a **helpful** policeman
a **forgetful** man
a **respectful** bow
a **graceful** dance
a **wonderful** holiday
a **joyful** smile
a **sorrowful** face

beautiful flowers
a **delightful** garden
a **successful** shot
cheerful children
powerful muscles
colourful clothes
a **useful** tool

a **skilful** juggler
a **peaceful** view
playful puppies
an **awful** mess
a **faithful** dog
a **painful** bruise

joy + ful

joy + less

*The vowel **u** in **useful** and **useless** sounds like the word **you**. These words sound as if they begin with the consonant **y**, so you use **a** before them, not **an**.*

 ISBN 978-81-8477-744-4

Nouns
Pronouns
Adjectives
Determiners
Verbs
Adverbs
Prepositions
Conjunctions
Interjections
Sentences
Phrases
Clauses
More about Sentences
Direct and Indirect Speech
Punctuation

Some adjectives end in -less.

a **meaningless** word	**flightless** birds	a **careless** boy
homeless refugees	a **fearless** soldier	a **joyless** life
a **hopeless** player	a **merciless** king	a **leafless** tree
a **sleeveless** dress	a **spotless** floor	a **lawless** town
harmless animals	a **cordless** phone	a **cloudless** sky
weightless astronauts	**seedless** grapes	a **useless** car

Word Power

- **The -ful endings usually mean full of, filled with or having a lot. For example:**

  powerful *means* having a lot of power
  joyful *means* full of joy

- **The -less endings usually mean without. For example:**

  leafless *means* without leaves
  fearless *means* without fear

Did you know?

- **You can also add -ful to nouns like spoon and cup to form new nouns to talk about amounts. For example, you can say:**

  a **spoonful** of medicine
  a **mouthful** of jelly
  a **pocketful** of coins
  a **handful** of beans
  two **cupfuls** of flour

Here are some pairs of adjectives that begin with the same word ending with -ful or -less. Sometimes you can use the -less adjective as the opposite of the -ful adjective.

Adjective + ful	Adjective + less	Adjective + ful	Adjective + less
careful	careless	colourful	colourless
cheerful	cheerless	fearful	fearless
faithful	faithless	fruitful	fruitless
harmful	harmless	hopeful	hopeless
joyful	joyless	meaningful	meaningless
merciful	merciless	powerful	powerless
painful	painless	useful	useless

Some adjectives end in -ous.

a **courageous** soldier	a **poisonous** snake	a **famous** author
an **adventurous** climber	**numerous** awards	a **serious** mistake
a **furious** customer	a **victorious** team	a **generous** gift
a **dangerous** place	a **ferocious** animal	a **notorious** gang
a **mountainous** area	a **glorious** victory	**studious** pupils
mischievous boys	a **rigorous** training	**precious** stones
nervous competitors	a **humorous** book	an **enormous** hat

 ISBN 978-81-8477-744-4

- Some adjectives end in **-y**. Many of these adjectives are formed by adding **-y** to a noun.

a **thirsty** runner
a **hairy** monster
a **gloomy** look
a **noisy** machine
a **dirty** street
sleepy passengers
baggy trousers
dusty furniture

a **rusty** anchor
a **sunny** day
a **misty** view
a **furry** kitten
a **muddy** road
a **funny** hat
a **smoky** room
healthy food

a **messy** bed
a **cloudy** sky
a **windy** day
a **stormy** sea
a **skinny** boy
a **witty** joke
juicy apples
rainy weather

Grammar Help

- You add **-y** to each of these nouns to form the adjective.

Noun	Adjective	Noun	Adjective	Noun	Adjective
cloud	cloudy	mess	messy	sleep	sleepy
dirt	dirty	mist	misty	storm	stormy
dust	dusty	rain	rainy	speed	speedy
health	healthy	rust	rusty	greed	greedy

- If the noun ends with a consonant, but with a vowel before it, you double the final letter before adding **-y** to form the adjective.

Noun	Adjective	Noun	Adjective	Noun	Adjective
bag	baggy	fun	funny	star	starry
fog	foggy	mud	muddy	sun	sunny
fur	furry	skin	skinny	smog	smoggy

- If the noun ends in **-e**, you usually take away the e before you add **-y** to form the adjective.

Noun	Adjective	Noun	Adjective
ease + y	easy	smoke + y	smoky
haze + y	hazy	stone + y	stony
juice + y	juicy	taste + y	tasty
lace + y	lacy	wave + y	wavy

- Some adjectives end in **-ing**.

chattering monkeys
disappointing results
matching clothes
an **interesting** book
an **outstanding** swimmer
shocking behaviour

a **refreshing** drink
a **daring** leap
a **rewarding** job
an **exciting** ride
a **flashing** light
running water
a **charming** smile

a **smiling** face
a **gleaming** car
a **swishing** tail
a **caring** nurse
loving parents
pouring rain
a **boring** story

Grammar Help

Words like **smiling**, **caring** and **pouring** are present participles. Many present participles can be used as adjectives.

 ISBN 978-81-8477-744-4

Some adjectives end in -ed.

satisfied customers
a **disappointed** person
worried passengers
an **abandoned** ship
escaped prisoners
classified advertisements

a **haunted** house
trained workmen
a **divided** nation
our **loved** ones
a **closed** door
a **painted** wall

reduced prices
boiled eggs
dried fruit
added value
wasted time
armed robbery

Grammar Help

The adjectives such as **haunted**, **closed** and **added** are **past participles** of the regular verbs **haunt**, **close** and **add**. Many past participles are used as adjectives.

Some adjectives end in -en.

a **wooden** table
a **woollen** sweater
frozen food

silken thread
a **golden** egg
a **hidden** picture

a **rotten** apple
a **drunken** soldier

Grammar Help

- Some adjectives ending with **-en** mean **made of something**, like **woollen**, **wooden** and **golden**.
- Others are the past participles of verbs, like **frozen**, from the verb **freeze**. Here are some more examples:
  - a **broken** leg (from **break**)
  - a **swollen** face (from **swell**)
  - a **woven** fabric (from **weave**)
  - **spoken** English (from **speak**)
  - **written** Chinese (from **write**)
  - **stolen** watches (from **steal**)

wool

woollen

wood

wooden

Some adjectives end in -al.

medical equipment
a **naval** commander
botanical gardens
musical instruments
a **traditional** dance
personal belongings

tropical fruits
electrical goods
national costumes
parental love
internal organs
a **natural** disaster

magical power
a **coastal** town
a **bridal** gown
a **loyal** friend
a **visual** display
virtual reality

 ISBN 978-81-8477-744-4

Some adjectives end in -ic.

a **gigantic** spider
a **volcanic** island
an **energetic** boy
the **metric** system
basic **arithmetic**
patriotic citizens
enthusiastic clapping
exotic fruits and plants
botanic gardens

a **heroic** act
a **majestic** arch
a **scenic** highway
comic books
a **drastic** action
fantastic food
artistic talent
a **magic** trick

a **public** place
a **tragic** accident
aerobic exercises

Word Power

You can say **botanic gardens** or **botanical gardens.**

Some adjectives end in -ive.

an **attentive** class
an **attractive** design
an **innovative** idea
collective nouns
festive decorations
a **massive** explosion
a **subjective** opinion
an **expensive** necklace
a **defensive** action
offensive weapons

talkative girls
creative pupils
defective goods
adhesive tape
captive animals
an **active** baby
an **objective** view
negative reply
a **positive** answer
an **effective** tool

*Another word for **expensive** is **costly.***
Subjective** is the opposite of **objective.
Offensive** is the opposite of **defensive.
Positive** is the opposite of **negative.

Some adjectives end in -ish.

a **British** police officer
a **lavish** wedding reception
a **Spanish** dance
a **Danish** pastry
a **sheepish** smile
a **youngish** man
a **sluggish** stream
childish behaviour

a **foolish** action
a **feverish** illness
a **smallish** person
girlish giggles

a **boyish** look
a **selfish** child
ticklish feet
stylish shoes

*You can add **-ish** to colour adjectives like **red, green, yellow, pink** when you want to say that something is slightly red or green or yellow or pink. For example, you can say:*
***yellowish** paper* ***pinkish** skin*

 ISBN 978-81-8477-744-4

Nouns
Pronouns
Adjectives
Determiners
Verbs
Adverbs
Prepositions
Conjunctions
Interjections
Sentences
Phrases
Clauses
More about Sentences
Direct and Indirect Speech
Punctuation

Some adjectives end in -ly.

a **yearly** inspection
a **daily** newspaper
an **elderly** woman

*Another word for **elderly** is **old**.*

a **sprightly** old lady
an **hourly** broadcast
a **weekly** magazine

a **cowardly** act
a **kindly** remark
a **leisurely** walk
a **costly** diamond
monthly meetings
a **deadly** weapon
a **lovely** garden
a **friendly** hug
motherly love

a **sickly** child
a **lonely** child
lively kittens

Did you know?
Many **adverbs** also end in **-ly**.

Some adjectives end in -able.

a **memorable** journey
a **comfortable** chair
a **dependable** staff
a **forgivable** mistake
a **reputable** company

a **readable** book
a **durable** watch
a **washable** dress
a **valuable** vase
a **capable** manager

a **curable** disease
a **lovable** koala

***Lovable** can also be spelt **loveable**.*

Some adjectives end in -ible.

a **terrible** mess
compatible software
a **credible** story
a **visible** improvement
edible mushrooms
inedible meat
legible handwriting
illegible handwriting
a **combustible** material
a **responsible** person
a **possible** solution
an **impossible** mission

a **horrible** smell
a **feasible** project
incredible speed
invisible ink

Word Power
Incredible is the opposite of **credible**.
Impossible is the opposite of **possible**.
Invisible is the opposite of **visible**.
Inedible is the opposite of **edible**.
Illegible is the opposite of **legible**.

Adjective endings

-ful -less -ous -y -ic -ing -ly
-en -ed -al -ish -ive -ible -able

 ISBN 978-81-8477-744-4

Kinds of Adjectives

There are several different kinds of adjectives.

- Some adjectives tell you the **colour** of things.

an **orange** balloon
an **amber** traffic light
a **blue** uniform
a **cream** blouse
green peppers

a **red** carpet
a **white** swan
a **grey** suit
a **purple** skirt
pink shoes

a **black** panther
a **brown** bear
a **yellow** ribbon
a **violet** scarf

- Some adjectives tell you about the **size** of people or things.

a **large** house
a **large** army
a **little** bird
a **little** hut
a **high** shelf
a **high** mountain
a **huge** sum of money

a **huge** ship
a **tall** building
a **tall** person
a **short** skirt
a **short** man
a **long** bridge
a **long** journey

tiny insects
tiny feet
small flowers
a **small** car
a **thin** slice
a **thin** boy

Grammar Help

- You use **tall** to describe people and narrow upright objects. For example, you can say:

  a **tall** girl　　a **tall** building　　a **tall** player　　a **tall** tree

- You use **high** to describe objects that reach a great height, or are a long way off the ground. For example, you can say:

  a **high** cliff　　a **high** wall
  She is not **tall** enough to reach the **high** bookshelf.

- Here are some more adjectives that describe the size of people or things.

a **big** box
a **big** crowd
a **broad** smile
broad shoulders
a **fat** parcel
fat sumo wrestlers
a **thick** piece of bread

a **thick** wall
a **thick** book
thick clothing
a **wide** road
a **wide** river
a **narrow** door
a **narrow** lane

a **low** fence
low prices
a **giant** balloon
an **enormous** house
a **large** amount of water
a **mini** dictionary
a **high** ceiling

 ISBN 978-81-8477-744-4

Some adjectives tell you what people or things are like. They describe their quality.

a **beautiful** princess	a **young** soldier	a **poor** family
a **successful** businessman	a **familiar** voice	a **rich** couple
an **important** person	a **popular** singer	a **deep** pool
a **handsome** prince	a **sharp** corner	a **flat** surface
anxious moments	a **strange** place	a **special** gift
a **warm** welcome	a **lucky** number	a **cold** winter
a **frank** discussion	**sweet** dreams	**fine** weather
a **common** plant	a **violent** temper	a **lovely** day

Nouns
Pronouns
Adjectives
Determiners
Verbs
Adverbs
Prepositions
Conjunctions
Interjections
Sentences
Phrases
Clauses
More about Sentences
Direct and Indirect Speech
Punctuation

Here are some more adjectives that describe quality.

a **great** composer	a **fierce** dog	a **busy** secretary
a **strong** man	a **clever** parrot	a **happy** face
a **wicked** witch	a **new** house	an **ugly** duckling
a **kind** fairy	an **angry** father	a **silly** clown
a **difficult** puzzle	a **simple** sum	a **nasty** smell
a **lazy** dog	a **proud** team	a **sad** look
	a **cheeky** boy	an **old** car

Grammar Help

Adjectives that describe shape, size or quality come **before colour** adjectives. For example:

a big **green** ball	a smart **grey** suit	a short **purple** skirt
little **red** berries	a fierce **black** dog	large round **blue** eyes

Some adjectives tell you which place or country a person or thing comes from or belongs to. They are called adjectives of origin.

a **Japanese** lady	an **Indian** temple	**Thai** boxing
a **Balinese** dancer	an **Italian** car	**Dutch** clogs
an **English** police officer	a **Filipino** dress	the **French** flag
a **Scottish** outfit	**Chinese** kungfu	a **Mexican** hat
Australian apples	a **Malay** kris	

Grammar Help

Adjectives that describe shape, size or quality come **before** adjectives of origin. For example:

a tall **English** police officer	a fat **American** cigar
a beautiful **Indian** temple	a fast **Italian** car
a colourful **Scottish** outfit	juicy **Australian** apples

 ISBN 978-81-8477-744-4

Some adjectives tell you what type of thing something is, or what material it is made of.

These are sometimes called classifying adjectives.

a **mathematical** problem
a **medical** centre
botanical gardens
wooden shoes
a **silk** dress
a **gold** ring
a **financial** report
a **chemical** formula
an **electric** guitar
plastic chairs
a **steel** knife
a **diamond** necklace

Grammar Help

Adjectives that describe size, shape or quality come **before** classifying adjectives. For example:

a long **financial** report
heavy **wooden** shoes
a difficult **mathematical** problem
an expensive **diamond** ring
extensive **botanical** gardens
a new **medical** centre

You can turn some adjectives into nouns when you add the before them.

the rich
the poor
the sick
the healthy
the strong
the living
the elderly
the weak
the young
the old
the disabled
the deaf
the faithful
the powerful
the unemployed
the blind
the lame
the homeless
the dead
the underprivileged
the privileged

Did you know?

These nouns refer to groups of people, so they are **plural nouns.** For example, you can say:

The rich (meaning rich people) have a duty to help **the poor** (meaning poor people).

The young (meaning young people) have a duty to help **the old** (meaning old people).

The strong (meaning strong people) have a duty to help **the weak** (meaning weak people).

 ISBN 978-81-8477-744-4

Adjectival Phrases

Some adjectives are made up of more than one word. They are called adjectival phrases.

a **two-year-old** child
a **five-cent** coin
a **ten-storey** building
a **seventy-foot** yacht
a **well-known** writer
a **well-dressed** lady
a **soft-spoken** person
a **wide-angle** lens

a **kind-hearted** boss
a **long-distance** call
a **long-legged** bird
a **leather-bound** book
a **user-friendly** computer
world-class athletes
third-year students
old-fashioned ideas

Did you know?

When an adjectival phrase is used before a noun, you join the words up with **hyphens**.

- **Some adjectival phrases that describe nouns come after them.**

The boy **on the bicycle** is riding too fast.
Do you see that girl **with long hair**?
I tried on a pair of shoes **with high heels**.
People **in flats** can't make too much noise.
My best friend lives in that house **across the road**.
Sally sits at the desk **next to mine**.
Which is the road **to Taipei**?
This is the main door **into the supermarket**.
I prefer books **with pictures** to books **without pictures**.
The lady **in the bookshop** is a friend of my Mum's.

Grammar Help

- All the phrases here begin with **prepositions**. The prepositions here are **in, with, on, across, next to, without, to** and **into**.
- Phrases that begin with prepositions can be called **prepositional phrases**.

 ISBN 978-81-8477-744-4

Synonyms and Antonyms

Synonyms are pairs of words that have the same or similar meanings.

Here are pairs of adjectives that are synonyms.

beautiful — pretty

***Attractive** also means the same as **beautiful**.*

rich — wealthy
active — lively
big — large

***Huge** and **enormous** also mean the same as **big**.*

expensive — costly
wide — broad
fast — quick
small — tiny

***Little** also means the same as **small**.*

old — elderly

simple — easy
good — admirable
able — capable
bad — naughty
bold — brave
circular — round
close — near
correct — right
crazy — mad
difficult — hard
neat — tidy
nice — pleasant
quiet — silent
sad — unhappy
silly — foolish
strong — powerful
clever — smart

Antonyms are pairs of words that have opposite meanings. Here are pairs of adjectives that are antonyms.

beautiful — ugly
bright — dark
deep — shallow
hard — soft
heavy — light
curved — straight
kind — cruel
loose — tight
quiet — noisy
rich — poor
simple — difficult
alive — dead
clever — stupid

cold — hot
cool — warm
different — similar
dry — wet
expensive — cheap
high — low
loud — soft
transparent — opaque
rough — smooth
straight — crooked
strong — weak
wide — narrow
wild — tame

 ISBN 978-81-8477-744-4

Nouns
Pronouns
Adjectives
Determiners
Verbs
Adverbs
Prepositions
Conjunctions
Interjections
Sentences
Phrases
Clauses
More about Sentences
Direct and Indirect Speech
Punctuation

Comparison of Adjectives

Adjectives have a form called the **comparative**. You use it when you are comparing two things or people. You add **-er** to the adjectives to make the **comparative** form.

Here are some adjectives with their **comparative** form.

	Comparative		Comparative
clean	cleaner	thick	thicker
dark	darker	warm	warmer
dear	dearer	broad	broader
deep	deeper	clear	clearer
firm	firmer	fair	fairer
high	higher	few	fewer
low	lower	grand	grander
old	older	hard	harder
poor	poorer	keen	keener
quick	quicker	neat	neater
soft	softer	proud	prouder
tall	taller	slow	slower

Grammar Help

You use the word **than** when you compare two things or people. For example, you say:

Nick is 12 years old.
Diana is 10 years old.
Nick is **older than** Diana.
Nick is **the older** of the two.

Mary is 1.37 m tall.
Helen is 1.40 m tall.
Helen is **taller than** Mary.
Helen is **the taller** of the two.

Adjectives have another form called the **superlative**. You use it when you are comparing **three or more** things or people. You add **-est** to the adjectives to make the **superlative** form.

Here are some adjectives with their **superlative** form.

		Superlative			Superlative
clean	cleaner	cleanest	warm	warmer	warmest
dark	darker	darkest	broad	broader	broadest
dear	dearer	dearest	clear	clearer	clearest
deep	deeper	deepest	fair	fairer	fairest
firm	firmer	firmest	fast	faster	fastest
low	lower	lowest	few	fewer	fewest
old	older	oldest	grand	grander	grandest
poor	poorer	poorest	hard	harder	hardest
quick	quicker	quickest	keen	keener	keenest
soft	softer	softest	neat	neater	neatest
tall	taller	tallest	proud	prouder	proudest
thick	thicker	thickest	slow	slower	slowest

Grammar Help

You often add **the** before the superlative adjective. For example, you say:

Mary is **tall**.
Helen is **taller** than Mary.
But Janet is **the tallest** of the three.

The horse is **fast**.
The deer is **faster** than the horse.
But the cheetah is **the fastest** of the three.

 ISBN 978-81-8477-744-4

Here are some adjectives with their **comparative** and **superlative** forms.

	Comparative	Superlative
bright	**brighter**	**brightest**
tough	**tougher**	**toughest**
cheap	**cheaper**	**cheapest**
long	**longer**	**longest**
clever	**cleverer**	**cleverest**
cold	**colder**	**coldest**
cool	**cooler**	**coolest**
kind	**kinder**	**kindest**
light	**lighter**	**lightest**
smooth	**smoother**	**smoothest**
short	**shorter**	**shortest**
rough	**rougher**	**roughest**
brave	**braver**	**bravest**

If the adjective ends in -e, you just add -r to form the comparative, and -st to form the superlative.

	Comparative	Superlative
close	**closer**	**closest**
fine	**finer**	**finest**
large	**larger**	**largest**
rude	**ruder**	**rudest**
safe	**safer**	**safest**
wide	**wider**	**widest**

Look at these adjectives. They have only one syllable, end with a consonant, and have a single vowel before the consonant. You double the last letter of these adjectives before adding **-er** to form the comparative, and **-est** to form the superlative.

	Comparative	Superlative
big	**bigger**	**biggest**
dim	**dimmer**	**dimmest**
fat	**fatter**	**fattest**
fit	**fitter**	**fittest**
flat	**flatter**	**flattest**

 ISBN 978-81-8477-744-4

	Comparative	Superlative
hot	hotter	hottest
mad	madder	maddest
red	redder	reddest
sad	sadder	saddest
slim	slimmer	slimmest
thin	thinner	thinnest
wet	wetter	wettest

- For some adjectives with **two syllables**, you add **-er** to the **comparative** form, and **-est** to the **superlative** form. If the adjective ends in **-e**, you just add **-r** to form the **comparative**, and **-st** to form the superlative.

	Comparative	Superlative
near	nearer	nearest
common	commoner	commonest
gentle	gentler	gentlest
narrow	narrower	narrowest
pleasant	pleasanter	pleasantest
polite	politer	politest
quiet	quieter	quietest
remote	remoter	remotest
shallow	shallower	shallowest
simple	simpler	simplest
stupid	stupider	stupidest

- Adjectives with two syllables that end in **-y** have a special rule for the comparative and superlative forms. You change the **y** to **i**, and then add **-er** or **-est**.

	Comparative	Superlative
busy	busier	busiest
dirty	dirtier	dirtiest
easy	easier	easiest
funny	funnier	funniest
noisy	noisier	noisiest
happy	happier	happiest
heavy	heavier	heaviest
juicy	juicier	juiciest
lovely	lovelier	loveliest
pretty	prettier	prettiest
tidy	tidier	tidiest

Did you know?

A **syllable** is a sound that makes a word or part of a word.

A word with two syllables has two sounds. For example:

clever	clev-er
polite	po-lite
common	com-mon
quiet	qui-et
simple	sim-ple
narrow	nar-row
stupid	stu-pid

Spell Well

Here are three adjectives which end with -y, but they don't all form comparatives and superlatives the same way:

dry	drier	driest
shy	shyer	shyest
sly	slyer	slyest

 ISBN 978-81-8477-744-4

- Most other adjectives with two syllables use **more** to form their comparative, and **most** to form their superlative.

	Comparative	Superlative
active	**more** active	**most** active
brutal	**more** brutal	**most** brutal
careless	**more** careless	**most** careless
charming	**more** charming	**most** charming
foolish	**more** foolish	**most** foolish
famous	**more** famous	**most** famous
hectic	**more** hectic	**most** hectic
precious	**more** precious	**most** precious
zealous	**more** zealous	**most** zealous
cheerful	**more** cheerful	**most** cheerful
harmful	**more** harmful	**most** harmful

- Adjectives with **three** or **more syllables** use **more** to form their comparative, and **most** to form their superlative.

	Comparative	Superlative
beautiful	**more** beautiful	**most** beautiful
capable	**more** capable	**most** capable
confident	**more** confident	**most** confident
difficult	**more** difficult	**most** difficult
delicious	**more** delicious	**most** delicious
expensive	**more** expensive	**most** expensive
fortunate	**more** fortunate	**most** fortunate
generous	**more** generous	**most** generous
poisonous	**more** poisonous	**most** poisonous
powerful	**more** powerful	**most** powerful
comfortable	**more** comfortable	**most** comfortable
competitive	**more** competitive	**most** competitive
disappointed	**more** disappointed	**most** disappointed
dissatisfied	**more** dissatisfied	**most** dissatisfied
embarrassing	**more** embarrassing	**most** embarrassing
imaginative	**more** imaginative	**most** imaginative
intelligent	**more** intelligent	**most** intelligent
interesting	**more** interesting	**most** interesting
reasonable	**more** reasonable	**most** reasonable
valuable	**more** valuable	**most** valuable

 ISBN 978-81-8477-744-4

Grammar Help

With some adjectives, you can use either the **-er, -est** forms, or the **more, most** forms. For example:

polite	polite**r**	polite**st**
polite	**more** polite	**most** polite
common	common**er**	common**est**
common	**more** common	**most** common
stupid	stupid**er**	stupid**est**
stupid	**more** stupid	**most** stupid

Did you know?

- These adjectives have three syllables:

beautiful	**beau-ti-ful**	expensive	**ex-pen-sive**
capable	**ca-pa-ble**	fortunate	**for-tu-nate**
confident	**con-fi-dent**	generous	**gen-e-rous**
delicious	**de-li-cious**	poisonous	**poi-son-ous**
difficult	**dif-fi-cult**	powerful	**pow-er-ful**

- These adjectives have more than three syllables:

comfortable	**com-for-ta-ble**	imaginative	**i-ma-gi-na-tive**
competitive	**com-pet-i-tive**	intelligent	**in-tel-li-gent**
disappointed	**dis-ap-point-ed**	embarrassing	**em-bar-ras-sing**
interesting	**in-te-res-ting**	dissatisfied	**dis-sat-is-fied**
reasonable	**rea-son-a-ble**	valuable	**val-u-a-ble**

- Here are some adjectives that have irregular comparative and superlative forms. You don't add **-er** or use **more** for the comparative; and you don't add **-est** or use **most** for the superlative.

	Comparative	Superlative
good	better	best
bad	worse	worst
many	more	most
much	more	most
little	less	least
far	farther	farthest

Word Power

Good is an adjective.

Goods is a noun, and is used in the **plural.**

good

better

best

Did you know?

- The comparative and superlative forms of **far** can also be **further** and **furthest.**
- You use **farther, farthest** for distance.

  Further, furthest can be used for distance and other meanings. For example:

  Which planet is **farthest** from the sun?
  Further instructions will be sent later.

 ISBN 978-81-8477-744-4

Numbers

It may surprise you, but a number is a kind of adjective too. It tells you how many people, things or animals there are.

one polar bear
two birds
three cats
four puppies
five ducks
six chicks
seven owls
eight rabbits
nine bats
ten butterflies
eleven pizzas

twelve months

*Twelve is a **dozen**.*

thirteen pens
fourteen hamburgers
fifteen books
sixteen rings
seventeen cups
eighteen caps
nineteen watches
twenty masks

Word Power

Here are some more numbers you need to know.

twenty-one	21
twenty-two	22
thirty	30
forty	40
fifty	50
sixty	60
seventy	70
eighty	80
ninety	90
one hundred	100
one thousand	1,000
ten thousand	10,000
one hundred thousand	100,000
one million	1,000,000
ten million	10,000,000
one hundred million	100,000,000
one billion (one thousand million)	1,000,000,000

*You spell **forty** without the **u**.*

Did you know?

When it is clear what noun a number refers to, you can leave out the noun. For example, you can say:

How many cats can you see? — Three.
Have we plenty of cups? — We have **seventeen**.

 ISBN 978-81-8477-744-4

- **Numbers like first, second, third are also adjectives. They tell you about the order of people and things when they follow one after the other. These numbers are called ordinal numbers.**

The **first** month of the year is January.
The **second** month of the year is February.
The **third** month of the year is March.
The **fourth** month of the year is April.
The **fifth** month of the year is May.
The **sixth** month of the year is June.
The **seventh** month of the year is July.
The **eighth** month of the year is August.
The **ninth** month of the year is September.
The **tenth** month of the year is October.
The **eleventh** month of the year is November.
The **twelfth** month of the year is December.

Did you know?

- **You can leave out the noun after an ordinal number if it is clear what noun you are referring to. For example, you can say:**

  Is August the seventh month of the year?
  No, it's the **eighth**.

- **When you talk about days of the week, you are referring to Sunday, Monday, Tuesday, Wednesday, Thursday, Friday and Saturday. For example:**

  What day is today? It's Monday.

- **When you talk about the day, the month, and sometimes the year, you are talking about the date. Here are some ways of asking for and giving dates:**

  What's the **date** today?
  The **date** today is 20th June.
  What **date** is it today?
  Today's **date** is the 20th of June.
  What **date** is your birthday?
  It's the 3rd of August.

Word Power

Here are some more ordinal numbers:

13th	**thirteenth**	19th	**nineteenth**
14th	**fourteenth**	20th	**twentieth**
15th	**fifteenth**	21st	**twenty-first**
16th	**sixteenth**	22nd	**twenty-second**
17th	**seventeenth**	23rd	**twenty-third**
18th	**eighteenth**		

 ISBN 978-81-8477-744-4

Exercise 1

Forming Adjectives (1)

- You often form adjectives by adding an ending to a **noun.**
- There are many different endings that form adjectives.

Choose an ending from the box to form adjectives from the nouns below. You will have to use some endings more than once. Two have already been done for you.

-able	-al	-ful	-ic	-ish
-ive	-less	-ly	-ous	-y

1. effect effective
2. leisure leisurely
3. music ______
4. self ______
5. rain ______
6. danger ______
7. dust ______
8. peace ______
9. week ______
10. artist ______
11. mass ______
12. home ______
13. comfort ______
14. success ______
15. person ______

Exercise 2

Put the adjectives into the gaps below, in the right order. One has been done for you.

1. a strange purple Indonesian fish **(purple, Indonesian, strange)**
2. ______ books **(academic, thick, big)**
3. a ______ tree **(narrow, dark-green, tall)**
4. ______ air hostesses **(Singaporean, charming, young)**
5. ______ clouds **(fluffy, small, white)**
6. some ______ tourists **(English, noisy)**

 ISBN 978-81-8477-744-4

7. a ______________________ box (**cardboard, square, large**)

8. a ______________________ pop group (**crazy, American**)

9. those ______________________ insects (**stinging, red, nasty, tiny**)

10. a ______________________ (**grey, stone, high**)

11. a ______________________ magazine (**geographical, new, wonderful**)

12. ______________________ leaves (**pointed, yellow, long**)

Exercise 3

Choose a synonym from the box to write beside each of the words in the list below. One has been done for you.

~~difficult~~	easy	extensive	firm
handsome	intelligent	noisy	slender
soft	splendid	studious	wide

1. hard difficult
2. clever ________
3. broad ________
4. marvellous ________
5. loud ________
6. thin ________
7. quiet ________
8. steady ________
9. good-looking ________
10. large ________
11. simple ________
12. hardworking ________

 ISBN 978-81-8477-744-4

Exercise 4

Choose an antonym from the box to write beside each of the words in the list below. One has been done for you.

slow	hollow	short	dull	gentle	graceful
light	narrow	early	thin	stingy	~~active~~

1. lazy	active	5. generous	________	9. late	________
2. bright	________	6. heavy	________	10. clumsy	________
3. rough	________	7. wide	________	11. tall	________
4. thick	________	8. fast	________	12. solid	________

Exercise 5

Fill in the correct form of the comparative or superlative in the following sentences.

1. The weather has been ________________ today than it was yesterday. **(good)**
2. Mike is the ________________ boy I know. **(handsome)**
3. The journey was much ________________ than we thought it would be. **(far)**
4. You're a lot ________________ than you used to be. **(thin)**
5. That's the ________________ joke anyone has told me for a long time! **(funny)**
6. The ________________ method of all is to book tickets through the Internet. **(simple)**
7. Watching a good video is the ________________ way to spend an evening. **(pleasant)**
8. Sally is the ________________ of all my friends. **(nice)**
9. Is lead ________________ than iron? **(heavy)**
10. That's the ________________ story I've ever heard. **(sad)**
11. Where is the ________________ place to cross the road? **(safe)**
12. The ________________ thing to say if someone thanks you is 'You're welcome!' **(polite)**

 ISBN 978-81-8477-744-4

4 DETERMINERS

Read the following passage. The items in bold are all types of determiners.

The sun and health

The usual message we get from medical experts is that **the** sun can be dangerous to **our** health. In **some** cases, we have been told, **its** rays can cause skin cancer. However, **an** article describing recent research conducted by an American team of experts at Harvard University gives an alternative message. The rays of the sun, **that** article suggests, can actually help to prevent cancer. These are two conflicting messages. **Which** message are we to believe?

For **several** years, **many** people have been acting on medical advice, either staying in the shade, keeping themselves covered, or rubbing **a lot of** sunscreen on **their** skin. They are mindful of the fact that **more** people are dying of skin cancer than ever before.

Of course, **some** people pay **little** or **no** attention to the advice and have gone on sunbathing without protection. **These** sunbathers are regarded as living dangerously, but will such an approach to the sun prove to be the right one after all? If so, **what** evidence is there for this?

The American report emphasizes the importance of vitamin D in the diet. It claims that an adequate level of vitamin D in **a** diet can reduce the risk of cancer by nearly a third. **What** connection does this have with sunbathing?

Well, the sun's rays play **an** important part in **our** production of vitamin D. Vitamin D is found in **some of** the food which **many of** us eat regularly—margarine, dairy products, eggs and oily fish. However, **most of** us, it appears, do not get **enough** vitamin D from our diet. We need the sun's contribution to make up the shortfall.

The solution to this dilemma is to adopt **a** middle course. Enjoy the sunshine for half-**an**-hour or so, but avoid over-exposure to **its** rays.

 ISBN 978-81-8477-744-4

There are some words called **determiners**, such as **this, my, some, a few, many,** which are used before nouns. They are a special kind of adjective.

The Articles

The **articles** belong to the class of words called **determiners.** The words **a, an** and **the** are the articles.

- The words **a** and **an** are called indefinite articles. You use **a** and **an** with singular count nouns.

Sam is reading **a magazine**.
Mum bought me **a dress** today.
Sssh! Can you hear **a bird** singing?
This is a picture of **an elephant**.
Who would like **an ice cream**?
Do you wear **a uniform** at school?
She looks like **a European**.
I live in **a house**, but **a mouse** lives in **a hole**.
Do you want **an apple** or **a pear** or **an orange**?
Bees live in **a hive** and build **a honeycomb**.
I have been waiting here for **an hour**.
I want to go to **a university** when I grow up.
The big book is called **an encyclopedia**.
An icon like this is called **an hourglass**.
Do you know what **a eucalyptus** tree looks like?
You write **a one** like this and you write **an i** like this.

Grammar Help

- Words for things that you can count are called count nouns. You use a before count nouns that begin with a consonant. The consonants are:
  b c d f g h j k
  l m n p q r s t
  v w x y z
- You use an before count nouns that begin with a vowel. The vowels are:
  a e i o u

Grammar Help

- The consonant h at the beginning of **hour** and **hourglass** is silent. **Hour** sounds the same as **our**, so you use an before it.
- The vowel u in **university** and **uniform**, and the vowels eu in **European** and **eucalyptus** sound like the word **you**. These words sound as if they begin with the consonant **y**. So you use **a** before them.
- The word **one** sounds as if it begins with the consonant **w**, so you use **a** before it.

 ISBN 978-81-8477-744-4

- **The word the is called the definite article.**
  You use the before a noun when you are talking about something or someone definite, and people know which thing or person you mean.

The telephone is ringing.
Granny is in **the garden**.
Who spilt juice on **the carpet**?
I have to go to **the dentist** today.
Tom has won **the race**.
The street is very busy today.
Shall I turn **the radio** on?
Dad is waiting in **the car.**
Where is **the cat**?
I think she's under **the bed.**
We are going to **the beach**.
Helen is laying **the table.**

Did you know?

- **The e in the has a short sound before words beginning with a consonant, like the words below:**

the carpet	the dentist	the television	the road
the nurse	the show	the sofa	the computer
the sitting room			

- **When you use the before a word beginning with a vowel, it has a different sound. You say it with a long e, like the sound in me or bee or tea.**

the umbrella	the apple	the orang-utan	the igloo
the exit	the abacus	the orange	the other hand
the ugly duckling			

- **The word university starts with a sound like the consonant y, so the e in the is short before university:**

  Mum teaches at the university.

- **The word one starts with a w sound, so the e in the is short before one:**

  Is this **the one** you wanted?

- **Here are some more sentences using a or the.**

Can someone open a **window**?
Please shut **the door.**
He is **the man** we are looking for.
The examination starts in five minutes.
Quiet! Here comes **the principal.**
The sea and **the sky** are grey today.
The sun has gone behind **a cloud.**
That's **a star** and that's **the moon.**
There's **a picture** on **the wall.**
A truck is blocking **the road.**
I won **a prize** in **the competition.**
I'd like **a book** about the beginning of **the world.**

 ISBN 978-81-8477-744-4

- **You can put adjectives between the articles and the nouns.**

That's **a** lovely **dress**.
Here's **a** sharp **pencil** for you.
Rex is **a** very lazy **dog**.
He is wearing **a** rather silly **hat**.
Is that **an** interesting **book**?
What **an** enormous **dog**!
Which of you is **the** best **runner**?
There is **a** beautiful **rainbow** in the sky.
The biggest **dinosaur** had a very small **head**.
Would you like **the** orange **mug**, or **the** blue **one**?
Who won **the** first **prize** in **the** writing **competition**?
Maggie was **the** only **person** who got **the** last **question** right.
They're building **a** new **bridge** to replace **the** old **one**.

Grammar Help

- You use **a** when there are several of the same kind of thing to choose from.
- You use **the** when there is only one.

- **Plural nouns can be used without an article.**

This is **a bee**.	**Bees** are **insects**.
This is **a cow**.	**Cows** are **animals**.
This is **a shark**.	**Sharks** are **fishes**.
This is **a parrot**.	**Parrots** are **birds**.
This is **a frog**.	**Frogs** are **amphibians**.
This is **a toy**.	**Babies** like **toys**.
This is **a statue**.	**Statues** are made by **sculptors**.
This is **a suit**.	**Suits** are made by **tailors**.
This is **a poem**.	**Poems** are composed by **poets**.
This is **a bridge**.	**Bridges** are built by **engineers**.

- **When you use the words my, your, his, her, its, our, their, or this, that, these, those with singular or plural nouns, they take the place of the.**

Our house is down **this road**.
Susan is combing **her hair**.
His bedroom is untidy.
Do **your grandparents** live in Singapore?
The cat is licking **its paw**.
This shirt is clean. **That shirt** is dirty.
Those vegetables are going mouldy. **These ones** are fresh.

 ISBN 978-81-8477-744-4

■ You can use the determiner **some** as the **plural** of the articles **a** and **an**.

Here is **a book**.
Here are **some books**.
There's **a horse** in the stable.
There are **some horses** in the field.
Sue's wearing **a flower** in her hair.
Have **a biscuit**.
I've bought you **some flowers**.
I found **some biscuits** in that tin.
Is that **a** spare **seat**?
No, but there are **some** spare **seats** at the back.

■ You usually use **any** instead of **some** after **not**, and you often use **any** in **questions** too.

I would like to buy **a melon**, please.

Sorry, we **haven't** **any melons** today.

I'd like **a ticket**.

Sorry, there **aren't** **any tickets** left.

There's **a picture** on the book cover.

Are there **any pictures** inside?

Isn't that **a** funny-looking **fly**?

I **can't** see **any flies**.

■ You can use **the** with **plural nouns** when you are referring to definite things, and people know which things you mean.

Let's open all **the windows**.
Marianne, please give out **the books**.
You've drawn **the eyes** too small and **the ears** too big.
The wheels are muddy.
We'd better wash **the dishes**.
I've just been making **the beds**.

■ You can also use the determiners **my, your, his, her, its, our, their, these** and **those** with **plural nouns**. If you use them with plural nouns, you don't use **the**.

Please hand in **your books**.
Now, where did I put **my running shoes**?
The mother bird is feeding **her babies**.
Will **his climbing boots** fit me?
Our grandparents live in Singapore.
These clothes are dirty.
Those clothes are clean.
Those vegetables are going mouldy. **These ones** are fresh.

 ISBN 978-81-8477-744-4

You don't use **a** or **an** with **uncount nouns.**

Water is wet.
Sugar is sweet.
We cannot live without **food**.
We get **wool** from sheep.
We get **milk** from cows.
We make **bread** from **wheat**.
Silkworms make **silk**.
Glass is made from **sand**.
Paper is made from **wood**.

Grammar Help

Uncount nouns are always **singular**. They are words for things you can't count.

You can use **some** and **any** with **uncount nouns.**

There's **some milk** in the fridge.
Thank you. I'd like **some bread** and **butter**.
Would you like **some food** before you leave?
Is there **any rice** left?
There isn't **any paper** in the printer.
I've got **some sand** in my shoes.

Wipe your feet.
I don't want **any mud** brought into the house.

We'll have **some wine** with our meal.
I don't think we've **any salt**.
I can't find **any glue**.
There's **some truth** in what you say.
How can you have **any doubt**?

Word Power

Here are some uncount nouns.

air	bread	cloth	dust	food	glass	milk	mud	paper
rice	salt	sand	silk	sugar	water	wine	wood	wool

You can use **the** with **uncount nouns** when you are talking about a particular lot of something, and people know what you are referring to.

Where's the **sugar**?
The butter is melting.
Put **the salt** on the table.
You haven't finished **the food**.
The cat has drunk **the milk**.
He has finished **the wine**.

Has **the mail** arrived?
The bread is stale.
May I use **the glue**?

 ISBN 978-81-8477-744-4

Nouns
Pronouns
Adjectives
Determiners
Verbs
Adverbs
Prepositions
Conjunctions
Interjections
Sentences
Phrases
Clauses
More about Sentences
Direct and Indirect Speech
Punctuation

- **When you are talking about people playing instruments, you usually put the before the instrument.**

Susan plays **the piano.**
Michael plays **the violin.**
Sara plays **the organ.**
John plays **the guitar.**
Henry plays **the trombone.**
Mary plays **the cello.**
Sally is playing a tune on **the clarinet.**

Peter is beating a rhythm on **the drums.**
Jim plays **the oboe** in the school orchestra.
I've always wanted to learn **the harp.**
My uncle is teaching me **the trumpet.**

- **You don't use the with the names of people or streets or places. But you use the before the names of rivers, seas, oceans, mountain ranges and important buildings and monuments.**

the Golden Gate Bridge
the Millennium Dome
the Straits of Gibraltar
the Statue of Liberty
the Atlantic Ocean
the Little Mermaid

the River Kwai
the Panama Canal
the Yellow Sea
the Taj Mahal
the Himalayas
the Pacific Ocean

the Rhine
the Nile
the Rockies
the Eiffel Tower
the Yangtze
the Alps

- **You often omit the before these words: home, school, work, church.**

We get the bus to **school** every morning.
What time does **school** begin?
Why isn't Tim at **school** today?
What time do you get home from **school**?
School finishes at 3.00 p.m.
Is your Dad at **home** ?
No, sorry. He is at **work**.
Mum goes to **work** every day.
She leaves for **work** at 7.30 a.m.
Mum isn't back from **work** yet.
Some people go to **church** on Sundays.
We left **church** at midday.

Grammar Help

In American English you can say somebody is home, instead of at home. For example:
Is your dad home?

 ISBN 978-81-8477-744-4

Demonstrative Determiners

The words this, that, these and those are determiners too. They are showing words. You use them to tell people which thing or person you mean. They are called demonstrative determiners.

You use this and that before singular nouns, and you use these and those before plural nouns.

James lives in **this** house.
This ice cream is delicious.
How much is **that** bag?
What is **that** animal?
Bring me **that** ball.
Stop **that** man!

Would you like **these** apples?
No, give me **those** apples.
These stamps are mine.
Who are **those** people?
I'm keeping **these** books.
I'm selling **those** books.

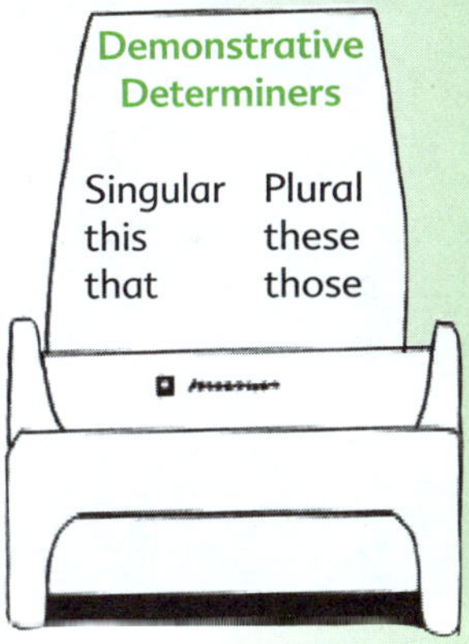

Interrogative Determiners

The question words what, which and whose are another set of determiners. You use them before nouns to ask about people or things. They are called interrogative determiners.

What time is it?
What size do you wear?
What colour is her hair?
What kind of bird is that?
What kind of clothes do you like to wear?

Which school do you go to?
Which doll is your favourite?
Which way leads to the zoo?
Which runner is the winner?
Do you know **which** train is going to London?

Whose footprints are these?
Whose baby is this?
Whose dog was barking in the middle of the night?

> **Grammar Help**
>
> **You can use which with of.**
> **For example:**
> Which of the mobiles do you prefer?

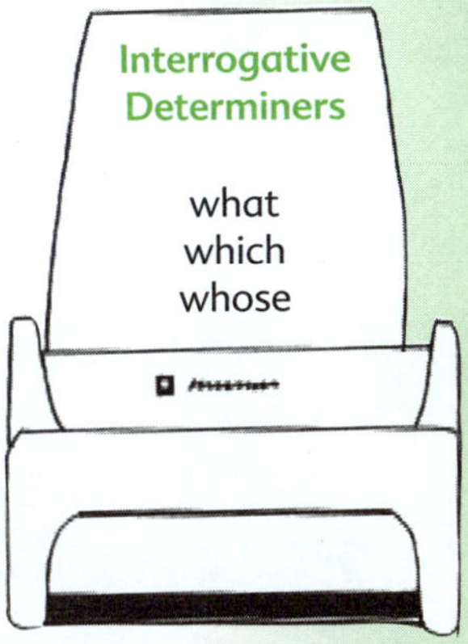

 ISBN 978-81-8477-744-4

Possessive Determiners

The words my, your, his, her, its, our, their are another set of determiners. They are called possessive determiners. You use them before nouns to say who something belongs to.

I lent Margaret **my** guitar.
Is this **your** house?
Robert, **your** handwriting is difficult to read.
Michael is showing **his** tortoise to his friends.
The dentist asked **his** patient to open **her** mouth.
My sister lost **her** way in the city.
The lion is chasing **its** prey.
We like **our** teacher, Miss Lee.
We always keep **our** classroom clean.
They are good at supporting **their** team.
The sailors put on **their** life jackets before jumping into the sea.

Did you know?

The possessive determiners my, your, his, her, its, our and their are also called possessive adjectives.

Grammar Help

- Here is a table to help you remember the **possessive determiners.**

	Singular	Plural
First person	my	our
Second person	your	your
Third person	his	their
	her	their
	its	their

- **Remember that the possessive determiners always come before a noun. For example:**

your pen　　my desk　　**her** case　　**our** seats

- **There is another way to say who owns something. You put an apostrophe (the ' sign) after a name or noun, and add s.**

When the noun is singular, the apostrophe comes before the s.

I took a ride in **John's** car.
Father is holding **Susie's** hand.
Jane is wearing her **mother's** shoes.
We're going to our **aunt's** house.
There is a **bird's** nest in that tree.
Our **dog's** collar is brown.
Is this **Singapore's** tallest building?

 ISBN 978-81-8477-744-4

- **When a name or a singular noun ends in -s, you use the same rule. You put the apostrophe first and then add another s.**

The **princess's** golden ball fell into a well.
A **rhinoceros's** skin is very thick.
A **hippopotamus's** legs are very short.
This is **James's** house.
Miss Lee is talking to **Charles's** parents.

- **For plural nouns that end in -s, you put the apostrophe after the -s.**

Birds' beaks are all different shapes and sizes.
This is my **parents'** wedding photo.
Dresses are upstairs in the **ladies'** department.
James goes to a **boys'** school.
The **girls'** changing rooms are over there.
Dr Kim parked his car in the **doctors'** car park.

- **Some plural nouns do not end in -s. With these plural nouns, the apostrophe comes before the -s.**

Dr Lee works in a **children's** hospital.
The **men's** changing room is occupied.
The newsagent sells newspapers, comics and **women's** magazines.
Doctors look after **people's** health.

Grammar Help

- You can refer to a **person's office or shop** by using a possessive form with an apostrophe. For example:

  I'll collect the bread from the **baker's**.
  I was reading a book at the **dentist's**.
  It's time you went to the **barber's**.

- You can also refer to **your friends' homes** like this too:

  I'm going round to **Peter's**. I stayed the night at **Susan's**.

- When you make a possessive form of **two people** joined by **and**, like **Peter and John**, or **Mary and Anne**, you put **'s** only after the second name. For example:

  Barbara and **David's** house Jill and **Micky's** party

- You can use these possessive forms of names and nouns without a following noun. For example:

  Which desk is **Susan's**? **George's** is on the back row.
  This room is my **brother's**.

 ISBN 978-81-8477-744-4

Quantifying Determiners

Quantifying determiners tell you about how many people or things there are without giving you the exact number or quantity.

a few cranes	**a lot** of animals	too **much** noise
a little ice cream	**a lot** of food	**not much** water
some pelicans	**lots of** fish	**no** bread
several kingfishers	**plenty of** fruit	Is there **any** milk?
There is **some** food left.	**too many** cars	

Grammar Help

- **You can use of after most quantifying determiners. For example, you can say:**

  I've used **some glue.** or I've used **some of the glue.**

- **You use many with count nouns. For example, you say:**

  Don't blow up too **many** balloons. How **many** buildings can you see?

- **You use much with uncount nouns. For example, you say:**

  I don't have **much** money. Don't add too **much** salt to the soup.

- **You can leave out the noun after a quantifying determiner when it is clear what noun it refers to. For example, you can say:**

  The mail has come.
  Yes, there's **one** for you.
  There are **some letters** for Mum and **some** for Dad.
  I expect there are **some** bills.
  Aren't there **any** for me?
  Yes, **a few**.

- **There are many possible ways of using quantifying determiners. This section shows you the range of possibilities for each determiner. The following determiners are used with plural nouns.**

few (means **not many**)

Few guests knew the real reason.
Few of the guests knew the real reason.
Few of them knew the real reason.
Few knew the real reason.

a few (means **several**)

A few students arrived.
A few of the students arrived.
A few of them arrived.
A few arrived.

 ISBN 978-81-8477-744-4

fewer

I ate **fewer** sweets than you.
I ate **fewer** of the sweets than you.
I ate **fewer** of them than you.
I ate **fewer** than you.

many

Many verbs are irregular.
Many of the verbs are irregular.
Many of them are irregular.
Many are irregular.

several

Several books are missing.
Several of the books are missing.
Several of them are missing.
Several are missing.

both (refers only to **two**)

Both twins have dark hair.
Both of the twins have dark hair.
Both of them have dark hair.
The twins **both** have dark hair.
They **both** have dark hair.
Both the twins have dark hair.
Mum hugged them **both**.

You can use these determiners with plural nouns or uncount nouns.

all

We've eaten **all** the honey.
We've eaten **all** of the honey.
We've eaten **all** of it.
We've eaten it **all**.
It is **all** eaten.
The students **all** passed.
All the students have passed.
All of the students have passed.
Have they **all** passed?
Yes, **all** of them.
We'll give them **all** a prize
All dogs should have a licence.

 ISBN 978-81-8477-744-4

half

Half the computers are being used.
Half of the computers are being used.
Half of them are being used
Half are being used.
Half the grass has been cut.
Half of the grass has been cut.
Half of it has been cut.
Half has been cut.

some

Some food has gone bad.
Some of the food has gone bad.
Some of it has gone bad.
Some has gone bad.
Some teachers are away today.
Some of the teachers are away today.
Some of them are away today.
Some are away today.

Grammar Help

- **You often use any instead of some in questions. For example, you say:**
  Is there **any** mail today?
  Were there **any** letters for me?
- **You use any instead of some after not. For example, you say:**
  There was **some** mail today, but there **weren't any** letters for you.

enough

I've got **enough** chips.
I've got **enough** of the chips.
I've got **enough** of them.
I've got **enough**.
I've eaten **enough** food.
I've eaten **enough** of the food.
I've eaten **enough** of it.
I've eaten **enough**.

a lot of

A lot of students can speak English.
A lot of the students can speak English.
A lot of them can speak English.
A lot can speak English.
A lot of paper was thrown in the bin.
A lot of the paper was thrown in the bin.
A lot of it was thrown in the bin.
A lot was thrown in the bin.

 ISBN 978-81-8477-744-4

lots of

Lots of children have computers.
Lots of the children have computers.
Lots of them have computers.
Lots have computers.
Lots of food was wasted.
Lots of the food was wasted.
Lots of it was wasted.
Lots was wasted.

more

There's **more** paint in that tin.
There's **more** of the paint in that tin.
There's **more** of it in that tin.
There's **more** in that tin.
Susan did **more** sums than me.
Susan did **more** of the sums than me.
Susan did **more** of them than me.
Susan did **more** than me.

most

Most lemonade contains sugar.
Most of the lemonade has been drunk.
Most of it has been drunk.
Most contain sugar.
Most children can use a computer.
Most of my friends play football.
Most of us play football.
Most play football.

plenty

There's **plenty** of paper in the cupboard.
There's **plenty** of the paper in the cupboard.
There's **plenty** of it in the cupboard.
There's **plenty** in the cupboard.
There are **plenty** of plates on the shelf.
There are **plenty** of the plates on the shelf.
There are **plenty** of them on the shelf.
There are **plenty** on the shelf.

 ISBN 978-81-8477-744-4

You use these determiners with **uncount nouns.**

little (means not much)

There was **little** food left.
There was **little** of the food left.
There was **little** of it left.
There was **little** left.

a little (means **a bit**)

Try **a little** fried rice.
Try **a little** of the fried rice.
Try **a little** of it.
Try **a little**.

much

I didn't use **much** paint.
I didn't use **much** of the paint.
I didn't use **much** of it.
I didn't use **much**.

less

I've got **less** ice cream than you.
I've got **less** of the ice cream than you.
I've got **less** of it than you.
I've got **less** than you.

These determiners refer to singular count nouns.

another

There's **another** taxi.
There's **another** of the yellow taxis.
There's **another** of them.
There's **another**.

every

Every hospital is checked regularly.
Every one of them carries a pager.
She has read **every** one of the Harry Potter books.
Some pupils have read **every** one of Enid Blyton's books.

 ISBN 978-81-8477-744-4

each

Each pupil has a grammar book.
Each of the pupils has a grammar book.
Each of them has a grammar book.
Each has their own grammar book.
The pupils **each** have a grammar book.
They **each** have a grammar book.
We gave them **each** a grammar book.

Grammar Help

You use a plural verb after each in sentences like these:

The dogs **each have** their own kennel.
They **each have** their own kennel.

either (refers only to **two**)

I can't find **either** twin.
I can't find **either** of the twins.
I can't find **either** of them.
I can't find **either**.
She was holding a book in **either** (means **each**) hand.

neither (refers only to **two**)

Neither twin has long hair.
Neither of the twins has long hair.
Neither of them has long hair.
Neither has long hair.

You can use these determiners with singular, plural, or uncount nouns.

any

Are there **any** stamps?
Are **any** of the stamps left?
Are **any** of them left?
Are there **any**?
Is there **any** paper?
Is **any** of the paper left?
Is **any** of it left?
Is there **any**?
Any child can do that.

 ISBN 978-81-8477-744-4

no

There are **no** apples left.
I had **no** difficulty finding the answer.
No child is allowed in without an adult.

other

He likes playing with **other** children.
There is no **other** way of doing this.
Isn't there any **other** work for me to do?
Jane, Philip and several **others** came.

the other

I like **the other** music better.
The other children laughed at her.
The others laughed at her.
I hurt this foot but **the other** is fine.
There was a bridge across to **the other** side.

Grammar Help

You often use other after another determiner before singular, plural, or uncount nouns. For example:
There is **no** **other** way of doing this.

Who? What? Which?

- You use **who, what** and **which** to ask questions. You use **who** for people and **what** for things. But you use **which** when you mean a person, thing or animal from a **group** of two or more.

Exercise 1

Fill in who, what or which in the following sentences. Two have been done for you.

1. Lisa and Mary are twins. ___Which___ of them is taller?
2. ___What___ is your name?
3. ________ is knocking at the door?
4. There are three schoolbags here. ________ is yours?
5. Can you tell me ________ the time is?
6. ________ wants to come for a walk with me?
7. ________ of these colours do you prefer?
8. ________ do you want to do this evening?

 ISBN 978-81-8477-744-4

9. I can see two blue books. __________ do you mean?
10. __________ did that funny drawing?
11. __________ is this switch for?
12. __________ are those people in the garden?
13. __________ do you like better — swimming or cycling?
14. __________ of my friends shall I invite to my party?

Exercise 2

Fill in that, who, whom or which in the following sentences. Two have been done for you.

1. Did you find the video ___that___ you were looking for?
2. A screwdriver is a tool with ___which___ you tighten screws.
3. The person to __________ the letter is addressed doesn't live here any more.
4. Dad has an exercise bike __________ he uses every morning.
5. A bank is a place from __________ people borrow money.
6. We all like people __________ make us laugh.
7. What was the joke __________ everyone was laughing at?
8. I'm standing on the very spot from __________ the photo was taken.
9. A kiwi is one of those birds __________ cannot fly.
10. Where is the magazine __________ I was looking at?
11. Lisa is the friend __________ I like playing with most.
12. George is a boy on __________ you can always depend for help.

That, Whom, Which

- You can use the relative pronoun **that** instead of **who, whom** and **which**, but you must use **whom** or **which**, not **that**, immediately after a preposition.

 ISBN 978-81-8477-744-4

Using the Articles

- You use **a** or **an** before singular countable nouns when you don't expect people to know which thing or person you mean.
- You use **the** before nouns when you expect people to know which thing or person you mean, or when there is only one you could mean.

Exercise 3

In the following story, choose a, an or the to fill in the gaps. Some have already been done for you.

Helen looked in ___the___ cupboard in ___the___ kitchen for ___a___ tablecloth to put on ___the___ dining table. She found ________ pretty cloth with red spots. She spread ________ cloth over ________ table, and then she went to find ________ knives and forks and spoons to lay on ________ table ready for ________ meal. 'Lay ________ extra place,' said her mother, 'because Simon has invited ________ friend.' Helen put mats round ________ table and laid each place with ________ knife, ________ fork and ________ spoon. Then she gave everyone ________ glass. 'Shall I put ________ candle in ________ middle of ________ table?' she asked. 'If you can find ________ nice one,' said her mother.

Everybody came in and sat down at ________ table. They talked about ________ things they had done during ________ day. Helen had been working on ________ project at school. Simon had had ________ piano lesson. Mum had been to ________ dentist. Dad had been at ________ office all day. Simon's friend had ________ part in ________ school play and he had been rehearsing. When they had finished ________ meal, they turned on ________ television and watched ________ news. Then they saw ________ programme about ________ disappearance of wild animals from ________ world.

 ISBN 978-81-8477-744-4

Exercise 4

Fill in a, an, some or any in the following sentences.

1. I made myself __________ toast for breakfast.
2. Would you like __________ boiled egg?
3. __________ egg is very good for you at breakfast time.
4. There isn't __________ milk in the fridge.
5. There are __________ jars of jam on the shelf.
6. You'll find __________ little bit of butter in this dish.
7. There aren't __________ clean cups.
8. Here's __________ clean one for you.
9. Is there __________ coffee in that pot?
10. There's __________ tea in this pot.
11. I like __________ spoonful of sugar in my tea.
12. Have __________ good breakfast!

More Practice with A, An, Some, Any

- You can use **some** as the plural of **a** or **an**. You can also use **some** before uncountable nouns. But in questions and in sentences with a negative word like **not** or **never** you usually use **any** instead of **some**.

 ISBN 978-81-8477-744-4

5 VERBS

Read the following passage. The bold items are verbs in various present and past tenses.

A proposed shopping complex

'I **hear** that they are going to build a big shopping centre at Whitehill,' said Bob.

'Who **told** you that?' **asked** Jim.

'My cousin Jack told me,' **replied** Bob. 'He **works** for the developer who **is going** to build the complex.'

'**Are** you sure about this, Bob?' asked Bill.

'I **am** perfectly sure,' **said** Bob. 'I **was** up at Jack's house last night. He **mentioned** it when we **were talking** about the traffic jams in the town centre. He **is working** on the plans for the complex now.'

'I **am** absolutely horrified to hear that,' said Jim. 'I **knew** that a developer **was seeking** planning permission but some of us **are getting** together a protest campaign. We **were** certain that they **would** not **get** planning permission.'

'Why **are** you **protesting**?' asked Bob. It's good to have a choice of shops.'

'There **is** already a big shopping complex at the other side of the town and this one is bigger,' said Jim. 'It **affects** the business of the traders in the town centre quite badly. Another one **is** likely to be disastrous. A development like that **kills** a town centre. We **want** to keep ours alive.'

'I **know** someone in the council planning,' said Bill. 'I'll give him a ring.'

Bill **left** to phone his friend. He **came** back, saying, 'My friend **says** that the planning committee **are considering** the application from the developer. The planning process **takes** a long time and no decision has yet been made.'

'Thank goodness for that,' said Jim. 'That **gives** us time to mount a protest campaign.'

In the end, the protest campaign **was** successful. The developer **lost** their fight to build a shopping complex at Whitehill. However, they just **moved** to another town and **put** in another planning application. That's what developers do.

 ISBN 978-81-8477-744-4

What is a verb?

A **verb** is a word that either describes an action or an event (what someone or something does) or else helps to describe a state or a condition (what someone or something is or is like).

- There are various kinds of verbs. If somebody asks you for a verb, you are likely to give tham an **action verb**.

eat	drink	walk
run	stand	swim
jump	hit	kick

- Other **action verbs** represent mental activities or states, rather than physical actions. Verbs that express a state of mind are sometimes called **stative** verbs.

know	think	worry
remember	forget	love
hate	wonder	guess

- Another important kind of verb is a **linking verb**. It has that name because it **links** the subject with an adjective or noun, or sometimes a prepositional phrase or adverb. The most important **linking verb** is the verb **be (am, is, are, was, were)**.

The walls **are** green.
Harry's dad **is** a doctor.
Their house **was** near the supermarket.
The taxi **is** outside.

- Other **linking verbs** include **become, grow, seem, feel, get, keep, look, taste, smell, sound.**

He **became** an artist.
It **grew** dark.
I **feel** happy.
The idea **seemed** silly.
Dinner **smells** exciting.
It is **getting** late.
Her name **sounded** foreign.

 ISBN 978-81-8477-744-4

Am, Is and Are

The words am, is and are belong to the verb be.

■ You use am with the pronoun I, and you use is with the pronouns he, she and it.

Here are some sentences with the verbs am and is.

I **am** David. I am twelve.
I **am** busy with my work.

He is a policeman.
He is always friendly to children.

She is a good swimmer.
She is good at tennis too.

It is a wild animal.
It is very fierce.
It is wet today.

> *Learn these short forms:*
>
> *I am → I'm (I'm Vid.)*
> *he is → he's (He's a policeman.)*
> *she is → she's (She's a good swimmer.)*
> *it is → it's (It's a wild animal.)*
>
> *You can also shorten* ***is*** *to* ***'s*** *after somebody's name. For example:* ***Bob's*** *twelve today.*

■ You use is with singular nouns too.

Ali **is** a lawyer.
Lucky **is** a clever dog.
The camel **is** a desert animal.
A duck **is** a kind of bird.
The wall **is** very high.
The playground **is** full of children.
The sea **is** rough today.
The road **is** wet and slippery.
My house **is** near the school.
Maths **is** an interesting subject.
Joe's handwriting **is** neat.
Dinner **is** ready.
This computer game **is** very expensive.
Switzerland **is** a beautiful country.
Singapore **is** a small country.

■ You use are with the pronouns we, you and they, and with plural nouns.

We **are** in the same team.
You **are** late again.
They **are** good friends.
These people **are** very busy.

 ISBN 978-81-8477-744-4

All the children **are** healthy.
Are your teeth bright and clean?
The sausages **are** in the pan.
Your photographs **are** lovely.
Modern computers **are** very fast.
How **are** you? **I'm** fine, thank you.
The guests **are** here. But where **is** the host?
What **is** David? He**'s** a doctor.

Learn these short forms:

you are	→	*you're (You're late again.)*
we are	→	*we're (We're in the same team.)*
they are	→	*they're (They're good friends.)*

You use **are** after two or more nouns joined with **and**.

Jenny **and** Mary **are** neighbours.
Dad **and** Mum **are** in the kitchen.
My friends and I **are** always together.
The King and the Queen **are** both very young.
Vegetables and fruit **are** good for the body.
Pizza **and** spaghetti **are** popular with Italians.
Maths **and** science **are** my best subjects.
Blue **and** red **are** my favourite colours.
Brazil, Peru **and** Argentina **are** in South America.

Here are some more sentences using **am, is** and **are.**

Who **are** you?
What **is** your name?
These **are** my friends – this **is** Emily and this is Jenny.
I **am** the youngest in the family.
The scenery here **is** very beautiful.
Lions **are** meat-eating animals.
It**'s** too hot.
You**'re** very smart today, Mary.
We**'re** all members of the youth club.
They**'re** in a hurry to catch the last train.

Grammar Help

Here's a table to remind you about the use of am, is and are.

	Singular	Plural
First person	I am	we are
Second person	you are	you are
Third person	he is	they are
	she is	they are
	it is	they are

 ISBN 978-81-8477-744-4

■ Here are some sentences using **am, is** and **are** with the word **not**.

I **am not** well today.
Peter **is not** a good driver.
David **is not** here yet.
A whale **is not** a fish.
These books **are not** mine.
Mum and Dad **are not** at home.
Mum **is** in the kitchen, **isn't** she?
Isn't this your jacket?
You're my sister's friend, **aren't** you?
Tom and Joe **are** twins, **aren't** they?
Aren't the flowers lovely?
I'm older than you, **aren't** I?
I'm not eleven yet.

Learn these short forms:
am not → aren't (only in questions)
is not → isn't
are not → aren't
*The only short form of **I am not** is **I'm not**.*

Grammar Help

- **It's is the short form of it is. It's is also the short form of it has.**
- **Its is a possessive determiner.**

■ You use **is** and **are** with **there** to say what you can see and hear.

There is a castle on the hill.
There is a beehive in the garden.
There is a fence around the school.
There is too much noise in the classroom.
There is a beautiful rainbow in the sky.
There is a traffic jam at the junction.
There are a lot of fish in the pond.
There are lots of flowers in the fields.
There are two pigeons on the roof.
There are too many books on the shelf.
There's a big dog sitting outside on the doorstep.
There's a clean pair of trousers for you on the bed.
There's plenty of paper on the shelf.
There're some pencils in the drawer.
There're two guards at the gate.
There're quite a few sharks in the bay.
Is there any food in the fridge?
How much rice **is there**?
How many kittens **are there**?
How many apples **are there** on the tree?
Isn't there any paper in the printer?
Isn't there any fruit in the bowl?
Yes, **there's** an apple and a banana.
Aren't there any mangoes left on the tree?
There are enough books for everyone, **aren't there**?

Learn these short forms:
there is → there's
there are → there're

 ISBN 978-81-8477-744-4

The Simple Present Tense

Verbs have different forms called tenses. The tense of a verb tells you when the action happens. If it happens regularly, or if it happens often or sometimes or never, you use the simple present tense.

We always **wash** our hands before meals.
Joe sometimes **lends** me his bicycle.
We never **cross** the road without looking.
I often **help** Dad to wash the car.
He **buys** a newspaper every day.
The sun **rises** in the east and **sets** in the west.
Most people **eat** three meals a day.
More and more people **use** computers to do their work.

- **When you are talking about facts, or saying something you know about a person or thing, you use the simple present tense.**

Tim **likes** bananas.
Mary **enjoys** singing.
Mum **hates** cockroaches.
Uncle Joe **wears** glasses.
Jenny **wants** to be a nurse.
The earth **goes** around the sun.
A river **flows** into the sea.
Plants **need** water and sunlight to grow.
Cows **eat** grass.
Ducks **love** water.
Pandas **feed** on bamboo shoots.
Penguins **live** in Antarctica.

- You use the **simple present tense** to talk about things that have been arranged **for the future**.

Melanie **starts** school tomorrow.
We **join** the senior school next year.
My big brother **leaves** school in July this year.
The new supermarket **opens** this Friday.
The new grammar book **comes** out in September.
Next week I **go** to summer camp.
Grandad **retires** next year.
We **fly** to London next Thursday.
The plane **lands** at 5.30.
The train **departs** in five minutes.
We **move** house in a month.
My big sister **begins** her holiday job at the library in a few days' time.

 ISBN 978-81-8477-744-4

- You often use the **simple present tense** when you are telling a story in the present, for example, when you are describing a series of pictures that tell a story.

Sally **knocks** at Granny's door.

Her Granny opens it. Sally **walks** in.

She **puts** down her schoolbag. Granny **gives** Sally a drink of juice and some biscuits.

Sally **sits** in the armchair. Granny **turns on** the television.

They both **watch** television.

Sally **gets** up. It **is** time to go home. She **picks** up her schoolbag.

She **goes** to the door.

She **calls**, "Thank you, Granny! Goodbye!"

 ISBN 978-81-8477-744-4

The Third Person Singular

You put -s at the end of a verb when you use the verb with the pronouns he, she and it, and with singular nouns. The -s form of the verb is known as the third person singular.

He **sings** well.
He **likes** ice cream.
He always **takes** the biggest piece.
She **enjoys** running.
Sally **hates** maths.
She **waters** her plants every day.
Don't mind the dog - it always **barks** at strangers.
It **looks** like rain.
Mum **helps** me with my lessons.
Uncle Joe **works** in a bank.
Jean often **talks** to her dolls.
The chef **cooks** delicious meals.
I know a dog that **climbs** trees.
A snake **moves** very quietly.
The traffic **stops** at the red light.
Glue **joins** things together.

Spell Well

Here are more third person singular verbs ending in -s.

bends	eats	jogs	plays	reads	talks
builds	falls	knits	pours	rides	thinks
digs	hides	opens	prays	shakes	travels
draws	hunts	paints	rains	stands	unites

For some verbs you add -es instead of -s for the third person singular.

Sue **brushes** her teeth after each meal.
She sometimes **watches** TV after dinner.
After school Joe **rushes** home to play video games.
Dad usually **reaches** his office very early.
A cat **arches** its back when it's angry.
Sally **goes** to school by bus.
Miss Lee **teaches** us English.
Uncle Joe **polishes** his shoes every day.
Jim sometimes **punches** his little brother.
Dad sometimes **does** the shopping.
A plumber is a person who **fixes** water pipes.

 ISBN 978-81-8477-744-4

A frog **catches** insects with its long tongue.
Tom **touches** his toes twenty times every morning.
A drink of water **quenches** your thirst.

Spell Well

Here are more **third person singular** verbs that end in **-es.**

bashes	clashes	faxes	kisses	munches	switches
brushes	crashes	fetches	marches	passes	thrashes
buzzes	dashes	finishes	misses	rushes	washes
cashes	dresses	hisses	mixes	stretches	wishes

- **You drop y and add -ies to form the third person singular of verbs that end in -y.**

A cat **carries** its kittens in its teeth.
Mike usually **fries** an egg for breakfast.
He **copies** all the questions into an exercise book.
The dog **buries** the bones in a corner of the garden.
The baby **cries** a lot.
Michael sometimes **bullies** the other children.
Alice **tries** hard at school.
Mr Thomas **hurries** to work every morning.
A plane **flies** to the island every day.
Washing **dries** very quickly in the sun.

Spell Well

- Here are more **third person singular** verbs that end in **-ies.**

apply + ies → applies
ferry + ies → ferries
marry + ies → marries
satisfy + ies → satisfies
study + ies → studies
terrify + ies → terrifies
tidy + ies → tidies
vary + ies → varies
worry + ies → worries

- **But for some verbs that end in y, you don't drop the y if there is the vowel a, e, o or u before it. You just add -s after the y.**

James always **buys** a magazine to read on the train.
Anna **stays** with her aunt at weekends.
Can you read what the notice **says**?
Mr Lee **pays** his bills with a credit card.
A good soldier always **obeys** orders.
A Muslim **prays** five times a day.
That noise **annoys** me.
The eagle **preys** on small animals.

Spell Well

- Here are more verbs that have a vowel before the **y**. You just add -s to form the **third person singular.**

bray → brays
fray → frays
lay → lays
enjoy → enjoys
employ → employs
sway → sways

 ISBN 978-81-8477-744-4

The Present Continuous Tense

You use the present continuous tense to talk about actions in the present, or things that are going on or happening now.

I am **learning** how to swim.
I am **cycling** outside the house.
I am **eating** my lunch.

She **is reading** a storybook.
He **is climbing** up the ladder.
Mum **is baking** a cake.
Dad **is jogging** in the park.
Sharon **is drawing** a horse.
David **is making** a puppet.
Uncle James **is polishing** his car.
The gardener **is mowing** the lawn.
The clown **is standing** on his hands.

The blackbird **is feeding** its young.
The crow **is building** a nest on top of the tree.
The leopard **is chasing** a zebra.
The stork is wading across the stream.

You **are singing** too loudly.
We **are playing** a computer game.
They **are catching** fish in a stream.
The firemen **are fighting** the fire.
The workmen **are building** a house.

Grammar Help

- You form the **present continuous tense** like this:

am	+	present participle
is	+	present participle
are	+	present participle

- You form the **present participle** by adding **-ing** to the verb. For example:

				Present Participle
learn	+	ing	→	learning
sing	+	ing	→	singing
read	+	ing	→	reading

- The words **am, is** and **are** are called **helping verbs**, or **auxiliary** verbs. They help to form the **present continuous tense** of the verb when you join them to the present participle.

 ISBN 978-81-8477-744-4

Spell Well

You must remember these two spelling rules.

■ **You have to double the last letter of some verbs before you add -ing.**

get	+	t	+	ing	→	getting
hit	+	t	+	ing	→	hitting
jog	+	g	+	ing	→	jogging
nod	+	d	+	ing	→	nodding
rob	+	b	+	ing	→	robbing
swim	+	m	+	ing	→	swimming
stop	+	p	+	ing	→	stopping
tap	+	p	+	ing	→	tapping

Look at these verbs. You will see four things about them:

- They are **short verbs.**
- They have only **one syllable.**
- They all end with a **consonant** such as **b, d, g, m, n, p, r, t.**
- They all have just one **vowel** (a, e, i, o, u) before the consonant.

■ **If the verb ends with e, you usually have to drop the e before you add -ing.**

chase	+	ing	→	chasing
cycle	+	ing	→	cycling
drive	+	ing	→	driving
ride	+	ing	→	riding
rise	+	ing	→	rising
shake	+	ing	→	shaking
shave	+	ing	→	shaving
smile	+	ing	→	smiling
take	+	ing	→	taking
wave	+	ing	→	waving

■ **If a verb ends with a single l, it is doubled in British English but not in American English:**

British	:	dial	dialling
		equal	equalling
		travel	travelling
American	:	dial	dialing
		equal	equaling
		travel	traveling

■ **Here are some more sentences in the present continuous tense.**

I **am writing** a letter to my pen-pal.
I'm playing chess with my friend.
She **is riding** a horse.
She**'s knitting** a sweater for Sally.
He **is taking** a walk in the park.
He's counting the money.
We **are practising** *tai chi.*
We**'re rushing** to the airport to meet Mr Lee.

 ISBN 978-81-8477-744-4

They **are** still **sleeping**.
They**'re swimming** in the sea.
Am I **jumping** or **hopping**?
Is the phone **ringing**?
What are they **doing**?
What's **happening**?
Why **aren't** you **doing** your homework?
Aren't I **sitting** up straight?
You **aren't wearing** a raincoat. **Isn't** it raining?

Learn these short forms:
what is → what's
who is → who's

You also use the **present continuous tense** to talk about things that you have planned to do **in the future.**

We **are going** camping tomorrow.
I'm starting piano lessons soon.
Jim's parents **are taking** him to Australia next week.
We **are having** a barbecue later on this morning.
All our friends **are coming**.
Who**'s bringing** the drink for the barbecue? I am.
Who**'s bringing** the potatoes? We are.
Who**'s bringing** the sausages? Jane and Anne are.
Who**'s bringing** the bread? You are, aren't you?

The Simple Past Tense

You use the simple past tense to talk about things that happened in the past.

Dinosaurs **lived** millions of years ago.
I **bought** a new camera last week.
Joe **learnt** to play the guitar very quickly.
We **drove** to the safari park last weekend.
The giant panda **gave** birth to a baby last night.
Yesterday Dad **took** me to the carnival.
The plane **landed** a few minutes ago.
The children **visited** a farm during the holidays.
Who **invented** the computer?

 ISBN 978-81-8477-744-4

- **You also use the simple past tense to talk about things that happened in stories.**

The little men in Lilliput **tied** Gulliver to the ground.
Jack and Jill **went** up the hill.
Pinocchio's nose **grew** longer every time he **told** a lie.
Little Red Riding Hood **wanted** to visit her grandmother.
The Three Bears **found** Goldilocks asleep in their house.
Jim hid in the apple barrel and **heard** the pirates talking.
Scrooge **decided** to buy the biggest turkey in the shop window.
Tom **dipped** his brush in the bucket of whitewash.

- **In unlikely wishes and in *if*-clauses about unreal situations in the present, you use a form of the verb that is the same as the simple past.**

I wish I **had** a million dollars.
We all wish we **knew** the answer.
If only I **earned** a bit more!
I would accept the offer if I **were** you. (But I'm not you.)

Grammar Help

This form of the verb that looks like the simple past is actually the past subjunctive. The only difference between the past subjunctive and the simple past is that with the verb be you use were, not was, with the first and third person:

I wish I **were** richer.
If only she **were** tidier!

Spell Well

There are two main **spelling rules** to remember.

- You have to **double the last letter** of some verbs before you add **-ed.**

drum + m + ed	→	drummed		pat + t + ed	→	patted
fan + n + ed	→	fanned		pin + n + ed	→	pinned
grab + b + ed	→	grabbed		rip + p + ed	→	ripped
nod + d + ed	→	nodded		slam + m + ed	→	slammed

Look at these verbs. You will notice four things about them:

- They are **short verbs.**
- They only have **one syllable.**
- They all end with a **consonant** such as **b, d, g, m, n, p, r, t.**
- They all have just **one vowel (a, e, i, o, u)** before the consonant.

- **With verbs that end in -y, you change the y to i before adding -ed.**

carry + i + ed	→	carried		hurry + i + ed	→	hurried
cry + i + ed	→	cried		spy + i + ed	→	spied
dirty + i + ed	→	dirtied		try + i + ed	→	tried

 ISBN 978-81-8477-744-4

Irregular Verbs

The simple past form of some verbs does not end in -ed or -d. Such verbs are called irregular verbs.

■ The simple past form of some **irregular verbs** does not change at all.

Mum opened the door and **let** us in.
Joe **cut** his finger yesterday.
He **hit** the ball over the net.
My ring **cost** only 10 dollars.
David **hurt** his foot when he jumped over the drain.
Dad **read** to us last night.
Mr Brown **split** the firewood with his axe.
I **put** some sugar in my coffee.

Word Power

■ **Here are some more irregular verbs that don't change for their simple past form:**

beat	broadcast	shed
slit	spread	upset

■ **Notice that read is pronounced red when it is the simple past form.**

Spell Well

■ **You usually form the simple past tense by adding -ed to the verb.**

cross + ed → crossed
jump + ed → jumped
laugh + ed → laughed
lift + ed → lifted
look + ed → looked
open + ed → opened
paint + ed → painted
walk + ed → walked

■ **If the verb ends with -e, you just add -d.**

agree + d → agreed
die + d → died
hate + d → hated
judge + d → judged
live + d → lived
pause + d → paused
queue + d → queued
race + d → raced
stare + d → stared

 ISBN 978-81-8477-744-4

- But most **irregular verbs** change to a different form for their simple past form.

Sam **bent** the stick in two.
I **lost** my pen on the bus.
We **sold** our car last week.
The baby **slept** right through the night.
Tom **shot** and scored a goal.
Peter **got** a watch for his birthday.
It **kept** fine for the match.
I **heard** a noise in the night.
A bird **flew** into the classroom.
He **brought** his mouse to school.
My book **fell** off the desk.

- Here are some more **irregular verbs** in the simple past form.

Mary **drew** a dog on the computer.
This is the house that Jack **built**.
They **sat** on the fence.
Jenny **hid** in the cupboard.
The dog **dug** a hole for its bone.
The man **blew** his nose loudly.
Sally **laid** the table for dinner.
Bob **ate** lots of vegetables for his dinner.
We **held** a party last night.
Everyone **sang** at the party.
The waiter **broke** some plates.
Dad **gave** us each ten dollars.
Sally **chose** a red dress.
Sue first **met** her uncle from Hong Kong five years ago.
He **woke** up in the middle of the night.
I **thought** you were a ghost.
Kelvin **left** the company for a better job.

Word Power

Here are more verbs that have a different simple past form:

Verb	Simple Past	Verb	Simple Past	Verb	Simple Past
begin	began	grow	grew	shine	shone
buy	bought	have	had	take	took
break	broke	know	knew	teach	taught
drink	drank	kneel	knelt	throw	threw
drive	drove	make	made	win	won
fight	fought	pay	paid	wear	wore
give	gave	run	ran	write	wrote

 ISBN 978-81-8477-744-4

Was and Were

The verbs was and **were** belong to the verb **be.**

- **Was** is the simple past form of **am** and **is.** You use **was** with the pronouns **I, he, she** and **it**, and with **singular nouns.**

Edison **was** a famous inventor.
Beethoven **was** a German composer.
The Brontosaurus **was** a huge creature.
Snow White **was** a beautiful princess.
Her stepmother **was** unkind to her.
The genie **was** happy to be free.
Sue **was** at a disco last night.
Mary **was** absent from school yesterday.
There **was** a terrible storm last night.
It **was** very wet on Monday.
It **was** six o'clock when we reached home.
Ten years ago I **was** only a baby.
When I **was** small, I liked dolls.
Was he behind the door all the time?
Was Peter late for school yesterday?
Was there enough soup for everybody at lunchtime?
Jack **was** not well yesterday.
There **wasn't** any petrol in the tank, so the car stopped.
Last year, I **wasn't** tall enough to reach the shelf.
Why **wasn't** Maggie at the gym last week?
It **wasn't** time to get up, so I stayed in bed.
Samantha **was** second in the race, **wasn't** she?
There **was** a terrible mess to clear up after the party, **wasn't** there?
She **wasn't** on holiday, **was** she?

- **Were** is the simple past form of **are.** You use **were** with the pronouns **you, we** and **they**, and with **plural nouns.**

The Romans **were** brave soldiers.
Dinosaurs **were** prehistoric animals.
Jack and his mother **were** very poor.
My Mum and Dad **were** at the station to meet me.
We **were** the champions last year.
They **were** last in the wheelbarrow race.
These fields **were** once covered with trees.

Learn these short forms:
was not → wasn't
were not → weren't

 ISBN 978-81-8477-744-4

Nouns
Pronouns
Adjectives
Determiners
Verbs
Adverbs
Prepositions
Conjunctions
Interjections
Sentences
Phrases
Clauses
More about Sentences
Direct and Indirect Speech
Punctuation

We looked for the bowls, but they **were not** in the cupboard.
There **weren't** any clouds in the sky.
Were you still in bed when I phoned?
How many dancing princesses **were** there in the story?
There **were** twelve, **weren't** there?
Weren't you cross when Jack beat you at chess?
Those **were** my best jeans.

Grammar Help

Here's a table to help you remember the use of was and were.

	Singular	Plural
First person	I was	we were
Second person	you were	you were
Third person	he was	they were
	she was	they were
	it was	they were

The Past Continuous Tense

You use the past continuous tense to talk about actions that were going on, or happening at a certain moment in the past.

Miss Lee **was cleaning** the chalkboard.
Peter **was making** a model of a bridge.
Ben **was finishing** his sums.
Sally **was putting** her books into her schoolbag.
Jenny and I **were tidying** the classroom.
The twins **were fighting** in the corner.
Bob **was stacking** the chairs.
The caretaker **was sweeping** the corridor.
Michael and John **were washing** the paint brushes.
Bill **was doing** his maths when I visited him.
Mum **was cooking** the supper when I came home.
Mary **was waiting** for the bus when Peter passed by.
We **were** all **enjoying** the party when suddenly the lights went out.
When I met Joe, he **was looking** for his dog.
You **weren't listening**, were you?
Why **were** you **looking** out of the window?
What **were** they **doing** when the bell rang?

Grammar Help

- **You form the past continuous tense like this:**

  was + present participle
  were + present participle

- **The words was and were are called helping verbs, or auxiliary verbs. They help to form the past continuous tense when you join them to the present participle of the verb. For example:**

  was drawing — was waiting
  were driving — were sleeping

 ISBN 978-81-8477-744-4

Read the following passage. Among the bold items are the verb have as an ordinary lexical verb and as an auxiliary verb for forming the perfect tenses, the verb be as an auxiliary verb, and a number of modal verbs, used for expressing the future or for other purposes.

A search for biological parents

Four years ago, my wife and I **had** a beautiful baby son. We now **have** two beautiful twin baby daughters. I **had been hoping** to have more children but my wife **has said** no. She **had** a lot of health problems when she was pregnant with the twins.

I **have** always **wanted** a large family. I **have assumed** that that is because I was an only child. I **had** no one to play with.

My Mum and Dad **have been telling** me the truth all my life. I **have known** since I was very young that I was adopted. **I have been wondering** about my biological parents ever since I was a teenager, but it was not until my son was born that I began to try to find them.

'You know that I **will** always **regard** you as my real parents and that I **will** always **love** you,' I told my adoptive parents, 'but I feel that I need to be able to tell my children something about their family background. They **will want** to know when they're grown up. If I do not look for my biological parents now, I **will regret** it.'

'We understand,' said my adoptive mother. 'We **are going** to do all we can to help you. We **shall be racking** our brains to think of ways that we can help. We **will let** you know if we come up with anything useful.'

My wife, however, said, 'If I were you,' she said, 'I **would forget** all about my biological parents. In any case, it's probably too late. If you **had started** when you were younger you **might have had** more success. They could be dead by now.'

I know she's right, but I regard my search as something I simply cannot give up.

 ISBN 978-81-8477-744-4

Have, Has and Had

The verbs have and has are used to show possession.

- You use **has** with the pronouns **he, she** and **it**, and with **singular nouns.**

He **has** a lot of stamps.
She **has** long hair.
Our apartment **has** large windows.
The eagle **has** sharp claws. It also **has** sharp eyes.
A guinea pig **has** no tail, **has** it?
An elephant **has** a long trunk, **hasn't** it?

- You use **have** with the pronouns **I, you, we** and **they**, and with **plural nouns.**

I **have** a kid brother.
You **have** a stain on your shirt.
We **have** a caring teacher.
They **have** a new car.
Monkeys **have** long tails.
Have you any brothers or sisters?
I **haven't** any brothers or sisters.
Bears **have** thick fur, **don't** they?

Grammar Help

Some people, especially Americans, use the verb **do** as a helping verb with **have** when it means **possess.** So you can say:

I **haven't** any brothers or sisters.
or
I **don't have** any brothers or sisters.
She **has** three sisters, **hasn't** she?
or
She **has** three sisters, **doesn't** she?

You can also say the same thing this way:
She **has got** three sisters, **hasn't** she?

- You use **have** or **has** to talk about **things you do,** or **things that happen to you.**

We **have** art lessons on Mondays.
I **have** a bike ride after tea.
The children always **have** a lot of fun at bedtime.
Some cows **have** calves every year.
I **have** a party on my birthday.
Have another try.
Peter **has** a sore knee.
Alice **has** toothache.
Dad often **has** a run before breakfast.
He **has** a shower every morning.
We **have** football practice on Fridays, **don't** we?
Granny usually **has** a nap after lunch, **doesn't** she?

Grammar Help

You usually use do as a helping verb with have when you use it to talk about things you do. So you say:

You usually **have** a shower after exercising, **don't** you?

 ISBN 978-81-8477-744-4

■ You can use **have** or **has** to talk about things you **eat** and **drink**.

We **have** breakfast at 7.00 am.
At supper time they **have** a glass of milk and an apple.
Jenny often **has** sandwiches for lunch.
He always **has** coffee after dinner.
The dog only **has** one meal a day, **doesn't** he?

Grammar Help

Also, when you use have to mean eat or drink something, you usually use do as the helping verb. So you say:
He usually **has** a fried egg for breakfast, **doesn't** he?

■ You also use **have to** or **has to** to talk about **things you must do.**

I **have** to get up at 7 o'clock.
We **have** to be very careful crossing the road.
You **have to** knock at the door before you enter someone's room.
They **have to** do their school work before watching television.
Mary **has to** go to bed at 9 o'clock.
We **have to** be quiet while people are sleeping, **don't** we?
She **has to** practise the violin every day, **doesn't** she?

Grammar Help

- **When you use have to to mean must, you use do as the helping verb. For example:**
  You **have to** restart the computer when you install a new program, don't you?
- **But some people say have got to instead of have to. For example, you can say:**
  You **have got to** finish your homework, **haven't** you?

■ **Had** is the simple past tense of **have** and **has**. You use **had** with **I, you, he, she, it, we** and **they**, and with **singular** and **plural nouns.**

I **had** lots of toys when I was small.
The Three Bears **had** a house in the forest.
Our dog **had** three puppies last week.
John and Joe **had** a quarrel yesterday.
Mum **had** a headache yesterday.
We **had** coffee after dinner.
The woodcutter **had** a sharp axe.
Harry Potter **had** a strange scar on his forehead, didn't he?

*You usually use **did** as the **helping verb** with **had**, even when you use it to talk about **possession**. So you say:*
*Cinderella **had** two ugly sisters, **didn't** she?*
*Harry Potter **had** a strange scar on his forehead, **didn't** he?*

 ISBN 978-81-8477-744-4

Nouns
Pronouns
Adjectives
Determiners
Verbs
Adverbs
Prepositions
Conjunctions
Interjections
Sentences
Phrases
Clauses
More about Sentences
Direct and Indirect Speech
Punctuation

The Present Perfect Tense

You use the verb **has** or **have** as a **helping verb** to form the **present perfect tense.** The **present perfect tense** connects the **past** with the present. You use it to talk about happenings in the past that affect the present.

■ Here are some sentences in the **present perfect tense.**

I **have made** you a cup of tea.
I**'ve lost** my wallet.
We **have seen** this film already.
We**'ve made** the bed.
You **have made** two spelling mistakes.
They **have moved** house.
Oh good! They**'ve mended** the fence.
Look! The hens **have laid** plenty of eggs.
She **has done** her school work.
He**'s cut** his finger.
Ali **has** already scored two goals.
John**'s gone** out.
It**'s been** very hot today.
There **has been** an accident.
The train **has** just **arrived.**
It **has not rained** for months.
Have you **found** your keys yet?
Who **has eaten** the sandwiches?
Where **has** the thief **hidden** the jewellery?
Hasn't Peter **come** home yet?

Learn these short forms:

I have	→	*I've*
you have	→	*you've*
we have	→	*we've*
they have	→	*they've*
he has	→	*he's*
she has	→	*she's*
it has	→	*it's*
have not	→	*haven't*
has not	→	*hasn't*

Grammar Help

You join have or has to the past participle of the verb to form the present perfect tense:

have + past participle
has + past participle

 ISBN 978-81-8477-744-4

The Present Perfect Continuous Tense

You use the present perfect continuous tense to talk about things that began in the past and are still continuing or having an effect.

He **has been living** in this country since 1998.
She **has been chatting** on the phone for an hour.
It **has been raining** since this morning.
Harry **hasn't been performing** his magic tricks again, has he?
Who**'s been sitting** in my chair?
The train**'s been standing** in the station for half an hour.
I **have been trying** to do this puzzle for the last two hours.
They **haven't been working** for a month.
I'm afraid I **haven't been practising** the piano lately.
The police **have been looking** for the man for a week.
You haven**'t been brushing** your teeth regularly, have you?
We**'ve been reading** A Tale of Two Cities at school.

- *Learn these short forms:*

  there has → there's
  who has → who's
  what has → what's

- *You can also shorten* ***has*** *to* ***'s*** *after somebody's name. For example:*
  Peter's ***come*** *home.*

Grammar Help

- You form the **present perfect continuous** tense like this:

have	+	been	+	present participle
has	+	been	+	present participle

- Here's a table to remind you about the use of **have** and **has**.

	Singular	Plural
First person	I have	we have
Second person	you have	you have
Third person	he has	they have
	she has	they have
	it has	they have

 ISBN 978-81-8477-744-4

Grammar Help

- The **past participles** of most verbs are the same as the simple past tense.

  If the simple past tense ends with **-ed**, the past participle ends with **-ed** too.

Present	Simple Past	Past Participle
attack	attacked	attacked
chase	chased	chased
close	closed	closed
defend	defended	defended
delay	delayed	delayed
flow	flowed	flowed
laugh	laughed	laughed
love	loved	loved

- Some **irregular verbs** have the same form for the simple past and the past participle.

Present	Simple Past	Past Participle
build	built	built
catch	caught	caught
keep	kept	kept
lay	laid	laid
put	put	put
send	sent	sent

- But some **irregular verbs** have different forms for the simple past and the past participle.

Present	Simple Past	Past Participle
break	broke	broken
draw	drew	drawn
drive	drove	driven
do	did	done
eat	ate	eaten
fly	flew	flown
go	went	gone
hide	hid	hidden
know	knew	known
see	saw	seen

The Past Perfect Tense

You use **had** as a **helping verb** to form the **past perfect tense.** When you are using the simple past, you use the past **perfect tense** to mention something that happened some time before.

The police arrived to arrest him, but he **had** already **left**.
Suddenly he remembered where he **had hidden** the money.
I noticed that he **had left** his books behind.
The clock struck eleven, and Maggie still **hadn't got** out of bed.

 ISBN 978-81-8477-744-4

When he reached the bus stop, the bus **had** already **left**.
He collected money for the people who **had lost** their homes in the earthquake.
My test results were much better than I **had expected** them to be.
Dad **had** just **reached** home when it started to rain.
We **hadn't been** at the party long when Jack arrived.
Dad **had** just **put** down the phone when it rang again.

Grammar Help

You form the **past perfect tense** like this:

had + past participle

The Past Perfect Continuous Tense

You use the past perfect continuous tense to talk about things that were going on in the past when something happened.

I **had been wondering** whether to telephone you when you rang me yourself.

I **had been working** at the hospital for three years when the trouble began.

Grammar Help

- You form the **past perfect continuous tense** like this:

had + been + present participle

- Here's a table to remind you about the use of **had**.

	Singular	Plural
First person	I had	we had
Second person	you had	you had
Third person	he had	they had
	she had	they had
	it had	they had

- Learn these short forms:

I had	→	I'd	we had	→	we'd
you had	→	you'd	they had	→	they'd
he had	→	he'd	had not	→	hadn't
she had	→	she'd			

 ISBN 978-81-8477-744-4

Nouns
Pronouns
Adjectives
Determiners
Verbs
Adverbs
Prepositions
Conjunctions
Interjections
Sentences
Phrases
Clauses
More about Sentences
Direct and Indirect Speech
Punctuation

The Future Tense

You can talk about future actions and happenings using the helping verbs shall and will.

- **You can use shall or will with the pronouns I and we when you are deciding or promising to do something, and to make forecasts.**

I **shall write** to Granny.
I **shall make** a list of everything I need for the holiday.
I **shall be** glad when the exams are over.
I **will take** the dog to the vet tomorrow.
We **shall miss** you when you leave.
We **will water** the plants every day while you are away.
Shall I **take** the dog for a walk?
Shall we **come** and **play** again tomorrow?
I **will not punish** you this time.
I **won't do** it again.

- **You can use will with you to ask about somebody's expectations, or to make forecasts.**

You **will enjoy** New Zealand.
When **will you** get your exam results?
You **won't forget**, will you?
You **will remember** to lock the door, won't you?
She **will be** free to talk to you in a few minutes.
He **will be** back for dinner.
It **will** soon **be** dark.
They **will get** their exam results tomorrow.
Plants **will die** without water.
I expect school **will close** early tomorrow.
When **will** the new road **be** ready to use?
Your parents **will be** very pleased with your marks, **won't they**?

Grammar Help

- **You form the future tense like this:**

shall + verb   or   will + verb

- **Here's a table to remind you about the use of shall and will.**

	Singular	Plural
First person	I shall	we shall
	I will	we will
Second person	you will	you will
Third person	he will	they will
	she will	they will
	it will	they will

 ISBN 978-81-8477-744-4

Grammar Help

- Learn these short forms:

I shall → I'll
I will → I'll
you will → you'll
he will → he'll
she will → she'll
it will → it'll
we shall → we'll
we will → we'll

Did you know?

- The basic meaning of **will** is **be willing**. It is still used like this in requests. **Will not**, or **won't** for short, is used in rude refusals. For example:

  Please **will** you **stop** playing that noisy music?
  No, I **won't**.

- You often use **won't** when you are talking about people and things that don't do what you want them to do. For example:

  I have told them to tidy up the mess, but they **won't**.
  The baby **won't** eat her food.
  The car **won't** start.

The Future Continuous Tense

You use the future continuous tense to talk about things that have been planned or are likely to happen. Sometimes these are continuous actions and sometimes single actions.

I **shall be sending** invitations for the concert to all your parents.
I'**ll be waiting** at the gate when you come out of school.
I expect I'**ll be having** a party for my birthday.
You **won't be needing** your laptop for the next few hours, **will** you?
We'**ll be starting** the new grammar book on Friday.
We certainly **won't be going** back to that restaurant!
You'**ll be working** hard next week while I go on leave.
We **shall be leaving** in ten minutes.
Will you **be staying** with your Granny during the holidays?
Will you **be seeing** Maggie at the weekend?
The new supermarket **will be opening** soon.
Auntie Jill **will be coming** to see us soon, **won't** she?

Grammar Help

You form the **future continuous tense** like this:

shall + be + present participle
or
will + be + present participle

 ISBN 978-81-8477-744-4

- **There is another way to talk about future actions and happenings. You can use going to.**

I'm **going to work** hard and pass my exams.
I haven't read that book yet, but I'**m going to.**
We **are going to make** a snowman.
We'**re all going to sing** in the concert, aren't we?
I hope someone **is going to fix** the television soon.
I think it'**s going to rain.**
Are you **going to go** to the match?
Aren't you **going to read** a story tonight?
The plane is just **going to take off.**
Hurry! The performance **is going to start** soon.
Mum and Dad **are going to get** me a computer.
There's **going to be** a barbecue tonight.

- **You can also use the simple present and the present continuous to talk about future happenings.**

Term **ends** on Friday.
The new supermarket **opens** on Friday.
Tomorrow **is** a public holiday.
My sister **is leaving** school soon.
We **are going** to the library tomorrow.

- **Another way to talk about an event that is happening very soon indeed is to use be + about to + verb.**

The plane is **about to take off.**
Hurry! The performance **is about to start!**
The bridge **is about to collapse.**
The movie **is about to start.**
I think it'**s about to rain.**
The supermarket **is about to close.**
We **are about to serve** dinner.

The Future Perfect Tense

You form the future perfect tense with will or shall and have, followed by the past participle of the verb.

The future perfect is used for saying that some happening or action will be probably over by a particular time.

When you get this message, **I shall have left** for Britain.
They'**ll have realized** by now that we're coming.

 ISBN 978-81-8477-744-4

I hope **I shall have lost** weight by the time the wedding takes place.
The first rehearsal is on Monday, but **I won't have had** time to learn my part.
In another hour, the sun **will have moved** quite a distance across the sky.
It's their golden wedding next month – they**'ll have been married** fifty years!
It's too early to telephone Robert – he **won't have got up** yet.
By the time we arrive, everybody **will have gone** home.
Will you already **have eaten** when you arrive? Yes, I **shall**.
Won't they **have heard** the news already from somebody else? Yes, I expect they **will**.
Susan **won't have received** her parcel from me yet, will she?
By six o'clock the sun **will have set, won't** it?
When do you think you **will have finished** that piece of work?
How **shall I have changed** in twenty years' time?

Grammar Help

You form the **future perfect tense** like this:

shall + have + past participle

or

will + have + past participle

Do, Does and Did

You use the verbs do, does and did to talk about actions.

- You use **do** with the pronouns **I, you, we** and **they**, and with **plural nouns**.

  You use **does** with the pronouns **he, she** and **it**, and with **singular nouns**.

Dad **does** the washing.
Mum **does** the cooking.
You **do** such interesting work.
We always **do** our exercises before breakfast.
The road **does** a detour round the city.
They **do** two performances every night.

 ISBN 978-81-8477-744-4

- **Did is the simple past form of do and does.**

Who **did** this drawing?
You **did** well in the test.
I **did** badly in my exam.
They **did** the dusting and cleaning.
Sally **did** her hair in front of the mirror.

Grammar Help

- **Here's a table to remind you about the use of the verb do.**

	Singular	Plural
First person	I do	we do
Second person	you do	you do
Third person	he does	they do
	she does	they do
	it does	they do

- **Here's a table to remind you about the use of the verb did.**

	Singular	Plural
First person	I did	we did
Second person	you did	you did
Third person	he did	they did
	she did	they did
	it did	they did

- **But you also use do, does and did as helping verbs.**

  You join do, does and did to other verbs to ask questions and to answer them.

Do you **like** cats? Yes, I **do**.
Do you **think** it's going to rain again? Yes, I **do**.
Does it **rain** every day here? Yes, it **does**.
Does he **enjoy** painting walls? Yes, he **does**.
Do these clothes **look** OK on me?
Yes, of course, they **do**.
Did it **snow** last night? Yes, it **did**.
Who wants to come to the zoo?
We all **do**!
Who broke this vase? Peter **did**!
Do you **have** an umbrella with you? Yes, I **do**.
Does he always **have** a run before breakfast? Yes, he **does**.
Where **did** you **find** that shell?
What **do** you **want** for lunch?
Why **did** they **leave** so suddenly?
How **did** you **get** up there?

Grammar Help

When the verb have means possess or carry, some people use the helping verb do with it. So there are two ways of saying the same thing:

Have you an umbrella with you?
Yes, I **have**.
or
Do you **have** an umbrella with you?
Yes, I **do**.

 ISBN 978-81-8477-744-4

■ You use **do not, does not** and **did not** to make other verbs negative.

Cats **do not like** water.
You **don't look** very happy.
Mum **does not enjoy** scrubbing the floor.
There **doesn't seem** to be any milk left.
Dad **did not catch** his train.
We **didn't remember** to bring our passports.
Don't you **have** a dictionary?
No, I **don't**.
Don't you **want** any breakfast?
Yes, I **do**.
Don't you like having your photo taken?
No, I **don't**.
The garden looks lovely, **doesn't** it?
Yes, it **does**.
Did you **see** the rainbow?
No, I **didn't**.
Didn't he **win**?
No, he **didn't**.
She usually has an egg for breakfast, **doesn't** she?
You **didn't hit** the ball very far, **did** you?

Learn these short forms:
do not → don't
does not → doesn't
did not → didn't

Grammar Help

Here are some ways of saying the same thing:

Don't you **have** a dictionary?
No, I **don't**.
or
Haven't you a dictionary?
No, I **haven't**.
or
Haven't you **got** a dictionary?
No, I **haven't**.

 ISBN 978-81-8477-744-4

Read the following passage. The bold items are all modal verbs or semi-modal verbs.

Travel Plans

'What are you going to do this summer, Jane?' asked Aunt Meg.

'I **may** take a gap year before going to university,' replied Jane. 'My brother did and my father thinks that I **should**, too.'

'Does he?' asked Aunt Meg. 'He never **used to** think like that. He once told your brother that he **must** not even think of it.'

'He thought that John **would** just waste time and money for a year,' said Jane, 'but he travelled a lot overseas and did voluntary work. John said that he saw lots of places that he **might** otherwise never have seen and Dad said that the experience matured John.'

'Is that something you **would** like to do?' asked Aunt Meg. 'I **must** say it **would** be wonderful to travel for a year. I **dare** say you **won**'t get such an opportunity again.'

'It **would** be marvellous to travel,' said Jane, 'although I **could**n't afford to do voluntary work. If I do decide to travel, I **need** to find paid work.'

'If John was able to do voluntary work, you **should** be able to do so, too,' replied Aunt Meg. 'How did John manage to do it if you **can**'t?'

'John didn't **need** to do paid work because he got some kind of travel grant from school. I thought that I **might** be able to do that too, but there are none available this year.'

'You father **would** help with your travel expenses, **would**n't he?' asked Aunt Meg.

'Unfortunately he **can**'t,' replied Jane. 'His business didn't do very well last year.'

'I **may** be able to help,' said Aunt Meg. 'I **dare**n't offer your father any money directly, but surely he **can**'t object if I give my goddaughter an airline ticket for her birthday.'

'Thanks, Aunt Meg,' said Jane. 'That **would** be wonderful!'

 ISBN 978-81-8477-744-4

Modal Verbs

There is a group of verbs called **modal verbs** or **modal auxiliary verbs.** These are a special kind of **auxiliary** or **helping verb.**

The main **modal auxiliary verbs** are: **can, could, will, would, shall, should, may, might, must, ought.**

The verbs **dare, need** and **used to** can be included in the group, because they too have uses like those of modal auxiliaries. They are known as **semi-modal verbs.**

- **Modal verbs** are used with the **base form** (the **infinitive without to**) of ordinary action verbs.

  Ought is an exception — it is always used with a **to**-infinitive.

I **can** swim. We **must hurry**.

- Modal verbs always keep the same form. They do not add **s** for the third person singular.

She **may** object. The bird **can't** fly.

- Most modal verbs have contracted negative forms: **can't, couldn't, won't, wouldn't, shan't, shouldn't, mightn't, mustn't, oughtn't, daren't, needn't.**

  Will and **shall** have the short form **'ll** and **would** has the short form **'d.**

We'**ll** help. We said we'**d** help.

- Some modal verbs have another modal verb as a past form:

Present	Past
can	could
may	might
shall	should
will	would

I **can** swim quite well now, but last year I **couldn't** swim at all.

What time **will** the others be here? They said they **would** arrive around three o'clock.

 ISBN 978-81-8477-744-4

But all these past forms have several other independent uses.

- The purpose of modal verbs is to add to the ordinary action verb a feeling of the action being, for example, **possible, likely, necessary, certain, compulsory, allowed** or **advisable.**

You **may start** writing now. (allowed)
You **must stop** writing now. (compulsory)
Dad **may phone.** (possible)
Dad **must be** delayed at the office. (likely)

- Modal verbs can't combine with each other; and they don't form **to**-infinitives or **-ing** forms. You avoid these difficulties by replacing modal verbs with other verbs.

  For example, you can use **be able to** instead of **can.**

The baby **will** soon **be able to** walk.
I want **to be able** to see my children.

- You can use **have to** instead of **must.**

I might **have to** leave early.
I don't like **having to** punish the children.

- Modal verbs can form questions and negatives, and are used in question tags and short answers and other shortened constructions.

Need you leave so early? No, I **needn't**, really.
I suppose he **can't** help it, **can** he?

Can and Could

The verbs **can** and **could** are both helping verbs, too.

- The modal verb **can** is used mainly to express the idea of **ability** and **possibility**.

  You use **can** and **could** with the pronouns **I, you, he, she, it, we** and **they**, and with **singular** or **plural nouns.**

He **can run** faster than me.
She **can swim** like a fish.
She **cannot afford** such an expensive ring.
They **can't find** their way out of the maze.
Can you **tell** the difference between these two pictures?

 ISBN 978-81-8477-744-4

- **You can use can for requests or asking or giving permission.**

Can you tidy your desks, please?
Can I open a window? Yes, of course, you **can**.
Can we use your computer? No, you **can't**.

> - *When you put **not** after **can**, you write it as one word: **cannot**.*
> - *Learn these short forms:*
>
> | | | |
> |---|---|---|
> | cannot | → | can't |
> | could not | → | couldn't |

- **Could is the past tense of can. You use could to express skills and abilities.**

Jack ran as fast as he **could**.
Gillian **could read** before she started school.
Mozart **could play** the piano when he was four years old.
I **could understand** why she was worried.

- **You can also use could for asking permission, making requests, making suggestions or wishes.**

Please **could** I **leave** early?
Please **could** you **show** me the way?
We **could eat** in that new restaurant this evening.
Perhaps I **could** train as a nurse.
I wish I **could speak** English better.

Would

- **You use would as the past tense of will.**

He said he **would come** early.
She said she **would bring** some sandwiches.
I said I **would help** Mum with her shopping.
I knew you **would enjoy** New Zealand.
The Prince said he **would only** marry a true princess.
We realized **we'd be** late if we didn't hurry.
We started running so that **we'd get** there in time.
John and Sue said **they'd meet** us at the station.
We were sitting in the car ready to go, but it **would not start**.
He promised he **wouldn't forget** her birthday.
My computer **wouldn't work** when I switched it on.
I asked them to help but they **wouldn't**.

Learn these short forms:

I would	→	I'd
we would	→	we'd
you would	→	you'd
they would	→	they'd
he would	→	he'd
she would	→	she'd
would not	→	wouldn't

 ISBN 978-81-8477-744-4

Nouns
Pronouns
Adjectives
Determiners
Verbs
Adverbs
Prepositions
Conjunctions
Interjections
Sentences
Phrases
Clauses
More about Sentences
Direct and Indirect Speech
Punctuation

- **It is polite to use would like when you are offering people things, or asking for something yourself.**

Would you **like** a cup of tea?
What fruit **would** you **like**?
I'm going for a walk.
Would you **like** to come with me?
I expect **you'd like** a shower straight away.
Wouldn't you **like** a sandwich?
You'**d like** a meal now, wouldn't you?
I am tired now. **I'd like** a rest.

Did you know?

When you are accepting an offer, you often use would love instead of would like. For example:

Would you like a chocolate?
Yes, please, I **would love** one.

- **You can use would when you are asking someone to do something.**

Would you please **stop** making that noise?
Would you please **close** the door?
Please would you **bring** me my spectacles?
Would you **draw** the curtain, please?
Would you **check** my spelling?
Please **would** you make a cup of tea?

- **You use would when you are wishing something, or talking about situations that don't exist at present.**

I wish he **would stop** talking.
I **would buy** a house with a swimming pool if I had a lot of money.
If I was musical, I **would learn** the bassoon.
If only those flies **would leave** me in peace.

- **Would is sometimes used to talk about a habit in the past.**

Every night, she **would set** her alarm clock for 6.00 am.
The twelve princesses **would dance** until their shoes wore out.
Sometimes she **would get** up in the night and make a cup of tea.

- **Would is used in questions and with not to talk about what is probable or unlikely.**

It **wouldn't hurt** a fly.
Would she **lie** to save herself?
They **would** never **do** anything dishonest.

Grammar Help

You can say:

If I was musical, I would learn the bassoon.
or
If I were musical, I would learn the bassoon.

 ISBN 978-81-8477-744-4

Should and Ought to

Should and **ought** are very close in meaning. Unlike other modal verbs, **ought** is always used with a **to**-infinitive. You use **should** and **ought to** to say what is right, normal or expected, and to give advice and ask for it.

You **should eat** plenty of fruit.
You **ought to take** plenty of exercise.
We **should** always **tell** the truth, **shouldn't** we?
We **ought not to tell** lies, **ought** we?
I don't feel well – **should** I **go** and see the doctor?
I feel sick – **ought** I **to go** back to bed?
You **should know** how to spell your own name by now.
He **ought to be** able to count to ten at his age.
Shouldn't I **switch off** the laptop when I'm not using it?
Yes, you **should**.
Who **should** I **invite**?
What **ought** I **to bring** with me?
Oughtn't you **to back up** the file you're working on?
Yes, I **ought** to.
You **should read** this book – I'll lend it to you when I've finished.
You really **ought to watch** the new 'Walking with Dinosaurs' series.
I posted your birthday card today; you **should get** it tomorrow.
My parents **ought to be arriving** in Britain about now.
When **should** the washing machine **finish** its programme?
When **ought** the cake **to be** ready to take out of the oven?
We had a great walk – you **should have come** with us.
We couldn't stop laughing at Jack's performance – you **ought to have been** there!

Learn these short forms:

should not → shouldn't
ought not → oughtn't

In American English, ***oughtn't*** *isn't used.*

Grammar Help

- You use **ought to** like **should**. **Ought** is always used with **to + verb**. For example:
  We all **ought to drink** more water.
  You **ought to know** how to spell your own name by now.
  Which course **ought** I **to choose**?

Did you know?

- Nowadays, **should** is not much used as the past tense of **shall**, but you will find it in older literature:
  I know I **shall** soon **be** well again.
  I knew I **should** soon **be** well again.
  Nowadays, people prefer to use **would**:
  I knew I **would** soon be well again.
- **Why should ...?** is sometimes used to express annoyance at a situation:
  Why should I **pick up** your belongings for you?
  Why should Helen **get** more pocket money than me?

 ISBN 978-81-8477-744-4

May and Might

The modal verb may is used for asking politely for permission or for giving permission.

May I **watch** television now? Yes, you may.
Please **may** we **have** a biscuit?
May I **borrow** your calculator?
May I **see** your ticket?
Please **may** I **feed** your fish?
May Jim **come** with us to the swimming pool?
Yes, he **may**.
Please **may** Sally **borrow** this video? No, she **may not**.
You **may come** in.
You **may go** home if you aren't well.
John **may leave** now, but you may not.

You also use may to talk about things being possible or likely.

Take an umbrella. It **may rain**.
If it continues to rain, there **may be** a flood.
I **may go** to Mary's birthday party if I'm free.
You **may fall** down if you aren't careful.
I **may not have** time to come round and see you tonight.
We're early. The bus **may not come** for quite a while.
Are you going to the match?
I don't know. I **may** or I **may not**.

Grammar Help

Can and may are both used for asking and giving permission. May is more formal and polite than can:

Can I use your mobile phone?
Yes, you **can**.
May I come in now?
Certainly you **may**.

Might is used as the past tense of may.

He realized he **might catch** the early train if he hurried.
I knew my Mum **might find** out.
I was afraid there **might be** trouble.
I thought you **might like** this present.
She said she **might call** this evening.

 ISBN 978-81-8477-744-4

■ **Might** is used as an alternative to **may** to say that things are **possible** or **likely**.

Do be careful! You **might fall**!
Put your purse away or someone **might steal** it.
It's too early to phone them — they **might not be** up yet.
They **might cancel** the match if it rains, **mightn't** they?
I suppose they **might**.
Might there **be** a chance of seeing you later in the week? There **might**.

Learn this short form:
might not → mightn't

I **might need to** reinstall the program on the computer.
The problem **might** or **might not be** caused by a virus.
You **might try** deleting that file and reloading it.
Are you going to take that computer course? No, I **might not**.
If you had worked harder, you **might have passed** your exam.
You **might have warned** me you were bringing a friend to supper.

Must

The modal verb must is used to say that something has to be done, because it is necessary, or right, or because there is a law or rule about it.

We **must** always **use** a dictionary for difficult words.
I **must post** the letter now.
I cannot hear you. You **must speak** louder.
Why **must** I **get** up so early?
You **must not play** with matches.
Hurry! We **mustn't be** late!

Learn this short form:
must not → mustn't

You **mustn't let** the cat sleep on your bed.
Go to bed now. Oh, **must** I?
We **must keep** the beach clean, **mustn't** we?
We **mustn't tell** lies, **must** we?
You **mustn't change** television channels without asking.

■ You also use **must** to talk about things that are **very probable** or **likely**.

David **must be** out. He isn't answering the telephone.
I thought you **must be joking** when you said I'd won the competition.
Margaret **must be** at least fifteen now.

Grammar Help

You can use must in 'reported speech' after a saying verb in the past tense:

Mum told Tim he must hurry.

Otherwise, you use had to as the past tense of must:

PRESENT: It's late — I must **hurry**.
PAST: It was late — I had to **hurry**.

 ISBN 978-81-8477-744-4

Hello! You **must be** Peter.
He **must have forgotten** the time.
You **must have worked** very hard to get all this done.
There **must be** at least a thousand spectators.

Dare, Need and Used to

The verbs dare, need and used to behave like modal verbs in some ways. This section shows some common ways of using these three verbs.

■ The verb **dare** is used mainly with negatives and after **if**.

Learn these short forms:
dare not → daren't
need not → needn't

I'm worried, but I **daren't** tell my parents the truth.
Sally **doesn't dare disobey** her father.
If he **dares interfere** again, I'll get very angry.
Don't you **dare mention** this to Mum!
How **dare** you **tell** me I'm lazy!
After being beaten, the poor dog hardly **dared to come out** of its corner.
I **didn't dare jump** the gap between the two rocks.
He **dared not look out** of the window.
Come on, try! I **daren't.**
I wanted to ask a question, but I **didn't dare.**

Grammar Help

- **dare** can be used like an ordinary action verb, with **do** as its helping or auxiliary verb:
  She **doesn't dare tell** the truth or She **daren't tell** the truth.
- **The auxiliary do is common in the past tense:**
  She didn't **dare tell** the truth.
  (more formal) She **dared not tell** the truth.
- **The 3rd person singular can have an s in the present tense:**
  If he **dares interefere** again .... or If he **dare interfere** again ...
- **You can have an infinitive with or without to after dare:**
  She **didn't dare (to) tell** the truth. If he **dares (to) interfere** again ...
  But you never have a to-infinitive after dare not, daren't or dared not:
  She **dared not tell** the truth.
- **You don't use a to-infinitive after the idioms How dare ...? and Don't you dare ...!:**
  How dare they complain? Don't you dare complain!
- **Although modal verbs do not usually combine with each other, you can use dare with other modals:**
  I **wouldn't dare** contradict my teacher. I bought this hat to wear at the wedding, but I **might not dare** to.

 ISBN 978-81-8477-744-4

■ The verb **need** is used to say that an action is necessary.

We **need to book** those tickets straight away.
Fred **needs to concentrate** more.
I **needed to think.**
I **don't need to leave** yet.
Do you **need to go** shopping this morning?
You **didn't need to send** me that report — I already had a copy.
You **needn't cook** a meal for me tonight — I'll be out.
He can e-mail me — he **needn't write** a letter.
Need you **spend** so much time on that project?
Miss Lee told us we **needn't do** all the exercises.
You **needn't have worried** about me — I was quite OK.
Thanks for waiting for me, but you **needn't have.**

Grammar Help

■ **In positive sentences, need is used as an ordinary action verb using do as its helping or auxiliary verb, and followed by a to-infinitive:**

I needed to concentrate.

But in negative sentences and questions, you can use need as a modal verb or an ordinary action verb:

You **needn't** wait.
You **don't need to** wait.
Need you **change** your password?
Do you **need to change** your password?

■ **Although modal verbs do not usually combine with each other, you can use need to with other modals:**

I might **need to** change my password.
Won't you **need to** change your password?

■ The verb **used to** is a **past-tense** verb only. You use it for talking about situations that existed, and activities that were regular, in the past.

I **used to wear** my hair very long.
We **used to walk** home from school every day.
This computer **used to belong** to my brother.
People **used to think** the world was flat.
He **used not to mind** being teased, **did** he?
There **used to be** a fountain in the square, **didn't** there?
We **didn't use to get** as much homework as this.
Didn't he **use to have** a moustache?

Grammar Help

In negative sentences, you can say either:

I **used not to care** about the environment.

or

I **didn't use to care** about the environment.

Negative questions are usually formed with didn't ... use:

Didn't he **use to be** a lot fatter?

 ISBN 978-81-8477-744-4

Read the following passage. The bold items include active and passive verbs, imperative verbs, present and past participles, to-infinitives and infinitives without to, gerunds (verbal nouns), and phrasal verbs.

The fight for donations

There are more and more charities **seeking** donations across the world. Everywhere we **go**, we **are besieged** by demands for money such as, 'Please **give** generously' or '**Help** now!'

We cannot **give** them all money. The bulk of the money which **is earned** by us goes **to feed** and house ourselves and our families. We have to **make up** our minds which charities **to contribute** to.

It **has been suggested** that people are beginning to suffer from compassion fatigue. If communities **are asked** to give to too many good causes, they will not be able to **cope with** the demands. They might then **turn away from** all the charities.

Then, there is the bad publicity that **is suffered** by some charities. Some are successful at **collecting** money, but not so successful at **distributing** it to the needy. Too much money **is being spent** on administration.

Running a charity is not an easy task. Organizers of charities, however big or small, face apathy, criticism and increased competition. A local committee that is trying **to raise** money for the homeless in the town is likely to have to **deal with** similar problems to those that **are faced** by large international charities. Indeed, the local committees **are** more likely to receive criticism since they are easier to contact.

Appeals for help do not always receive the **deserved** response. However, this was not true in the case of the terrible tsunami disaster of December 2004. Not only governments, but also individual people in many countries, gave considerable sums of money to help the victims. This was a tragedy on such a huge scale that it affected a great many different nationalities. It touched the hearts of people all over the world and they responded by **giving** generously to the appeals. Fortunately, there was no sign of compassion fatigue then.

 ISBN 978-81-8477-744-4

Transitive and Intransitive Verbs

A verb which has an object is called a transitive verb.

Here are some sentences with transitive verbs. The words in colour are the object of each verb.

Birds **have** feathers.
The children **love** their pets.
He **owns** three cars.
I **saw** Sue yesterday.
Mum, Sally **hit** me!
They **are playing** chess.
Sue **has bought** a hat.
She **is typing** a letter on her computer.
He **is eating** an apple.
A ball **hit** Joe on the head.
The potter **has made** a beautiful jug.
Who **knows** the answer?

- **Some transitive verbs can have two objects.**

  The thing you give or do for someone is called the direct object. The person who receives the thing is called the indirect object.

  In these sentences, the indirect object is in colour and the direct object is in *italics*.

Dad **bought** James *a bike*.
Miss Lee **handed** John *his test paper*.
The bank **lent** him *money*.
Please **get** me *some coffee*.
Play us *a tune*, Simon.
Sue **is making** her doll *a dress*.
Mum **is reading** Jenny *a story*.
I **am writing** Grandma *a letter*.
I've **left** you *some food* in the fridge.
I'll **cook** you *a meal*.
Can you **fetch** me *a knife and fork*?

 ISBN 978-81-8477-744-4

- **A verb which does not have an object is called an intransitive verb.**

  Here are some sentences with intransitive verbs.

The soldiers **knelt** down when the emperor came in.
They **went** out for a walk.
Anne **stood** behind Susan.
Sally went upstairs and **dressed** for the party.
John **jogs** every day.
Maggie **looks** pretty today.
Lots of people **cycle** to work in China.
The boys **are playing** in the garden.
The hunter **was hiding** behind a tree.

Grammar Help

- **The object of a verb is the noun or pronoun that receives the action of the verb. For example:**
  Jack **kicked the ball.**
  The object of the verb **kicked** is **the ball.**
- **The indirect object comes before the direct object of the transitive verb.**

- **Some verbs can be either transitive or intransitive.**

Transitive	Intransitive
The pilot **is flying** a jet.	The eagle **is flying** freely in the sky.
Mr Lee **is driving** his new car.	Mr Lee **is driving** carefully.
The umpire **blew** the whistle to end the game.	The wind **blew** strongly.
They **are playing** dominoes.	They **are playing** in the garden.
He **studied** medicine.	The students **studied** hard.
Tim **is walking** his dog in the park.	Tim **is walking** briskly in the park.
He **runs** his own company.	He **runs** very fast.
They tried hard but **lost** the competition.	They took part in the competition but **lost**.

 ISBN 978-81-8477-744-4

Scholastic Active Grammar For Classes 6 to 8
Answer Key

1 Nouns

Page 32
Exercise 1

1. some, a
2. any
3. some, a
4. any
5. a, some
6. any
7. some
8. some, an
9. a, some
10. a, any
11. some, some
12. some, an, some

Page 33
Exercise 2

2. stationery
3. news
4. fruit
5. furniture
6. information
7. equipment
8. work
9. advice
10. clothing

Page 34
Exercise 3

1. the Eiffel Tower
2. Mount Fuji
3. Lake Superior
4. the Leaning Tower of Pisa
5. the United Kingdom
6. the Statue of Liberty
7. Great Britain
8. the Grand Canyon
9. the Black Sea
10. New Delhi
11. Tiananmen Square
12. the Brahmaputra
13. the Tower of London
14. the Merlion
15. the Indian Ocean
16. the Philippines
17. the North Pole
18. the Gulf of Mexico
19. the Andes
20. the Arctic Circle

2 Pronouns

Page 47
Exercise 1

2. third person singular
3. second person plural
4. third person plural
5. second person singular
6. third person singular
7. third person singular
8. first person plural
9. first person singular
10. third person singular
11. first person plural
12. third person plural

Page 48
Exercise 2

2. he
3. they
4. her
5. you
6. it
7. she
8. I, you
9. we
10. I, us
11. them
12. him

Page 49
Exercise 3

2. myself
3. themselves
4. ourselves
5. yourselves
6. herself
7. yourself
8. itself
9. myself
10. itself
11. themselves
12. himself

3 Adjectives

Page 69
Exercise 1

3. musical
4. selfish
5. rainy
6. dangerous
7. dusty
8. peaceful
9. weekly
10. artistic
11. massive
12. homeless
13. comfortable
14. successful
15. personal

Page 69
Exercise 2

2. big thick academic
3. tall narrow dark-green
4. charming young Singaporean
5. small fluffy white
6. noisy English
7. large square cardboard
8. crazy American
9. nasty tiny red stinging
10. high grey stone
11. wonderful new geographical
12. long pointed yellow

Page 70
Exercise 3

2. intelligent
3. wide
4. splendid
5. noisy
6. slender
7. soft
8. firm
9. handsome
10. extensive
11. easy
12. studious

Page 71
Exercise 4

2. dull
3. gentle
4. thin
5. stingy
6. light
7. narrow
8. slow
9. early
10. graceful
11. short
12. hollow

Page 71
Exercise 5

1. better
2. handsomest
3. farther or further
4. thinner
5. funniest
6. simplest
7. pleasantest
8. nicest
9. heavier
10. saddest
11. safest
12. politest

4 Determiners

Page 88
Exercise 1

3. Who
4. Which
5. what
6. Who
7. Which
8. What
9. Which
10. Who
11. What
12. Who
13. Which
14. Which

Page 89
Exercise 2

3. whom
4. which
5. which
6. who
7. that
8. which
9. who
10. that
11. whom
12. whom

Page 90
Exercise 3

Helen looked in _the_ cupboard in _the_ kitchen for _a_ tablecloth to put on _the_ dining table. She found _a_ pretty cloth with red spots. She spread _the_ cloth over _the_ table, and then she went to find _the_ knives and forks and spoons to lay on _the_ table ready for _the_ meal. 'Lay _an_ extra place,' said her mother, 'because Simon has invited _a_ friend.' Helen put mats round _the_ table and laid each place with _a_ knife, _a_ fork and _a_ spoon. Then she gave everyone _a_ glass. 'Shall I put _a_ candle in _the_ middle of _the_ table?' she asked. 'If you can find _a_ nice one,' said her mother.

Everybody came in and sat down at _the_ table. They talked about _the_ things they had done during _the_ day. Helen had been working on _a_ project at school. Simon had had _a_ piano lesson. Mum had been to _the_ dentist. Dad had been at _the_ office all day. Simon's friend had _a_ part in _the_ school play and he had been rehearsing. When they had finished _the_ meal, they turned on _the_ television and watched _the_ news. Then they saw _a_ programme about _the_ disappearance of wild animals from _the_ world.

Page 91
Exercise 4

1. some
2. a
3. An
4. any
5. some
6. a
7. any
8. a
9. any
10. some
11. a
12. a

5 Verbs

Page 145
Exercise 1

3. cycles
4. breathe
5. knows
6. are blowing
7. make
8. Susan's keying

ISBN 978-81-8477-744-4

9. want
10. are appearing
11. forgets
12. loves
13. I'm trying
14. Mum's doing
15. think it's raining

Page 146
Exercise 2

3. was staring, noticed
4. was still sleeping, landed
5. were wandering, spotted
6. were all running, walked
7. were you going, met
8. came, was still getting
9. were watching, heard
10. was cutting, began
11. called, was just finishing
12. was thinking, struck

Page 147
Exercise 3

2. will
3. shall
4. won't ~~not~~
5. will
6. will
7. won't ~~not~~
8. Will
9. shall
10. will
11. shan't ~~not~~
12. shall, won't ~~not~~
13. won't ~~not~~
14. will
15. Shall
16. won't ~~not~~

Page 148
Exercise 4

3. must finish
4. must have
5. mustn't alter
6. don't have to get up
7. must tell
8. had to wait
9. mustn't leave
10. had to open
11. must write
12. didn't have to wear

Page 149
Exercise 5

2. tell (V), me (IO), the whole story (DO)
3. hand (V), me (IO), that list (DO)
4. send (V), Granny (IO), a postcard (DO)
5. sing (V), us (IO), his favourite song (DO)
6. give (V), everybody (IO), a piece of cake (DO)
7. build (V), his rabbit (IO), a hutch (DO)
8. lend (V), Peter (IO), his bicycle (DO)
9. play (V), her teacher (IO), the new piano piece. (DO)
10. read (V), me (IO), the second question (DO)
11. fetch (V), me (IO), another pack of paper (DO)
12. cook (V), her friends (IO), a delicious meal (DO)

Page 150
Exercise 6

2. St Paul's Cathedral was designed by Sir Christopher Wren.
3. The part of the wicked uncle was played by Vincent.
4. This poem was written by Wordsworth.
5. The school is opened at 8.00 am. by the caretaker.
6. The football team is trained by Mr Kwo.
7. I was stung on the arm by a bee.
8. Singapore was founded by Sir Stamford Raffles.
9. These books were collected by my grandfather.
10. This apartment block is owned by the government.
11. In 1941, the house was destroyed by a bomb.
12. I was knocked off my bike by a taxi.

Page 151
Exercise 7

2. to leave
3. to take
4. to travel
5. to hurt
6. to train
7. to meet
8. to sing
9. to hold, to rain
10. to walk
11. to listen
12. to write

6 Adverbs

Page 160
Exercise 1

2. neatly
3. loudly, quietly
4. carefully
5. comfortably
6. angrily
7. musically
8. easily
9. suddenly
10. gradually, brightly
11. briskly
12. clearly

Page 161
Exercise 2

2. earlier
3. farther (or further)
4. most imaginatively
5. harder
6. later
7. more tidily
8. better
9. longest
10. sooner
11. more
12. worst

7 Prepositions

Page 178
Exercise 1

2. through (the door)
3. into (me)
4. in (Tokyo)
5. to (Julia)
6. of (Cinderella)
7. by (Shakespeare)
8. against (Peter)
9. in (it)
10. than (Joe), than (me)
11. over (the wall)
12. with (his brother)
13. from (the corner), for (Miss Lee)
14. at (this strange insect), on (my hand)

Page 180
Exercise 2

2. in, against
3. except
4. of
5. at, of
6. without
7. on
8. by
9. instead of
10. with
11. at, of
12. on
13. with
14. on
15. like

8 Conjunctions

Page 188
Exercise 1

2. and
3. and
4. or
5. or
6. but
7. or
8. but
9. and
10. or
11. but
12. or

Page 188
Exercise 2

2. so that (or in order that)
3. so that (or in order that)
4. so as to (or in order to)
5. so that (or in order that)
6. so that (or in order that)
7. so as to (or in order to)
8. so as to (or in order to)
9. so that (or in order that)
10. so as to (or in order to)

Page 189
Exercise 3

2. so
3. so
4. such a
5. such a
6. so
7. such a
8. such
9. so
10. such

9 Interjections

Page 192
Exercise 1

1. Shh, I can hear someone at the door.
2. Oh, how I wish it would rain.
3. David wanted to play football with his friends, but alas, he twisted his ankle.
4. 'Oh dear!' yelled Mom. 'How did your clothes get so dirty?'
5. It is indeed time for the opera to begin.
6. Phew! I am never riding that roller coaster again.
7. 'Excuse me,' said Mrs Lee. 'Could you tell me the way to the supermarket?'
8. Ouch! Don't step on my foot.
9. Sorry, I didn't see your foot there.
10. Goodnight, Grandma. I will see you in the morning.

10 Sentences

Page 196
Exercise 1

1. Statement
2. Question
3. Imperative/Command
4. Imperative/Request
5. Statement

 ISBN 978-81-8477-744-4

Page 196
Exercise 2

1. Matthew (S) slept for ten hours last night (P).
2. The nib of the pen (S) is broken (P).
3. The teacher (S) asked Tanya to redo her homework (P).
4. My cat (S) laps up her milk in no time (P).
5. Maria (S) told her friend John that she would not be able to go to his party (P).

11 Phrases

Page 201
Exercise 1

1. Put your maths textbooks away, please.
2. I'm giving you some grammar Exercise s for your English homework.
3. We're performing Macbeth, one of Shakespeare's plays.
4. I found some pretty shells on the beach and added them to my large collection.
5. Mary, my cousin from London, is visiting us soon.
6. Lucy examined the curious purple envelope carefully before opening it.
7. Look at these splendid red apples that I bought at the local supermarket.
8. Joe gave his last coin to a ragged child.
9. Yesterday I met Mark, an old friend of mine.
10. There are three good reasons why I can't play in Saturday's match.

Page 201
Exercise 2

1. In my opinion, she behaved extremely sensibly.
2. For once, the train arrived on time.
3. We shall be leaving at four o'clock.
4. Dad explained the process in great detail.
5. Come and sit beside me.
6. Watch once again, a bit more carefully.
7. We played tennis until half past six.
8. He walks very slowly with a stick.
9. We're going abroad during the vacation.
10. At least I played my part pretty well in the play.

Page 202
Exercise 3

2. She's a two-month-old baby.
3. We're a two-car family.
4. We had a two-hour delay.
5. It's an eight-page booklet.
6. They use up-to-date methods.
7. It's horrible-smelling cheese.
8. It is an eighteenth-century house.
9. It's a very odd-looking building.
10. It was a three-day journey.

12 Clauses

Page 214
Exercise 1

1. the grammar is difficult
2. I had to sing a solo at the concert
3. you aren't successful
4. he's still in good health
5. you think it sounds silly
6. We started the second book
7. Everybody's welcome to join the course
8. she's only ten herself
9. she's good at drawing horses
10. Mum usually laughs

Page 215
Exercise 2

3. The doctor who (or that) treated my injury was from Thailand.
4. The umbrella Anna lent me is hanging over there.
5. The strange noise that (or which) woke us in the night was the foghorn.
6. The friend I was trying to contact was away on holiday.
7. The passengers we made friends with were Scottish.
8. The hair-dryer Jane bought was faulty.
9. The armchair you're sitting in was my mother's.
10. The man who (or that) opened the door was tall and thin.

Page 216
Exercise 3

2. the apartment would be available in two weeks' time
3. he can't win
4. the plan will succeed
5. you were looking for me
6. you painted that picture yourself
7. he just died in his sleep
8. it's right to kill insects
9. you don't want to listen to all that nonsense
10. you were going out tonight

13 More About Sentences

Page 224
Exercise 1

1. Complex	2. Compound	3. Simple
4. Complex	5. Compound	6. Compound
7. Complex	8. Simple	9. Complex
10. Complex		

Page 224
Exercise 2

1. Ali has not won a scholarship.
2. The dog did not wag his tail when he saw me.
3. Joan cannot write very well.
4. The students never finish their homework on time.
5. It doesn't look like it's going to rain.
6. The books have not been dispatched to Australia.
7. Sam will not be in office tomorrow.
8. The hurricane did not cause a lot of damage to the town.
9. Tina does not want to go on a month-long holiday.
10. Weather forecasts do not say that this summer will be very hot.

Page 225
Exercise 3

1. Does Sheela work in a restaurant?
2. Do I have to catch the 8 pm bus if I want to see the movie?
3. Is the phone working anymore?
4. Does Misha drive to school every day?
5. Can Tom play any musical instrument?
6. Are the shoes too tight for Tanya?
7. Has Kim learnt how to swim yet?
8. Do I need to make a left at the intersection?
9. Is it advisable to eat fast food regularly ?
10. Over how many months is the language course taught?

Page 226
Exercise 4

1. We should leave before it gets dark, shouldn't we?
2. You will enjoy watching this movie, won't you?
3. Bonnie doesn't like eggs for breakfast, does she?
4. The school will be closed tomorrow, won't it?
5. The traffic at this hour is very bad, isn't it?
6. The town is full of historical monuments, isn't it?
7. I don't have to make a class presentation, do I?
8. Joe will see you tomorrow for lunch, won't he?
9. The doctor said there was nothing to worry about, didn't he/she?
10. Your new job is in another country, isn't it?

 ISBN 978-81-8477-744-4

14 Direct and Indirect Speech

Page 232
Exercise 1

3. would
4. would
5. couldn't
6. should
7. was, won't
8. hated
9. couldn't
10. had

Page 233
Exercise 2

2. she was, his
3. was, her there
4. she didn't
5. her, was
6. they had seen
7. they had taught
8. her, was hurting
9. she would
10. he won't be able to, tomorrow

Page 234
Exercise 3

2. not to leave her
3. to halt
4. to take a week's holiday
5. from entering
6. to help her with the beds
7. to be careful on the steps
8. to stay till tomorrow
9. not to look at the answers
10. to wipe our feet

15 Punctuation

Page 244
Exercise 1

1. Tom had an extra helping of ice cream.
2. Is there anything I can do to help?
3. What are you going to do with that?
4. What you did was a complete waste of time.
5. There's enough for everyone, isn't there?
6. Help! I'm drowning!
7. She asked him what he was intending to do.
8. Good morning! (or Good morning.) How are you today?
9. You idiot! You've broken my favourite vase.
10. What I want to know is whether or not you're willing to help us.
11. Do you think you could move over a bit?
12. Stop that at once!

Page 244
Exercise 2

1. Could I have another glass of water, please?
2. Excuse me, madam. Is that your purse on the floor?
3. Please, John, don't do that.
4. Oh, I'm so glad you managed to come, my dear.
5. Come along, children. Yes, you too, James.
6. No, no, no, not these ones! I want those pink ones over there.
7. I'm feeling very well, thank you.
8. Yes, that's the right answer. Well done, lad.
9. Well, here you are at last! You know, Liz, you really ought to try to be more punctual.
10. Believe me, it's no fun sleeping in a bus shelter in a thunderstorm.

Page 245
Exercise 3

1. He was followed into the room by a dirty, long-haired, nasty-looking dog.
2. This is a sure cure for coughs, colds, chills, fevers(,) and all sorts of aches and pains.
3. On the shelf were an odd assortment of boxes, bottles and tins.
4. The official languages of Singapore are English, Malay, Mandarin and Tamil.
5. With eating, drinking, talking, singing and dancing, the evening passed all too quickly.
6. He was wearing a brown and grey jacket, grey trousers(,) and green boots.
7. I heard a loud, eerie, almost despairing cry.
8. She spoke rapidly, excitedly, with eyes flashing.
9. Let's eat, drink and be merry.
10. Peter, John and I are going to the football match tomorrow.

Page 246
Exercise 4

1. I'll be back in a moment. Don't go away. We've some things to discuss about next week's concert.
2. She doesn't know what she's supposed to do.
3. They've spent a lot of money on their children's Christmas presents.
4. It's a lovely little dog, isn't it?
5. I'm so glad you've come.
6. It's no wonder that the dog's scratching its ears. It's got fleas.
7. Let's go inside. I'll put on the kettle and we'll have a nice cup of tea.
8. The teachers searched through every student's locker.
9. The teachers searched through both boys' lockers.
10. Could you tell me where the men's department is, please?
11. I suppose that's some people's idea of fun, but it certainly isn't mine.
12. There's at least three weeks' more work to do here.

Page 247
Exercise 5

There was a table set out under a tree in front of the house, and the March hare and the hatter were having tea at it. A dormouse was sitting between them, fast asleep, and the other two were using it as a cushion, resting their elbows on it and talking over its head. "Very uncomfortable for the dormouse," thought Alice. "Only as it's asleep, I suppose it doesn't mind."

The table was a large one but the three were all crowded together at one corner of it. "No room! No room!" they cried out when they saw Alice coming. "There's plenty of room!" said Alice indignantly, and she sat down in a large arm-chair at one end of the table.

 ISBN 978-81-8477-744-4

Active Voice and Passive Voice

- When the **subject** of a verb is **doing** the action, you say the verb is in the **active**.

Peter **drew** the picture.
Dad **parked** his car in the drive.
A Singapore company **published** this book.
Susan **read** the next story.
Asians **eat** rice.
Australia **produces** apples and oranges.

- When the **subject** of a verb **receives** the action, you say the verb is in the **passive**.

The picture **was drawn** by Peter.
The car **was parked** in the drive.
This book **was published** by a Singapore company.
Apples and oranges **are produced** in Australia.
Joe's hands **are covered** in paint.
All the hotel rooms **are cleaned** once a day.
These computers **were manufactured** in Taiwan.
The town **was hit** by a typhoon yesterday.
The train **was filled** with commuters.
Kangaroos **are** only **found** in Australia.

Grammar Help

- **Verbs that you can use in the passive are transitive verbs.**
- **The prepositions by, with or in are often used to say who or what causes the action. For example:**

The play **was written** by Sheridan.
All the books **are covered** in dust.
The air **was filled** with birdsong.

- **Some sentences in the passive voice may not tell you who does the action.**

The illegal immigrants **were taken** to the police station.
He **was fined** $100 for a traffic offence.
We **were warned** about the approaching storm.
The room **was painted** last week.
It **is said** that a cat has nine lives.
It **is believed** that he died in India.
You **are asked** to attend a meeting tomorrow.
The workers **are paid** very little for their work.
Breakfast **is served** between 7.00 and 9.00 am.

Did you know?

When you use **it is said** or **it is believed**, you mean the same as **people say**, or **people believe**.

Here are three ways of saying the same thing:
It was said that she was a genius.
or
People said that she was a genius.
or
She was said to be a genius.

 ISBN 978-81-8477-744-4

- Some sentences are used only in the **passive voice.**

George **was born** in 1990.
My house **is situated** in a quiet part of the town.

- For the **simple present tense,** you use **am, is** or **are** with a **past participle** to form the **passive voice.**

Active Voice	Passive Voice
The caretaker **locks** the doors.	The doors **are locked** by the caretaker.
Miss Lee **teaches** us ballet.	We **are taught** ballet by Miss Lee.
Ben **conducts** the orchestra.	The orchestra **is conducted** by Ben.
Students often **borrow** library books.	Library books **are** often **borrowed** by students.

- For the **simple past tense,** you use **was** or **were** with a **past participle** to form the **passive voice.**

Active Voice	Passive Voice
Dad **drove us** home.	We **were driven** home by Dad.
The army **built** this bridge.	This bridge **was built** by the army.
A dog **bit** him.	He **was bitten** by a dog.
Columbus **discovered** America.	America **was discovered** by Columbus.

Grammar Help

Here is a table to remind you about the passive voice.

For simple present tense			**For simple past tense**		
am	+	past participle	was	+	past participle
are	+	past participle	were	+	past participle
is	+	past participle			

- For the **present continuous tense,** you use **am, is** or **are** with **being,** followed by a **past participle,** to form the **passive voice.**

Active Voice	Passive Voice
The waves **are washing** away the sandcastle.	The sandcastle **is being washed** away by the waves.
Our teacher **is scolding** us.	We **are being scolded** by our teacher.
I am producing the school play this year.	The school play **is being produced** by me this year.

 ISBN 978-81-8477-744-4

- For the **past continuous tense**, you use **was** or **were** with **being**, followed by a **past participle**, to form the **passive voice.**

Active Voice	Passive Voice
Miss Lee **was making** our costumes.	Our costumes **were being made** by Miss Lee.
The police **were chasing** the thief.	The thief **was being chased** by the police.
Class 2A **were organizing** a jumble sale.	A jumble sale **was being organized** by Class 2A.

Grammar Help

Here is a table to remind you about the **passive voice.**

For present continuous tense

am + being + past participle
is + being + past participle
are + being + past participle

For past continuous tense

was + being + past participle
were + being + part participle

- For the **future tense**, you use **shall** or **will** with **be**, followed by a **past participle**, to form the **passive voice.**

Active Voice	Passive Voice
We **shall present** the prizes to the winners.	The prizes **will be presented** to the winners by us.
The girls **will visit** the old folks next week.	The old folks **will be visited** by the girls next week.
Jane **will play** the role of the Princess in the play.	The role of the Princess in the play **will be played** by Jane.
Peter **will lead** the team in the procession.	The team **will be led** by Peter in the procession.
The nurse **will look** after him.	He **will be looked** after by the nurse.
The choir **will sing** the next hymn.	The next hymn **will be sung** by the choir.
The couple **will cut** the cake before the speeches.	The cake **will be cut** by the couple before the speeches.
The boss **will make** a speech at the dinner.	A speech **will be made** by the boss at the dinner.
I **shall welcome** all of you personally.	All of you **will be welcomed** by me personally.

Grammar Help

Here is a table to remind you about the **passive voice** for the future tense.

shall + be + past participle
will + be + past participle

 ISBN 978-81-8477-744-4

Nouns
Pronouns
Adjectives
Determiners
Verbs
Adverbs
Prepositions
Conjunctions
Interjections
Sentences
Phrases
Clauses
More about Sentences
Direct and Indirect Speech
Punctuation

- For the **present perfect tense**, you use **have** or **has** with **been**, followed by a **past participle**, to form the **passive voice.**

Active Voice	Passive Voice
Ali **has scored** two goals.	Two goals **have been scored** by Ali.
The workmen **have painted** the house.	The house **has been painted** by the workmen.
The gardener **has swept** away the leaves.	The leaves **have been swept** away by the gardener.

- For the **past perfect tense**, you use **had** with **been**, followed by a **past participle**, to form the **passive voice.**

Active Voice	Passive Voice
The big bad wolf **had blown** down the house of straw and the house sticks.	The house of straw and the house of sticks **had been** blown down by the big bad wolf.
The hunters **had caught** a fox.	A fox **had been caught** by the hunters.
Snow White's stepmother **had poisoned** her.	Snow White **had been poisoned** by her stepmother.

Grammar Help

Here is a table to remind you about the passive voice.

For present perfect tense	For past perfect tense
have + been + past participle	had + been + past participle
has + been + past participle	

Verb Agreement

When you write a sentence, you have to make sure that the subject and the verb match each other.

- If the subject is a **singular noun**, or the pronoun **he, she** or **it**, you need a **singular verb.**

The earth **moves** around the sun.
She **shares** her toys with her friends.
He **enjoys** music.
Dad always **drives** carefully.

 ISBN 978-81-8477-744-4

The postman **is delivering** a parcel.
The zookeeper **is feeding** the animals.
She **was looking** out of the window.
The radio **was playing** loud music.
The fisherman **has caught** a lot of fish.
Mum **has bought** a dress for Sally.
It **is snowing**.
Is it **raining**?
Does everyone **know** the tune?

- If the subject is a **plural noun**, or the pronoun **we**, **you** or **they**, you need a **plural verb**.

The two girls always **walk** home together.
The stars **shine** brightly on a clear night.
All birds **lay** eggs.
Mum and Dad **love** us.
Clouds **are racing** across the sky.
The children **are playing** on the swings.
Both of them **have worked** hard.
We **have finished** our game of tennis.
These stamps **don't stick** very well, **do** they?
Do you all **know** the words?

Grammar Help

Matching the verb with the subject is called **verb agreement** or **concord.**

- **Group nouns** are usually singular, but can be used with a singular or a plural verb.

The audience **are laughing**.
The audience **is laughing**.
Our team **have won**.
Our team **has won**.
My family **come** from Hong Kong.
My family **comes** from Hong Kong.
My class **were** sent home early.
My class **was** sent home early.
The crowd **were watching**.
The crowd **was watching**.
The choir **were cheered** by the audience.
The choir **was cheered** by the audience.
The band **are playing**.
The band **is playing**.

Grammar Help

Remember some plural nouns, such as **people**, **cattle**, **police**, don't end with **-s**. You always use a **plural verb** with such plural nouns. For example:

People **like** getting presents.
The cattle **are** in the field.
The police **have found** the thief.

 ISBN 978-81-8477-744-4

Nouns
Pronouns
Adjectives
Determiners
Verbs
Adverbs
Prepositions
Conjunctions
Interjections
Sentences
Phrases
Clauses
More about Sentences
Direct and Indirect Speech
Punctuation

The Imperative

When you are giving orders or commands or instructions to one person or a group of people, you use the base form of the verb. This use of the verb is called the imperative.

Stand, everyone!
Tidy your bedroom immediately!
OK, children, **open** your books at page 25.
Always **stop** and **look** both ways before crossing.
Read the next chapter for your homework.
Choose a partner!
Eat plenty of vegetables.
Find some nice round pebbles.
Come back soon!
Have a biscuit.
Take a sandwich.
Come and **look** at this, Tom!

Grammar Help

Another firm way of telling people to do or not to do something is to use are + to + verb. For example:

You **are to sit** quietly!
You **are not to touch** that switch!

When you tell people not to do something, you use the helping verb do with not, or you can shorten it to don't. For example:

Do not remove this trolley from the supermarket.
Don't remove this trolley from the supermarket.
Do not cry, Anna!
Don't cry, Anna!

- **Imperatives are a very direct way of telling people to do something. You can make an imperative sound politer by using do or please before it.**

Please come in.
Do sit down.
Do check these figures again.
Please help yourselves to some food.
Please don't change anything on my computer.

Grammar Help

Remember that you can also use the helping verb would to sound polite. For example:

Please would you clear the table?
Would you please talk more quietly?
Would you please not change anything on my computer?

 ISBN 978-81-8477-744-4

Gerunds

There are two kinds of words ending with **-ing** that are formed from verbs. One kind of **-ing** form is the **present participle.** The present participle is used in forming the **continuous tenses.** It can also be used as an adjective.

The other kind of **-ing** form is called a **gerund** and you use it as a noun. It is also called a **verbal noun.** Here are some examples.

You're good at **drawing**.
He loves **dancing** and **singing**.
Have you ever tried **skating**?
Doing exercise is important.
I don't like **waiting in queues**.
We enjoyed **meeting you**.
I'm looking forward to **seeing him**.
It's no good **getting upset**.
No **talking in class**, please!
You need a shower after **exercising**.
Running is a good way to keep fit.
She hasn't started **writing her essay** yet.
His sister prefers **reading** and **watching videos**.
Read the agreement carefully before **signing it**.

> **Grammar Help**
>
> Gerunds or verbal nouns are often used **before** another noun like an adjective. For example:
>
> **washing** powder
> **running** shoes
> **reading** glasses
> a **sleeping** bag
> a **jogging** suit
> a **sewing** machine

The Infinitive

The **infinitive** is the base form of a verb. It is often used with **to** before it. Infinitives with **to** before them are called **to-infinitives.** There are lots of ways of using **to-infinitives.**

■ You use **to-infinitives** after some **verbs.**

David and I **agreed to meet** at 4 o'clock.
I'll **arrange to see** the dentist straight away.
I **hope to go** to university.
We **intend to move** house soon.
I **like to get up** early in the mornings.
Maggie **began to cry**.
Joe **has decided to buy** a puppy.
Paul **has learnt to swim**.
I **didn't mean to hurt** you.
It**'s starting to rain**.

 ISBN 978-81-8477-744-4

- Some verbs have an **object** before the **to-infinitive.**

Miss Lee allowed **us to leave** early.
Sue asked **me to help** her.
The policeman asked **us to wait.**
Anne persuaded **me to join** her choir.

Grammar Help

You can use the word not with a to-infinitive. You usually put it before to. For example:

Promise **not to tell** any one.
She told me **not to turn off** the computer.

- You use **to-infinitives** after some **adjectives.**

Julie was **afraid to cross** the road.
I'm so **glad to see** you.
He's the **first to arrive.**
Helen was the **last to leave.**
Science movies are so **interesting to watch.**
Are these nuts **good to eat?**
English verbs are not very **easy to learn.**
Those maths problems were **difficult to work out.**
They are all **keen to be** in the team.
He is **likely to win.**
You're **welcome to come** with me.

- You use **to-infinitives** after some **nouns and pronouns to express the idea of purpose.**

Take **a book to read** in case you get bored.
I phoned for **a taxi to take** us to the airport.
Bring **a mat to sit** on.
Have you all got **something to eat?**
I've got **nothing to wear.**
Isn't there **anything** else **to watch?**

- You often use **to-infinitives** in sentences beginning with **it is.**

It is very silly **to put** hot food in the fridge.
It's good **to be** back.
It's a good idea **to check** in early.
Is it time **to go?**

 ISBN 978-81-8477-744-4

To-infinitives sometimes follow words like **how, what, which** and **where,** after verbs that are to do with asking, knowing, learning or instructing.

Dad told me which key **to press**.
Sue asked me where **to buy** the best computer.
I can't think what **to write**.
Let me know how many copies **to print**.

I had no idea who **to ask**.
The nurse told him which pills **to take**.
Helen is learning how **to drive**.
I didn't know what **to do**.

Infinitives that come after helping verbs like **do, will, shall, would, should, can, could, may, might** and **must** do not have the word **to** before them.

I can **swim**.
He will **win** the race.
Can you **help** me, please?
May I **come** in?
We shall all **go** to Paul's party.

Don't **wait** for me.
It might **rain**.
You must **try**.
Should I **apply**?
I would **like** a copy.

Grammar Help

You can sometimes use the word to of the to-infinitive alone, if the meaning is clear. For example:

You can borrow these videos if you would like **to**.
She told me to turn off the computer but I didn't know how **to**.

Phrasal Verbs

A phrasal verb is a phrase consisting of a verb and a particle like on, of or at. The particle may be an adverb or a preposition, and gives the verb a special meaning.

They can't **agree with** each other about which road to take.
William Tell **aimed at** the apple on his son's head.
This house **belongs to** a rich man.
She is **blowing out** the candles on the cake.
The soldiers **blew up** the bridge.
His car **broke down** in the middle of the road.
A fire **broke out** yesterday.
A burglar **broke into** our house last night.
A heavy storm **brought down** the trees.
I was **brought up** in Singapore.

 ISBN 978-81-8477-744-4

A fire **burnt down** the whole village.
The boy **was beaten** up by some bullies.
The referee had to **call off** the match because of the fighting.
He is trying to **cover up** his mistake.
The frog **changed into** a handsome prince.
John and Joe are friends. They **get along** well.
He is **cutting down** the tree with an electric saw.
Baby birds have to **depend on** the mother bird for food.
Jane **dressed up** as a princess.
The passengers are **getting off** the bus.
Jim doesn't let the older boys **push** him **around**.

Here are some more sentences with phrasal verbs.

When the train arrived, a lot of people **got on**.
The doctor advised him to **give up** smoking.
I want to be a lawyer when I **grow up**.
Hurry up, or you will miss the bus.
The students listened and **jotted down** notes.
Little Helen can't **keep up** with her sister.
Keep off the grass.
Danger! **Keep out**!
Doctors and nurses **look after** patients.
Dad is **looking for** his watch.
Some of the older pupils **look down** on the younger ones.
Everyone is **joining in** the discussion.
Everyone was **laughing at** the emperor's new clothes.
The children are **lining up** for the school assembly.
She has **made up** her mind to study nursing.
I'm always **mixing up** the twins.
The children have **messed up** the room.
I **picked** him **up** from the station.
He has **put on** a lot of weight.
The firemen have **put out** the fire.
Mike is **rushing off** home after school.
We have **run out** of tea.
Tell him to **shut up**.
She was **showing off** her bracelet.
Watch out! There's a car coming!
Don't waste water! **Turn off** the tap.
He **took off** his hat when he entered the room.

 ISBN 978-81-8477-744-4

Exercise 1

Choose either the simple present or the present continuous to fill the blanks in these sentences. Use short forms where you can. Two have already been done for you.

1. The moon ___gets___ its light from the sun. (**get**)
2. We ___are learning___ about Brazil today. (**learn**)
3. Dad __________ to his office every day. (**cycle**)
4. Humans and animals __________ oxygen. (**breathe**)
5. Miss Lee __________ a lot of facts. (**know**)
6. Look! The trees __________ about in the wind. (**blow**)
7. Blue and red __________ purple. (**make**)
8. Susan __________ an e-mail message to Sally. (**key**)
9. I __________ to be an actor. (**want**)
10. Lots of dark clouds __________ over the horizon. (**appear**)
11. The head teacher never __________ anybody's name. (**forget**)
12. The baby __________ chocolate ice cream. (**love**)
13. I __________ to do this sum. (**try**)
14. Mum __________ her hair in front of the mirror. (**do**)
15. I __________ it __________ again. (**think, rain**)

 ISBN 978-81-8477-744-4

Simple Past and Past Continuous

- WHAT WERE YOU DOING WHEN ... ?
- You often use the past continuous to say what **was going on** (past continuous) when something **happened** (simple past).

Exercise 2

Fill in the past continuous and the simple past in each of the following sentences. Two have already been done for you.

1. I ___was washing___ the dishes when the doorbell ___rang___. (**wash, ring**)
2. What ___was___ he ___doing___ when you ___saw___ him? (**do, see**)
3. George ________ out of the window when he ________ something odd. (**stare, notice**)
4. Dad ________ still ________ when the plane ________. (**sleep, land**)
5. We ________ through the woods when we ________ a ring on the ground. (**wander, spot**)
6. The pupils ________ all ________ round the classroom when in ________ the head teacher. (**run, walk**)
7. Where ________ you ________ when we ________ you? (**go, meet**)
8. When Susan ________ to fetch me, I ________ still ________ dressed. (**come, get**)
9. My family and I ________ television when we ________ a loud bang. (**watch, hear**)
10. Mum ________ the grass when the hurricane ________. (**cut, begin**)
11. When Miss Lee ________ 'Stop writing!', I ________ just ________ the last question. (**call, finish**)
12. I ________ of nothing in particular when an idea ________ me. (**think, strike**)

 ISBN 978-81-8477-744-4

Exercise 3

Fill in will or shall in the following sentences; use shall for I and we, and use won't and shan't where you can. One has been done for you.

1. I ____shan't____ ~~not~~ be able to meet you at the station.
2. This colour __________ go better with your curtains.
3. We __________ all miss our cousins when they go home.
4. I hope you __________ not be late tonight.
5. The new ring road __________ make a big difference to the city-centre traffic.
6. The senior school __________ feel strange at first.
7. It __________ not be long before the baby's walking.
8. __________ you see Janet later today?
9. My brother and I __________ arrange accommodation for you.
10. Everybody __________ want to read the new Harry Potter book.
11. We __________ not be upset if we don't win.
12. I __________ send you your tickets – there __________ not be any problems.
13. The dictionary __________ not be published till September.
14. That bed __________ break if you jump on it like that.
15. __________ I start the washing machine?
16. The computer __________ not work if you don't turn it on.

Shall or Will?

- You can use **shall** or **will** with **I** and **we**.
- You use **will** with **you, he, she, it, they**, and with plural or singular nouns.
- You can shorten **shall not** to **shan't** and **will not** to **won't**.

 ISBN 978-81-8477-744-4

Exercise 4

Fill in must, mustn't, had to, don't have to or didn't have to, choosing a verb from the box below. Two have already been done for you.

alter	buy	catch	finish	forget
get up	have	leave	meet	open
tell	wait	wear	write	

1. I ___must catch___ the 7.30 train or I'll be late for my meeting.
2. Miss Lee found me a spare copy of the book, so I ___don't have to buy___ one.
3. Dad told us he ________________ some work for his boss.
4. I'm very tired. I ________________ some sleep.
5. You ________________ anything on my computer because it will cause problems.
6. It's still early. We ________________ yet.
7. You ________________ me all about your trip.
8. I'm sorry I'm late. I ________________ an hour for the bus.
9. You knew you ________________ the school grounds without permission.
10. We ________________ all our cases when we came through the customs.
11. You ________________ clearly in your exam.
12. The weather was hot and dry in London, so we ________________ our raincoats at all.

 ISBN 978-81-8477-744-4

Exercise 5

Pick out the verb, the direct object and the indirect object. You can use V for verb, DO for direct object, and IO for indirect object. One has been done for you.

1. Mum is making Susie a party dress.
   make (V), Susie (IO), a party dress (DO)
2. Tell me the whole story.
3. Could you hand me that list?
4. Have you sent Granny a postcard yet?
5. James sang us his favourite song.
6. Helen gave everybody a piece of cake.
7. Charlie is building his rabbit a hutch.
8. George lent Peter his bicycle.
9. Anna played her teacher the new piano piece.
10. Read me the second question.
11. Please fetch me another pack of paper from the cupboard.
12. Jean is going to cook her friends a delicious meal.

Two Objects

- Some transitive verbs can have two objects, a direct object and an indirect object. The indirect object comes before the direct object.

Mum gave **me** two dollars. The **direct object** of **give** is **two dollars** and the **indirect object is me.**

Miss Lee read **her pupils** a story. The **direct object** of **read** is **a story**, and the **indirect object** is **her pupils.**

 ISBN 978-81-8477-744-4

Exercise 6

Turn the following sentences into the passive. One has been done for you.

1. Anna takes the children to the park every afternoon.
   The children are taken to the park by Anna every afternoon.

2. Sir Christopher Wren designed St Paul's Cathedral.

3. Vincent played the part of the wicked uncle.

4. Wordsworth wrote this poem.

5. The caretaker opens the school at 8.00 am.

6. Mr Kwo trains the football team.

7. A bee stung me on the arm.

8. Sir Stamford Raffles founded Singapore.

9. My grandfather collected these books.

10. The government owns this apartment block.

11. In 1941, a bomb destroyed the house.

12. A taxi knocked me off my bike.

 ISBN 978-81-8477-744-4

Exercise 7

Fill in the gaps with a *to*-infinitive using the verbs in the box. One has been done for you.

come	hold	hurt	leave	listen
meet	rain	sing	take	train
travel	walk	write		

1. Do you want _to come_ to the shops with me?
2. You don't need __________ yet, it's not late.
3. Don't forget __________ your umbrella with you.
4. My parents are planning __________ abroad.
5. I didn't mean __________ your feelings.
6. Joe hopes __________ as a doctor.
7. Mum has arranged __________ the head teacher next week.
8. The birds woke me up when they began __________.
9. We intended __________ a barbecue, but it started __________.
10. Has the baby learnt __________ yet?
11. I'm trying __________ to the radio.
12. I promise __________ to you every week.

To-infinitives

- Many verbs can be followed by **to** + the infinitive (the base form) of another verb: He **decided to leave** school early. Granny **learnt to use** a computer very quickly.

 ISBN 978-81-8477-744-4

6 Adverbs

Read the following passage. The items in bold are all adverbs and adverbial phrases of various kinds.

A travel journal

We left France **on Wednesday** and **yesterday** we started our Italian trip. **At first**, my parents intended to spend all the time in Rome. **However**, they **then** decided to visit Naples and the surrounding area **first** and go to Rome **after that**.

Earlier today, we went to see the remains at Pompeii and Herculaneum.

They were buried when the volcano Mount Vesuvius **all of a sudden** erupted **in AD 79**. I was **in a state of excitement all last night**. I was **extremely** anxious to see such famous remains.

On our arrival, a **very** funny thing happened. My father **suddenly** shouted **angrily**, '**Where** did that come from?' He was cleaning some **rather** sticky white stuff **from his jacket**. The guide said **apologetically**, 'I'm afraid it's pigeon droppings. The birds come **here all the time** and they make a **terribly** unpleasant mess. **Unfortunately**, some of the visitors feed them.'

She **next** told us, **rather sadly,** that the pigeon droppings cause **absolutely** dreadful damage to ancient monuments and that they cause such damage **in a great many parts of the world**.

She said that the Herculaneum authorities had been trying **hard for many years** to rid the area **completely** of the pigeons. **Just recently**, she said **more hopefully**, they had been trying out something **entirely** new by bringing in two large hawks.

'**Why** did they do that?' asked Dad, sounding **quite** surprised.

She said that that the hawks were **there** to frighten off the pigeons and to prevent them from nesting **in the ruins** and from corroding them **with their droppings**.

We had an **utterly** fascinating day **at the ruins**. **In fact**, I have **never** been **anywhere** so **incredibly** interesting. I liked them **best** of all the places we visited.

PS Dad got home **safely** without being hit **accidentally** by any more pigeon droppings!

 ISBN 978-81-8477-744-4

An **adverb** is a **describing word**. It often **describes** or **modifies** actions or **verbs**. It tells you the way someone does something.

Because adverbs may consist of several words, the general term **adverbials** is sometimes given to the whole adverb class. It may, however, be convenient for you to think of single-word adverbs just as **adverbs**, and perhaps use the term **adverbials** for adverbs that consist of several words. Alternatively, you can call them **adverbial phrases** or, if they begin with a preposition, **prepositional phrases**.

- A lot of adverbs end in **-ly**. You form these adverbs by adding **-ly** to adjectives.

I can run **quickly**.
She jumped **bravely**.
He bowed **politely**.
He writes **neatly**.
The nightingale sings **beautifully**.
The tortoise moves **slowly**.
The tiger roared **fiercely**.
The baby's yelling **loudly**.
We waited **patiently** in the queue.
She always rides **carefully**.
They waved goodbye **sadly**.
They are reading quietly in the **library**.
She **wisely** decided not to cross the road.
Are you sitting **comfortably**?

Grammar Help

Not all words that end in **-ly** are adverbs. Some **adjectives** end in **-ly** too. For example:
a **costly** diamond
elderly folks
lively children
a **lovely** dress
a **lonely** boy
friendly neighbours

- When the adjective ends with **-y**, you change the **y** to **i** before you add **-ly** to form the adverb.

She shouted **angrily**.
They are playing **happily**.
He yawned **sleepily**.
She frowned **gloomily**.
They are talking **noisily**.
He won the race **easily**.
She put her clothes away **tidily**.
They were singing **merrily**.

Spell Well

- This is how you form adverbs from adjectives:

Adjective	Adverb	Adjective	Adverb
brave	bravely	fierce	fiercely
patient	patiently	sad	sadly
beautiful	beautifully	loud	loudly
polite	politely	slow	slowly
careful	carefully	neat	neatly
quick	quickly	wise	wisely
quiet	quietly	comfortable	comfortably

Notice that you just change the **e** of **comfortable** to y to form the adverb.

Spell Well

- Here are some **adverbs** formed from **adjectives** ending in **-y**.

Adjective	Adverb
angry	angrily
merry	merrily
easy	easily
noisy	noisily
happy	happily
sleepy	sleepily
gloomy	gloomily
tidy	tidily

Notice that you change the **y** of these words to **i** and add **-ly**.

 ISBN 978-81-8477-744-4

Nouns
Pronouns
Adjectives
Determiners
Verbs
Adverbs
Prepositions
Conjunctions
Interjections
Sentences
Phrases
Clauses
More about Sentences
Direct and Indirect Speech
Punctuation

Adverbs of Manner

Adverbs of manner tell you the way people do things. They answer the question how?

They crossed **safely**.
The driver braked **suddenly**.
He drove **carelessly**.
He cycled **speedily** down the road.
She plays **skilfully**.
Sally is behaving **selfishly**.
Mike is behaving **foolishly**.
Mrs White dresses **fashionably**.
The twins dress **differently**.
I looked **cautiously** round the corner.
She **thoughtfully** fetched Granny's walking stick.
He **hastily** hid the comic under his pillow.
The teacher explained the sum **clearly**.
Please speak **clearly**.
Please write **legibly**.
Look **closely** at the picture.
You have all done the sum **correctly**.
You can buy everything **cheaply** in this shop.
The villagers live **peacefully** together.
William Tell shot his arrow **accurately**.
The sun is shining **brightly**.
Animals can run about **freely** in the forest.
The dog jumped up **playfully**.

Word Power

Here is a list of common adverbs of manner.

safely	brightly
suddenly	clearly
carelessly	closely
speedily	cheaply
skilfully	freely
differently	playfully
correctly	peacefully

Adverbs of Time

Adverbs and adverbials of time tell you when someone does something, or when something happens. They answer the question when?

John's trousers were too large **last year**.
They fit him **this year**.
They will be too small **next year**.
It rained **last night**.
It's fine **this morning**.
Get up **now**, or you'll miss the bus.
The children are **still** playing computer games.
Everyone arrived **early**.
Joe arrived **late**.
I'll see you **soon**.

The plane has **just** taken off.
The train has **already** left.
Haven't you finished that sum **yet**?
The mother bird started to build her nest **yesterday**.
She is continuing to build it **today**.
She will finish it **tomorrow**.

Word Power

Here is a list of common adverbs of time.

yesterday	this morning
today	last night
tomorrow	now
this year	next year
still	early
late	soon
already	

Adverbs of Place, Direction and Distance

Adverbs and adverbials of place, direction and distance tell you the place of action, the direction of movement, the distance between things, or the distance travelled. They answer the questions where?, where to?, how far?

It's cooler to stay **inside** on a hot day.
Seagulls are circling **overhead**.
The dictionary is **on the top shelf.**
My cousins live in **Shanghai**, but I've never been **there** myself.
I must have dropped my keys **somewhere**.
These weeds grow **everywhere**.
Everybody assembled **outdoors** for fire drill.
We stood **at the side of the pitch** and cheered.
I've often seen him **on television**.
The apartment **upstairs** is empty.
The queue of people **outside** was getting longer and longer.
The pupils **in the next classroom** are making a dreadful noise.
I'm not going **anywhere special** this evening.
Please take this rubbish **outside**. The men will take it **away**.
We hurried **indoors** when it began to rain.
Could you put your books **over there**?
Poor Timothy was taken **to hospital**.
Ruth and Mark are spending a year travelling **round the world**.

 ISBN 978-81-8477-744-4

A strange smell was coming **from the kitchen.**
Nowhere is there a greater variety of cuisines than in **Singapore.**
Here comes the bus!
Where's the glue? **There** it is.
We walked a **long way** yesterday, but we didn't walk **far** today.

Nouns
Pronouns
Adjectives
Determiners
Verbs
Adverbs
Prepositions
Conjunctions
Interjections
Sentences
Phrases
Clauses
More about Sentences
Direct and Indirect Speech
Punctuation

Adverbs of Frequency

Adverbs or adverbials of frequency tell you how often someone does something, or how often something happens. They answer the question how often?

Jill **always** goes to school by bus.
The bus is **often** crowded.
Tom is **frequently** late for school.
Jim **usually** cycles to school.
Mum **normally** goes shopping on the way home.
Sometimes Mike skates to school on his roller skates.
We **occasionally** go to the cinema.
Many people exercise **regularly.**
Mary is **seldom** late.
I shall **never** do it again.
Have you **ever** ridden on an ostrich?
The radio broadcasts news **hourly.**
The newspaper is delivered **daily.**
The magazine comes out **weekly.**
We visit our grandmother **every week.**
They meet **fortnightly.**
They go for outings **monthly.**
The festival is held **annually.**
I go to the dentist once **every six months.**
I won't make the same mistake **twice.**

Word Power

Fortnightly means **once in two weeks.**
Another word for **annually** is **yearly** (once a year).
Another way of saying **once every six months** is **twice a year.**
Every week means the same as **weekly** or **once a week.**
Here is a list of common adverbs of frequency.

sometimes	often	always	monthly	hourly	ever	once
frequently	seldom	usually	weekly	daily	never	twice
fortnightly	annually					

 ISBN 978-81-8477-744-4

Adverbs of Duration

Adverbs or adverbials of duration tell you how long somebody does something for, or how long something lasts. They answer the question how long?

I haven't seen Helen **for two years.**
The storm lasted **for three days.**
They talked on the phone **for an hour.**
I stayed awake **all night.**
I won't be away **long.**
You were away **a very long time.**
Sandra stopped briefly to look in **a shop window.**
The telephone is **temporarily** out of use.
Use the public telephone **for the time being.**
Stand still **for a moment** and make sure the road is clear.
We waited **for ages** for a bus.

Word Power

Here is a list of common adverbs of duration.

briefly	long	temporarily	forever
for ages	all day	all night	a long time

Emphasizing Adverbs

Not all adverbs modify verbs. Some adverbs can be used before adjectives or other adverbs to emphasize them.

He is **really** strong.
That's **utterly** impossible.
That's a **fairly** good mark.
You have done **quite** well.
That's **completely** untrue.
It's an **exceedingly** silly play.
This is an **extremely** easy sum.
The news is **simply** unbelievable!
I am **absolutely** sure that Ken is not coming.
The children are behaving **very** nicely.
The characters in this book are **entirely** fictitious.
They were **totally** disappointed with the game.
It was a **truly** memorable experience.
The conditions they live in are **just** terrible.

Word Power

Here is a list of common emphasizing adverbs:

really	simply
very	exceedingly
fairly	truly
quite	extremely
just	utterly
completely	absolutely

 ISBN 978-81-8477-744-4

Nouns
Pronouns
Adjectives
Determiners
Verbs
Adverbs
Prepositions
Conjunctions
Interjections
Sentences
Phrases
Clauses
More about Sentences
Direct and Indirect Speech
Punctuation

Intensifying Adverbs

Intensifying adverbs (or **intensifiers**) are words such as **very, extremely, highly** and so on. You use them to increase the force of the adjective, adverb or verb they are used with.

I'm **extremely** sorry about the mistake. (with adjective)
Some **highly** confidential documents have been stolen. (with adjective)
You performed **exceedingly** well. (with adverb)
Break the eggs very **carefully** into the pan. (with adverb)
You've **really** grown! (with verb)
I **strongly** recommend this book. (with verb)

Interrogative Adverbs

The question words **where, when, why** and **how** are adverbs too. They are called **interrogative adverbs.** You use them to ask questions.

Where is the National Library?
Where do you live?
When did you last visit New York?
When are you going to finish your homework?
Why is the girl crying?
Why do snakes flick their tongues?
How deep is the river?
How did you know?

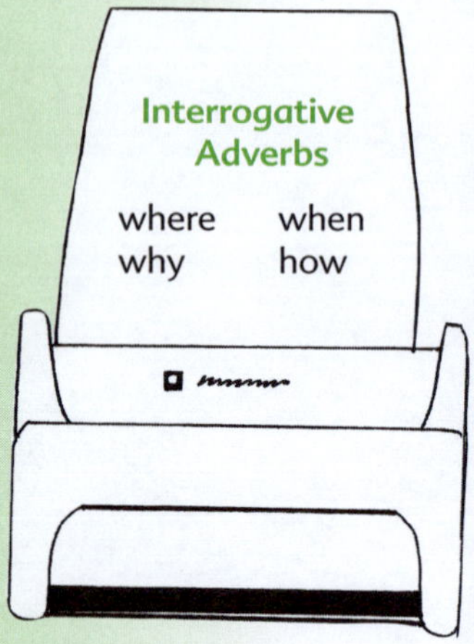

Comparison of Adverbs

Like adjectives, adverbs have a comparative and a superlative form. You use them for comparing the way people do things.

You use **more** to make the comparative form of an adverb. You use **most** to make the superlative form.

The thrush sings **beautifully**.
The lark sings more **beautifully**.
The nightingale sings the most **beautifully**.

The wolf runs **swiftly**.
The deer runs more **swiftly**.
The cheetah runs the most **swiftly**.

A candle shines **brightly**.
An electric light shines more **brightly**.
The sun shines the most **brightly**.

 ISBN 978-81-8477-744-4

- **With adverbs that don't end with -ly, you add -er and -est to form the comparative and superlative.**

A bike goes **fast**.
A car goes **faster**.
A plane goes the **fastest**.

John worked **hard**.
Peter worked **harder**.
James worked the **hardest**.

How **high** can you jump?
You can jump **higher** than that!
Dave can jump the **highest**.

Jill arrived **late**.
Susan arrived **later**.
Mary arrived the **latest**.

- **Here are some adverbs with irregular comparative and superlative forms. You don't add -er or -est to form the comparative or superlative.**

Susan sings **well**.
Maggie sings **better**.
Diana sings the **best**.

I played **badly**.
Mike played **worse**.
Peter played the **worst**.

I didn't cycle **far**.
Alice cycled **farther**.
Jane cycled the **farthest**.

Cats don't like swimming **much**.
Ducks like swimming **more**.
Fish like swimming the **most**.

This baby cries **a little**.
This baby cries **less**.
This baby cries **the least**.

Grammar Help

You often put **the** before a superlative adverb.

 ISBN 978-81-8477-744-4

Connectors

When you are giving an account of a situation, or telling a story, or even taking part in a conversation, you use linking words called connectors, as you go along, to show what the connection is with what has already been said. Connectors may be adverbs such as however, consequently, then, therefore or conjunctions such as but, so, therefore and yet.

Our sales figures have not been very good this year. **However**, I don't want to sound too gloomy. The market keeps changing, **therefore** there are bound to be disappointing years from time to time. **Nevertheless,** we must make a big effort to improve our sales in the coming year. **Consequently,** I am asking everybody to think hard about new and attractive — **yet** thoroughly practical — ways to market our products. We must **also** think about ways of cutting costs. The task before us is, **therefore,** a double one — to improve sales and to economize **as well. But** with everybody pulling their weight, we'll achieve our goals. You are a dedicated team, and an enthusiastic one **too. So,** the message is cheerful and positive: keep smiling and do your best to help the joint effort! It is **then** just a question of time before our sales achieve their former level, **though** we may have to be patient in the meantime.

Exercise 1

Choose an adjective from the box and turn it into an adverb to fill the gaps in these sentences. One has been done for you.

angry	bright	brisk	careful
clear	comfortable	easy	~~gentle~~
gradual	loud	musical	neat
quiet	sudden		

1. Mum laid the baby gently in his cot.

2. Write your name ____________ at the top of the page.

 ISBN 978-81-8477-744-4

3. You're talking too ____________. Please speak ____________.

4. Carry those dishes very ____________.

5. If you're all sitting ____________, I'll begin the story.

6. The man shook his fist ____________ at us.

7. Diana plays the piano very ____________.

8. Laura is a clever girl and passes all her exams ____________.

9. It happened so ____________ that we all got a surprise.

10. The clouds ____________ disappeared and the sun began to shine ____________.

11. Miss Lee was walking ____________ across the playground.

12. Say your name ____________ so that we can all hear what it is.

Formation of Adverbs

- Adverbs belong with the verb of a sentence, and often describe it: She coughed **noisily.**
- A lot of adverbs end in **–ly**. You form them by adding **-ly** to adjectives, for example: brave, brave**ly**, beautiful, beautifu**lly**.
- But remember that adjectives ending in **-y** change **y** to **i** before **-ly**, for example, noisy, nois**ily**.
- Adjectives that end with **-le** after another consonant, change **e** to **y**: double, doub**ly**.

Exercise 2

Put in the correct comparative or superlative form. Some of the adverbs are -ly adverbs. One has been done for you.

1. Art was the ____least____ difficult of all my exams. **(little)**

2. Andrea got here ______________ than we did. (**early**)

3. Joe jumped ______________ than me in the long jump. (**far**)

 ISBN 978-81-8477-744-4

Comparison of non-ly Adverbs: faster, fastest

- Adverbs that do not end in -ly have -er and -est endings:

  Harry ran **fast**. George ran **faster**. I ran the **fastest**.

  They'll arrive **soon**. They arrived **sooner** than we expected.

- These five adverbs have irregular comparatives and superlatives:

  badly (worse, worst); far (farther, farthest, or further, furthest), little (less, least), much (more, most), well (better, best).

4. Whose was the ______________ written essay? **(imaginative)**

5. I've worked ______________ this week than ever before. **(hard)**

6. Why do we always arrive ______________ than anybody else? **(late)**

7. Charles had folded his clothes ______________ than usual. **(tidy)**

8. You'll find that you can speak English ______________ than you think. **(well)**

9. I made my ice lolly last the ______________. **(long)**

10. Your schooldays come to an end ______________ than you expect. **(soon)**

11. I enjoy maths lessons ______________ than I used to. **(much)**

12. Really! That competition was the ______________ organized event I've ever attended. **(badly)**

 ISBN 978-81-8477-744-4

7 PREPOSITIONS

Read the following passage. The bold items are all prepositions.

Saved by a transplant

We have just arrived **at** our holiday cottage. We came **by** car. The cottage is right **by** the sea and the children are already **on** the beach. It is wonderful watching the three **of** them chasing **after** each other, particularly seeing Sue keeping up **with** her younger brothers. I still cannot believe that she is **out of** hospital.

For the past two years, Sue has been spending a lot **of** time **within** the kidney unit **in** the local hospital. She had to put up **with** having dialysis several times a week. She got very depressed **about** it.

Sue was a very healthy child **until** her 13th birthday. Then she was suddenly taken **to** hospital. We sat **beside** her bed, sick **with** worry. She was diagnosed **with** severe kidney disease. She would have to depend **on** regular dialysis for the rest **of** her life to keep her healthy.

She was very angry **about** her situation at first. However, she had just got used **to** it when things got worse **for** her and **for** us. We were told that our daughter's condition was deteriorating. Indeed, her life was **in** danger. The only thing that could save her **from** an early death was a transplant operation.

We thought that this problem could be solved **by** one **of** the family. One **of** us would donate a kidney **to** Sue. Unfortunately, none **of** us proved to be suitable donors. We had to hope that they could find a suitable donor **from** the general public.

They did – the young victim **of** a traffic accident. We are so grateful **to** her parents **for** giving their consent **to** the transplant. We urge everyone to carry a donor card giving permission **for** their healthy organs to be used **in** the event **of** their death. That saves lives.

 ISBN 978-81-8477-744-4

Prepositions are little words like **at**, **in** and **on**. There are many kinds of prepositions.

- Some prepositions are used to **show place**, or where something happens.

Some children are playing **on** the beach.
Some children are hiding **behind** the rock.
Some children are sliding **down** the slide.
Some children are reading **in** the shade.
Some children are resting **under** a tree.
Some children are chasing **after** each other.
Some children are sitting **round** the sandcastle.

- Some prepositions are used to **show time**, or when something happens.

The meeting starts **at** nine o'clock.
Shops close **on** Sundays.
Christians celebrate the birth of Jesus **on** 25 December.
Tom was born **on** 5 February 1990.
They were married **in** 1990.
The traffic is very heavy **in** the morning.
There are very few people in the streets **after** midnight.
They visited Paris **during** the school holidays.

- Some prepositions are used for **other purposes.**

Many people travel **by** train.
Everybody is looking **at** her.
They are talking **about** the football game.
Peter is walking home **with** Tom.
The Owl danced **with** the Pussy Cat.
They are always quarrelling **with** each other.
Bob was late and the bus left **without** him.
Bill has egg and ham **for** breakfast.

 ISBN 978-81-8477-744-4

Grammar Help

Prepositions are always followed by a noun, or **noun phrase**, or **pronoun**.

	Preposition	Noun/Noun phrase
Some children are playing	**on**	the beach.
Some children are hiding	**behind**	the wall.
Some children are sliding	**down**	the slide.
Some children are reading	**in**	the library.
Some children are eating	**under**	a tree.
Some children are chasing	**after**	each other.
Some children are sitting	**round**	the table.
The meeting starts	**at**	nine o'clock.
They visited Paris	**during**	the school holidays.
They were married	**in**	1990.
Many people travel	**by**	train.
Everybody is looking	**at**	her.
They are talking	**about**	the football game.
The Owl danced	**with**	the Pussy Cat.
They are always quarrelling	**with**	each other.
Bob was late and the bus left	**without**	him.
Bill has egg and ham	**for**	breakfast.

Prepositions of Place

Here are some prepositions that you use to show place, position or direction.

upon
on

Upon *means the same as* ***on****.*

at
from

beside
by

By *means the same as* ***beside****.*

down
underneath
beneath
under

Underneath *means the same as* ***under*** *and* ***beneath****.*

past
outside
below
across

around
round

Round *means the same as* ***around****.*

within
inside

Within *means the same as* ***inside****.*

against
behind

between
along
off
over
opposite
into
about
beyond
up
near
above
to
towards

aboard
in
through
among
after

 ISBN 978-81-8477-744-4

The prepositions we have looked at so far are all single words. Some prepositions are made up of a group of words.

ahead of
close to
away from
in between
near to
in front of

*You can use **close by** like **close to**.*

***Near to** means the same as **near**.*

all over
on to
out of
on top of
on board

*You can write **on to** as a single word: **onto**.*

***On board** means the same as **aboard**.*

Here are some sentences using the prepositions we have just looked at.

aboard, on board

How many people are **on board** the train?
There are 200 people **on board** the plane.
The crew were **aboard** the ship for a month.

above

He hung the picture **above** the fireplace.
Our plane is flying **above** the clouds.
Your eyebrows are **above** your eyes.

across

There is a new bookshop **across** the street.
We rowed **across** the lake.
There are two bridges **across** the river.

after

Tom is running **after** his dog.
Which letter comes **after** P in the alphabet?

against

Sara is leaning **against** the wall.
I am playing **against** John.

Grammar Help

Aboard, on board, above, across, after can also be used as adverbs, without a following noun. For example:

There were 60 passengers **aboard** (or **on board**).
We looked up at the stars **above**.
We got into the boat and rowed **across**.
Jack fell down and broke his crown and Jill came tumbling **after**.

 ISBN 978-81-8477-744-4

along

George is walking **along** the seashore.
We're sailing **along** the canal.
The cinema is further **along** the street.
There are bookshelves all **along** the wall.

among

There is a goat **among** the sheep.
The thieves divided the money **among** themselves.

You can also say:
*The thieves divided the money **between** themselves.*

around, round, about

May is wearing a string of beads **round** her neck.
I need a map to find my way **about** the city.
Draw a square and then draw a circle **round** it.
The moon goes **around** the earth.
They built a fence **around** their house.
Tom left his clothes lying **around** his room.
We are all sitting **around** the table.
He runs **round** the field every morning for exercise.

*You can use **round** instead of **around**. For example:*
*We are all sitting **round** the table.*
*The moon goes **round** the earth.*
*You can sometimes use **about** instead of **around**. For example:*
*Tom left his clothes lying **about** the room.*

at

There's a long queue **at** the bus stop.
What time does the ferry arrive **at** the jetty?
Is Peter **at** home?
Did you enjoy yourself **at** the party?
He lives **at** 20 Adam Road.

behind

Tom is hiding **behind** the tree.
There must be a lot of dust **behind** the bookcase.
Mary is **behind** Helen in the queue.

below

Your mouth is **below** your nose.
Ali lives in an apartment **below** ours.

beneath

The saucer is **beneath** the cup.
Most of the iceberg is **beneath** the water.
Who is hiding **beneath** the bed?

*You can also use **underneath** or **under** instead of **beneath**. For example, you can say:*
*The saucer is **underneath** (or **under**) the cup.*
*Most of the iceberg is **underneath** (or **under**) the water.*
*Who is hiding **underneath** (or **under**) the bed?*

Grammar Help

- **Along, around, round and about can also be used as adverbs, without a following noun. For example:**

  We're having a party. Why don't you come **along**?

  I can find my way **around** without a map.
  I'm having a friend **round** tonight.
  Don't leave your clothes lying **about**.

- **Behind and below can also be used as adverbs, without a following noun. For example:**

  I nearly left my coat **behind**.
  They looked down from the top of the hill to the valley **below**.

 ISBN 978-81-8477-744-4

Nouns
Pronouns
Adjectives
Determiners
Verbs
Adverbs
Prepositions
Conjunctions
Interjections
Sentences
Phrases
Clauses
More about Sentences
Direct and Indirect Speech
Punctuation

beside

Tom is standing **beside** Jill.
There's a tree **beside** the house.

between, in between

Jill is sitting **between** her parents.
There is a wall **between** our garden and the neighbours' garden.
When you walk on the beach, the sand gets **in between** your toes.

beyond

Beyond the fields there is a lake, and **beyond** the lake there are mountains.
When it's foggy, you can't see **beyond** the fence.

by

Granny is sitting **by** the fire.
We stayed in a hotel **by** the sea.
I often pass **by** your house on my way to the shops.

You can also use ***beside*** *instead of* ***by****. For example, you can say:*
Granny is sitting ***beside*** *the fire.*
We stayed in a hotel ***beside*** *the sea.*

down

The snowball is rolling **down** the hill.
The king was walking **down** the stairs.
The rabbit disappeared **down** a hole.

from

Sue took a magazine **from** the rack.
I received a letter **from** Sara.
He got a bicycle **from** his parents on his birthday.
Where do these people come **from**?
Are they **from** outer space?
The giant panda comes **from** China.

from...to

Dad walks **from** the station **to** his office every morning.
It's half a metre **from** one footprint **to** the next.

in

Peter is **in** bed.
The manager is **in** his office.
The Great Wall is **in** China.
This car is made **in** the US.
I read the story **in** a magazine.

Grammar Help

- **In between, beyond and by can also be used as adverbs, without a following noun. For example:**

  A sandwich consists of two slices of bread with some food **in between**.
  We looked out at the fields and the mountains **beyond**.
  Just then Susan passed **by**.

- **Down and in can also be used as adverbs, without a following noun. For example:**

  The birds flew **down** and landed on a branch.
  Jack fell **down** and broke his crown.
  Is the manager **in** today?
  The bus stopped and we got **in**.

 ISBN 978-81-8477-744-4

in front of

The teacher is standing **in front of** the class.
Helen is **in front of** Mary in the queue.
The tourists are taking photos of each other **in front of** the monument.
John is several metres **in front of** the other runners.

inside

It's better to be **inside** the house when it's raining.
Please stay **inside** the school grounds.

into

John is diving **into** the pool.
The rat ran **into** its hole.
How did the thief get **into** the house?
She is getting **into** bed.
Mum is getting **into** the car.

near

Our hotel was very **near** the beach.
Don't go too **near** the edge of the cliff.
They live **near** the bridge.
He moved his chair **nearer** the fire.

*You can use **close to** or **near to** instead of **near**. For example, you can say:*
*Our hotel was very **close to** the beach.*
*Our hotel was very **near to** the beach.*

off

Don't let the baby fall **off** the chair.
The passengers are getting **off** the plane.
Another button has come **off** my coat.
Please keep **off** the grass.

on

Susan is sitting **on** her bed.
The cat is sleeping **on** a chair.
There's a computer **on** his desk.
Dad is carrying Jimmy **on** his shoulders.
There are a lot of books **on** the shelves.
There's a funny programme **on** television.
Sally spends hours **on** the phone.
Put the pan **on** the stove.
There is a mole **on** his face.
The picture is **on** page 78.
On his head, he wore a pointed hat.

on top of

The bottle of shampoo is **on top of** the cupboard.
The books are piled one **on top of** the other.
She wears her hair in a knot **on top of** her head.

Grammar Help

- **Inside and near can also be used as adverbs, without a following noun. For example:**

  We took the lid off the box and looked **inside**.
  Where's Tom? He's **inside**, doing his homework.
  The bull may be dangerous. Don't go too **near**.

- **Off and on can also be used as adverbs, without a following noun. For example:**

  He took his coat **off**.
  Humpty Dumpty sat on the wall and fell **off**.
  Turn the television **off**.
  He put his hat **on**.
  Turn the television **on**.

 ISBN 978-81-8477-744-4

on to

The baby is trying to climb up **on to** the chair.
They are using a crane to unload goods **on to** the quay.
Peter is getting **on to** the train.
Sally is sewing the missing button back **on to** her coat.

*You can also say: Sally is sewing the missing button back **on** her coat.*

opposite

We live **opposite** the supermarket.
Peter and Sara are sitting **opposite** each other.
The hotel was built **opposite** a lake.

out of

John is getting **out** of the pool.
The rat is looking **out** of its hole.
The burglar is climbing **out** of the window.
Sue is getting **out** of bed.
Miss Lee took a book **out** of the bookcase.
Mum is getting **out** of the car.

outside

The delivery man has left the parcel **outside** the door.
Dad is waiting **outside** the school gate.
The ball went **outside** the court.

over, all over

Our plane is flying **over** Hong Kong.
There is a bridge **over** the river.
Mum is leaning **over** the baby's crib.
Tom fell **over** the cat.
Eva has spilt fruit juice **all over** her dress.

past

We are driving **past** the castle.
The soldiers saluted as they marched **past** the platform.
I live on Park Road, just **past** the local church.

through

We are driving **through** a tunnel.
They are going **through** the checkout.
We struggled **through** the crowd to reach the entrance.

Grammar Help

- **Opposite** and **outside** can also be used as **adverbs**, without a following noun. For example:
  I sat on one side of the table and Peter sat **opposite**.
  He went **outside** to play.
- **Over, past** and **through** can also be used as **adverbs**, without a following noun. For example:
  I accidentally knocked the vase and it fell **over**.
  The soldiers saluted as they marched **past**.
  The tunnel was very narrow but we managed to crawl **through**.

 ISBN 978-81-8477-744-4

to

John handed his homework **to** Miss Lee.
I'm writing **to** Granny.
Who are you sending this parcel **to**?
David takes the bus **to** school every day.
Miss Lee is talking **to** her class.
I don't like going **to** the dentist.

under

The cat ran **under** a chair.
Danny keeps his toys **under** his bed.
She hides her money **under** her pillow.
We rowed **under** the bridge.
Strange plants grow **under** the water.

up

We're pushing the pram **up** the hill.
I'm going **up** the stairs.
The fireman is climbing **up** the ladder.
The flag was hoisted **up** at 10.00.
I am going for a walk **up** the market.
The kite is flying high **up** in the sky.

upon

The bird landed **upon** a branch.
Some people are lying **upon** the grass.
Jane put her laptop **upon** her knees.
She wore a red bow **upon** her dress.
He was sleeping with the opened book **upon** his face.
Kate spilled the coffee **upon** the mattress.

*You usually use **on** instead of **upon**. For example, you can say:*
*The bird landed **on** a branch.*

Grammar Help

Under and up can also be used as adverbs, without a following noun. For example:

There was scarcely a ripple on the surface as the submarine went **under**.
Sally dropped her pencil and Jane picked it **up**.
We climbed **up** to see the view.

 ISBN 978-81-8477-744-4

Nouns
Pronouns
Adjectives
Determiners
Verbs
Adverbs
Prepositions
Conjunctions
Interjections
Sentences
Phrases
Clauses
More about Sentences
Direct and Indirect Speech
Punctuation

Prepositions of Time

Here are some prepositions that you use to show time, or when something happens.

at	about	after	around	before	between
by	during	for	from	in	to
on	past	since	till	until	from ... to

Here are some sentences using the prepositions we have looked at.

after

After my exams, I'm going to London.
John felt tired **after** his game of football.
We always brush our teeth **after** meals.
We all went home **after** the party.
I'm allowed to watch television **after** doing my homework.

around, about

I'll call you **around** five o'clock.
The movie starts **around** 7.30 pm.
Dad gets home **about** six in the evening.

at

Dad has his breakfast **at** seven o'clock.
The train arrived **at** noon.
At night, the sky is full of stars.
All our family gets together **at** New Year.
You must eat quietly **at** meals.

before

Mum cleans the whole house **before** ten o'clock.
Dad goes jogging **before** sunrise.
We always wash our hands **before** meals.
I have to finish my homework **before** watching television.
You must be home **before** dark.

between, between ... and

Sometimes Miss Lee lets us play **between** lessons.
Between 1995 **and** 1998, we lived in Tokyo.
The post office is closed **between** 1.00 **and** 2.00.

*You can also use **from...to** instead of **between...and**.*
For example:
***From** 1995 **to** 1998, we lived in Tokyo.*

 ISBN 978-81-8477-744-4

by

Please return all your library books **by** next Monday.
I have to hand in my assignment **by** nine o'clock tomorrow.
Send in your answers **by** 29 January.
The workmen promised to finish the work **by** June.

for

Could I borrow your video **for** a week?
We have lived in this house **for** five years.
I have been waiting at the bus stop **for** half an hour.
It has been raining **for** several days.
David is going abroad **for** six months.

from, from...to

Breakfast is served **from** seven o'clock.
The museum is open **from** Monday **to** Saturday.
The show lasted **from** eight o'clock **to** ten thirty.
We attend junior school **from** the age of six **to** the age of eleven.

*You can also use **from...till** instead of **from...to**. For example:*
*The supermarket is open **from** 8.00 am **till** 10.00 pm.*

during

Many people go to the seaside **during** the school holidays.
The street is always crowded **during** the day.
The trees lose their leaves **during** the autumn.
A lot of trees were blown down **during** the storm.
I had a ride on a camel **during** my visit to Egypt.
Some animals hunt **during** the night and sleep **during** the day.

*You can use **by...by** instead of **during**. For example:*
*Some animals hunt **by** night and sleep **by** day.*

in

We all go jogging **in** the evening.
It gets very hot **in** the afternoon.
We have our holidays **in** June.
It snows **in** winter.
We go for picnics **in** the summer.
This bridge was built **in** 1900.
You must finish the test **in** two hours.
Peter made his puppet **in** a week.

 ISBN 978-81-8477-744-4

Nouns
Pronouns
Adjectives
Determiners
Verbs
Adverbs
Prepositions
Conjunctions
Interjections
Sentences
Phrases
Clauses
More about Sentences
Direct and Indirect Speech
Punctuation

on

The baby was born **on** 6 July 1998.
Christmas Day falls **on** 25 December.
Some people have to work **on** Sundays.
I'm going to the dentist **on** Thursday.
We have a special feast **on** New Year's Day.
She got a lot of presents **on** her birthday.
We go home early **on** the last day of term.

past

The next bus arrives at ten **past** nine.
Mary leaves the house at twenty **past** seven.
It's a quarter **past** eight.
I have to go to a meeting at half **past** ten.

You can say:
*It's **quarter past** eight.*
or
*It's **a quarter past** eight.*
*It's **quarter to** eight.*
or
*It's a **quarter to** eight.*

to

It's a quarter **to** eight.
I leave the house at ten **to** seven.
I have to catch a train at five **to** three.

until

We watched the World Cup **until** midnight.
Dad works in his office **until** ten o'clock.
We have to attend school **until** the age of 16.
The car won't be ready **until** Friday.

*You can use **till** instead of **until**. For example, you can say:*
Dad works in his office till ten o'clock.

upon

Passengers go through immigration **upon** arrival.

*You can use **on** instead of **upon**. For example, you can say:*
*Passengers go through immigration **on** arrival.*

since

We have lived in Taiwan **since** 1995.
I've been waiting for the bus **since** eight.
This year, our school's exam results were the best **since** 1990.
Tom hasn't had his hair cut **since** January.
He has been much more careful **since** his accident.

Grammar Help

Since can also be used as an **adverb**, without a following noun. For example:

He had an accident last year and he has been much more careful ever **since**.

 ISBN 978-81-8477-744-4

Prepositions with Special Uses

There are lots of prepositions that are used in other special ways. Here are some of them.

by	in	on	without	of	at	as
like	than	with	for	except	instead of	

You use **by**, **on** and **in** to say how people and things travel.

Goods are brought to Singapore **by** sea.
Business people travel to London **by** air.
Mary goes to school **on** foot.
Peter goes to school **on** his bicycle.
Philip goes to school **on** the train.
Sue goes to school **on** the bus.
Sara goes to school **in** Dad's car.

*You often use **by** to show how people and things travel. For example, you can say:*
*Peter goes to school **by** bicycle.*
*Sue goes to school **by** bus.*

You use **by**, **with** and **without** to say how things are done, and who does them.

The problem was solved **by** computer.
This picture was painted **by** John.
Sue is drawing a picture **with** her coloured pens.
The cook is stirring the porridge **with** a wooden spoon.
We eat **with** chopsticks.
Grandad has to walk **with** a stick.
The patient can walk **without** help.
Animals cannot live **without** water.

***Without** is the opposite of **with**.*

You use **with** and **without** to describe people and things and actions.

I live in a house **with** large windows.
The emperor had a nightingale **with** golden feathers.
Who is the man **with** the beard?
Tom came home **with** torn trousers and a dirty face.
Cross the bridge **with** great care.
Those birds **with** long legs are wading birds.
Cats **without** tails are called Manx cats.

 ISBN 978-81-8477-744-4

Here are some ways of using in and on.

Tom is **in** the football team.
I'm going to be **in** the school play.
That bird is **in** danger.
Peter is **in** difficulties.
We're going **on** holiday soon.
There are some interesting pictures **on** show.
I do lots of my work **on** the computer.
We listen to the news **on** the radio.

Here are some ways of using at.

Mum is driving **at** 60 km per hour.
The train is travelling **at** high speed.
The plane is flying **at** 8,000 metres.
He left school **at** sixteen.
Most people stop work **at** 60.

Here are some ways of using of.

I bought a kilo **of** lychees and a litre **of** milk.
Mary is carrying a basket **of** flowers.
Peter is bringing in a jug **of** fruit juice.
Would you like a cup **of** tea?
Most **of** us have dark hair.
Maggie is a member **of** the photographic club.
I need a piece **of** paper.
Tom ate a whole bar **of** chocolate.
Are there more ways **of** using the word **of**?

Here are some ways of using for.

Here is a present **for** you.
Mum made a cake **for** my birthday.
There's room **for** another person here.
We're going to the US **for** our holidays.
What's this switch **for**?
This sum is too difficult **for** me.

Here are some ways of using except and instead of.

Everyone **except** Peter is swimming in the sea.
I like all kinds of vegetables **except** carrots.

 ISBN 978-81-8477-744-4

The shop is open every day **except** Monday.
You should eat fruit **instead of** chocolate.
You can go to the match **instead of** me.
Do something useful **instead of** sulking.

- **You use like, as and than for comparison.**

Jenny looks **like** her mother.
Tom walks **like** his father.
John rides his bike **like** a champion.
Is this dress the same **as** that one?
Mary is **as** tall **as** Margaret.
My ice cream is bigger **than** John's.
Jim is taller **than** Jenny, but Dad is taller **than** Jim.
The planet Jupiter is ten times bigger **than** the earth.

Grammar Help

- **You use like with what to ask for a description of a person or thing. For example, you can say:**

  What's she **like**?
  She is tall with long black hair.
  What's Jill's apartment **like**? It's quite large and looks modern.

- **You often use like to mean 'for example':**

  big cities **like** Bangkok or Seoul

- **You use prepositions with some adjectives.**

Tom is **angry with** his little brother.
Sue is very **fond of** her doll.
I'm **interested** in this programme.
Everyone was **afraid of** the giant.
I'm **bad at** maths.
May's **good at** singing.
Your diagram is **different from** mine.
The cupboard is **full of** toys.
Your shoes are **covered with** mud.
Dad is always **kind to** us.
Miss Lee is **pleased with** our test results.
Be **polite to** Granny.
I'm **sorry for** people without homes.
We are **used to** the noise.
What's **wrong with** the television?
Janet is **keen on** reading.

 ISBN 978-81-8477-744-4

You use prepositions with some **nouns.**

Congratulations on winning!
What's the **answer to** this sum?
Traffic causes **damage to** the environment.
Keep **control over** your dog.
What is the **reason for** the hold-up?
Here's a good **example of** the right style.
What is the best **cure for** toothache?
What's the **matter with** you?

You use prepositions with some **verbs.**

Sam is **aiming at** the target.
Do you **believe in** fairies?
Does this bag **belong to** you?
Tom **borrowed** the guitar **from** Jim.
Jim **lent** his guitar **to** Tom.
Tell me **about** your trip.
Dad's **looking after** the baby.
I **agree with** you.
We are **listening to** the story.
He has **escaped from** prison.
Ask the policeman **for** help.
Grandad is **looking for** his spectacles.
George is **paying for** the meal.
I'm going to **enter for** the competition.
Can you **think of** the right answer?
The lion has to **depend on** the mouse to save him.
Mary **cut** her cake **into** ten pieces.

Exercise 1

Write down the prepositions and put their objects in brackets. One has been done for you.

1. Sheila walked up the stairs.
   up (the stairs)
2. Dave came through the door.

 ISBN 978-81-8477-744-4

3. George bumped into me.

4. Dad is in Tokyo just now.

5. Give this package to Julia.

6. You all know the story of Cinderella.

7. Is this play by Shakespeare?

8. I'm playing against Peter in the finals.

9. We opened the box and found nothing in it.

10. I'm taller than Joe, but Dave is taller than me.

11. The ball bounced right over the wall.

12. Danny is always quarrelling with his brother.

13. Kate fetched a chair from the corner for Miss Lee.

14. Look at this strange insect on my hand.

Prepositions have Objects

- Prepositions are always followed by a noun, noun phrase or pronoun.

  We drove across **Paris**.

  We drove across **the old bridge**.

  We drove across **it**.

- The noun, noun phrase or pronoun that follows a preposition is its **object**.

 ISBN 978-81-8477-744-4

Exercise 2

Choose a preposition from the box to fill the gaps in each sentence. You will have to use some prepositions more than once. One has been done for you.

against	at	by	except	for
in	instead of	like	of	on
with	without			

1. I've bought a nice present for Mum's birthday.
2. Are you playing __________ the match __________ St Andrew's School?
3. Everyone is going to the match __________ Peter. He has a cold.
4. Ken passed round his bag __________ sweets.
5. The plane is flying __________ a height __________ 10,000 metres.
6. Plants will die __________ water.
7. Is there anything good __________ the radio?
8. The play was written __________ an Australian writer.
9. Why don't you do something sensible __________ crying?
10. A giraffe is an animal __________ a very long neck.
11. Most children start school __________ the age __________ five.
12. The school timetable is now done __________ the computer.
13. Mum was digging the flower bed __________ a spade.
14. Our neighbours are away __________ holiday.
15. That looks __________ salt, not sugar.

 ISBN 978-81-8477-744-4

8 Conjunctions

Read the following passage. The items in bold are all conjunctions.

A change in Tom

'Have you noticed **that** Tom is a bit quiet these days?' Mr Brown asked his wife.

'Yes, **and** I've been worried. I wonder **if** he's ill in some way,' replied Mrs Brown. 'He's usually very cheerful **and** outgoing, **but** he's now very moody, silent, **and** very nervous. I do wish I knew what was wrong with him.'

'He's never around **when** I come in after work these days, **or** I would ask him **whether** there's anything wrong,' said Mr Brown.

'He goes upstairs to his room **as soon as** he comes in,' said Mrs Brown. 'He says that's **because** he has such a lot of homework, **and** he certainly has to study hard this year, **but** I think there's some other reason. I've asked him to wait **until** you get home **before** he has his evening meal, **but** he won't. He **either** has a quick meal at the kitchen table **or** he takes something up to his room.'

'Also, I must admit **that** I've been coming home later than usual **because** I've been so busy at work,' said Mr Brown. 'I shouldn't have to work late any more for a while **unless** there's some kind of emergency. I can spend time with Tom, **provided** he wants to spend time with me. At the moment, he's acting **as if** he doesn't even like me.'

'I've asked Bill to talk to him **while** he's home from university,' said Mrs Brown.

Tom's old brother Bill was able to tell his parents **that** the reason for Tom's quietness and nervousness was **that** he was being bullied at school. Their parents were then able to talk the matter over with Tom's teachers. **Since** the school had an effective policy for dealing with bullying, the problem was soon solved successfully **and** Tom became his old self again. His parents were **as** pleased **as** they possibly could be.

 ISBN 978-81-8477-744-4

Conjunctions are **linking words**. They join words, phrases or clauses together. The commonest conjunctions are **and**, **but** and **or**.

■ The conjunction **and** links words or phrases that are **similar** in sense, or go together in some other way.

Tom and Joe are twins.
Fruits and vegetables are good for you.
We buy **eggs and rice** at the supermarket.
The train took us past lots of **towns and villages**.
He is **short and fat**.
She is **tall and thin**.
It is **cold and windy** today.
Yesterday it was **hot and sunny**.
This sofa is **soft and comfortable**.
Cross the bridge **slowly and carefully**.
Say your name **loudly and clearly**.

Grammar Help

The conjunctions and, or, but, yet, so are called co-ordinating conjunctions.

■ You can use the conjunction **but** to link words that have **different** or **contrasting** meanings.

Sue writes **fast but neatly**.
The elephant is a **large but gentle** animal.
Ants are **small but strong**.
Rock-climbing is **difficult but fun**.
The path is **short but steep**.
Today the weather is **sunny but cold**.
Yesterday it was **cloudy but warm**.
Slowly but surely the waves are coming towards us.

■ You can use the conjunction **or** to show a **choice**.

Which would you like, **ice cream or popcorn**?
You can have **an apple or an orange**.
I didn't know whether to **laugh or cry**.
I don't like **carrots or tomatoes**.
There's a choice of **coffee or tea**.
Is a spider **an insect or an animal**?
You press a button to go **up or down** in the lift.
Should we turn **right or left**?
What is this white stuff? Is it **sugar or salt**?
It isn't **clever or sensible** to throw stones.

Grammar Help

The conjunction or is also used instead of the conjunction and after a negative word like not. For example, you say:
I like apples **and** pears.
I do not like pineapples **or** guavas.

 ISBN 978-81-8477-744-4

The conjunctions and, but and or can link groups of words called phrases as well as single words.

Bring **a swimming costume** and **a beach towel**.
The Chen family have **two parrots** and **four pigeons**.
Sue's Dad has **a big car** and **a small one**.
Mum bought some jeans for **my older sister** and **me**.
I like getting **new clothes** and **dressing up smartly**.
The river is **very deep** and **very wide**.
My teddy is **rather dirty** and **a bit torn**.
My penknife is **very old** but **still useful**.
Danny works **very fast** but **rather carelessly.**
Sue is **taller than Jim** but **shorter than Mike**.
Sue and Jane are **at the same school** but **in different classes**.
Are we going **on foot** or **by bus**?
Is this **a thick piece of string** or **a thin piece of rope**?

When you have a list of more than two words or phrases, you put a comma (,) between them, and you put the conjunction and or or between the last two.

You need **scissors, a pencil, a rubber, a piece of paper** and **some glue**.
On Mondays we have **maths, English, music** and **computer studies**.
In the evening I have to **do my homework, practise the piano** and **tidy my room**.
We haven't got any **milk, bread, butter, eggs** or **tea**.
We can get to London by **car, bus** or **train**.
Shall we **play football, watch a video** or **play computer games**?

Conjunctions are also used to join two sentences together to make one sentence.

Jim is singing. Sue is playing the piano.
Jim is singing **and** Sue is playing the piano.

Dad is working in the garden. Mum is busy in the kitchen.
Dad is working in the garden **and** Mum is busy in the kitchen.

I invited Mike to my party. He couldn't come.
I invited Mike to my party **but** he couldn't come.

The fox is trying to attack the hedgehog. The hedgehog knows how to defend itself.
The fox is trying to attack the hedgehog **but** the hedgehog knows how to defend itself.

 ISBN 978-81-8477-744-4

Hurry up! You will miss the train.
Hurry up, **or** you will miss the train!

Would you like to go swimming?
Would you prefer to rest?
Would you like to go swimming **or** would you prefer to rest?

> **Grammar Help**
>
> A sentence that is made by joining two sentences together with **and**, **but** or **or** is called a **compound sentence**.

Nouns
Pronouns
Adjectives
Determiners
Verbs
Adverbs
Prepositions
Conjunctions
Interjections
Sentences
Phrases
Clauses
More about Sentences
Direct and Indirect Speech
Punctuation

■ **You use both ... and as a pair for emphasis.**

Both James **and** Sarah thought I was right.
We saw **both** oil palms **and** traveller's palms along our route.
The plan was **both** sensible **and** practicable.
A few people **both** aboard the plane **and** on the ground were slightly injured.
Sam could **both** read **and** write before he was five.

■ **The pair not only ... but (also) is used as a strong form of both ... and.**

Sam could **not only** read, **but also** write, before he was five.
The plan was **not only** sensible, **but** practicable.

■ **The pairs of conjunctions either ... or and neither ... nor are used to give more emphasis to alternative.**

The baby will be called **either** James after his grandfather **or** John after his father.
Frances drinks **neither** tea **nor** coffee.
It's **neither** clever **nor** sensible to throw stones.
I must have left the keys **either** in the car **or** at the office.
I'll **either** phone later **or** send you an e-mail.

■ **or else is an emphatic form of or.**

I'll phone later **or else** send you an e-mail.

■ **The conjunctions if, yet, though, although, therefore and so can link words and phrases.**

Our neighbours were very friendly, **if** (= 'though') rather talkative.
He painted an interesting, **though** very gloomy, picture of the situation.

Charlie is a nice enough little boy, **though** rather a mischievous one.
They own a handsome, **although** rather disobedient, dog.
I have one more obvious, **yet** important, point to make.
The idea was simple **yet** elegant.
She spoke kindly **yet** firmly to the children.
At night your brain is tired, **so** less efficient.
It was an eye-catching, **therefore** effective, advertisement.

Here are some more conjunctions that you use to say when something happens. They are called conjunctions of time.

Notice that there are two verbs, one on each side of the conjunction.

Look both ways **before** you cross the road.
I always brush my teeth **after** I have my breakfast.
Dad was frowning **as** he came in.
She feeds the cat **as soon as** she gets up.
You have grown **since** I last saw you.
Wait here **until** I get back.
Take all your belongings **when** you leave the plane.
Jim listens to pop music **while** he does his sums.

The conjunctions as, because, since and in case are called conjunctions of reason.

They are used to say why something happens, or why somebody does something, or why you are suggesting something.

As it's late, we'd better take a taxi.
I bought an ice cream **because** I was hungry.
Because there's full moon, it's very bright tonight.
You can set the table **since** you have nothing to do.
Since we don't know the way, we should look at the map.
Take your umbrella **in case** it rains.

The conjunctions so, so that, in order that, so as to and in order to are called conjunctions of purpose.

They are used to say what the purpose is of doing something.

Write down the number **so** you don't forget it.
Stand still **so that** I can brush your hair.

Grammar Help

So far, we have been looking at **co-ordinating conjunctions.** When they join two sentences or 'clauses' together, the two clauses are independent.

Conjunctions of time, reason, purpose, concession, condition, manner and comparison, which we are looking at next, are **subordinating conjunctions.** They introduce a clause that is dependent on the main clause.

 ISBN 978-81-8477-744-4

Children should be given lots of vegetables **so that** they keep healthy.
In order that everyone gets a piece of cake, please take only one piece each.
We trained hard **in order to** win the race.
We started off early **so as to** get to the theatre in good time.

- The conjunctions **although, even if, even though** and **though** are called **conjunctions of concession** or **conjunctions of contrast.**

  You use them to add something rather surprising or unusual about what you are saying.

Mary kept on walking **although** she felt very tired.
Although they are only five, they're good at using the computer.
I shall enjoy the race, **even if** I don't win.
They were pleased with their picnic, **even though** the weather wasn't very good.
You're doing quite well, **though** I think you could try harder.

- The conjunctions **if, as long as, providing** and **unless** are called **conjunctions of condition.**

  You use them to say what follows a certain happening, or what must come first before a certain thing happens.

I'll lend you my trainers **if** you lend me your video game.
If it rains, the match will be cancelled.
If you have finished that exercise, go on to the next one.
I'll tell you some news, **as long as** you agree to keep it secret.
You can go home now, **providing** you have tidied your desk.
We wouldn't be able to stay on the earth **unless** it kept on rotating.
You won't pass your exams **unless** you work hard.
Unless people take exercise, they get fat and stiff.

- The conjunctions **as, as if, as though, just as** and **the way** are called **conjunctions of manner.**

  You use them to talk about the way people behave or do things.

The children won't do **as** they are told.
I telephoned Mum **as** she had asked me to, to say I was OK.
He was running along **as though** he was in a terrible hurry.

 ISBN 978-81-8477-744-4

She was walking down the street **as if** she had nothing better to do.
I'd like to do my hair **the way** Maggie does hers.
Granny was looking out of the window for me, **just as** she always does.

- **The conjunctions as ... as and than are called conjunctions of comparison. You use them for comparing.**

I don't dance **as** well **as** Gillian does.
We don't see my auntie **as** often **as** we'd like.
I've walked **as** far **as** I can.
The sky is almost **as** dark **as** it is at night.
I can swim much further **than** my little brother can.
The train is going more slowly **than** it usually does.

Did you know?

- In very formal English, you use **as...as** or **than** like this:

  I can jump as high **as he** can.
  I can jump as high **as he.**
  I am taller **than he is.**
  I am taller **than he.**

- In more **natural English**, people say:

  I can jump as high **as him.**
  I am taller **than him.**

- **Here are some more examples of conjunctions used for various purposes.**

The road was flooded, **so** we couldn't drive any further.
We can't walk on water **nor** can we fly in the air.
The piano was **so** big **that** we couldn't get it through the door.
Now that you're all quiet, we'll begin the lesson.
Jim told me **that** he was going to move house.
I'm not certain **if** Liz has any brothers or sisters.
We'll have dinner **when** Dad gets home.
We waited with the injured man **till** the ambulance came.
This is the office **where** Mr Lee works.
Nobody knows **whether** Peter is coming.
Sally makes friends **wherever** she goes.
You can dress **however** you like for my party.
You may use the library **whenever** you want to.
Whatever you do, don't fall into the river.

 ISBN 978-81-8477-744-4

Exercise 1

Put in one of the conjunctions—and, but, or. One has been done for you.

1. Miss Lee is kind ___but___ quite firm with her pupils.
2. The sea looked calm __________ flat.
3. In England, we visited a lot of castles __________ palaces.
4. We didn't see many factories __________ offices.
5. Would you like an ice cream __________ an ice lolly?
6. George works fast __________ very accurately.
7. Is this lift going up __________ down?
8. The game was very strenuous __________ good fun.
9. I'm making a cake __________ sandwiches for tea.
10. I'm not sure whether to go right __________ left.
11. The dancer was rather fat __________ quite graceful.
12. What does he look like? Is he dark __________ fair?

Purpose: In order that, So that, In order to, So as to

- After the conjunctions **in order that** and **so that**, there has to be a subject and verb: Let's hurry **so that** (or **in order that**) **the others don't eat** all the food.
- After the conjunctions **in order to** and **so as to**, you have the infinitive (base form) of a verb only: Let's hurry **in order to** (or **so as to**) **get** there first. You use **in order to** and **so as to** when the subject of the verb after the conjunction is the same as the subject of the verb before it.

Exercise 2

Put in in order that, so that, in order to or so as to. One has been done for you.

1. I went to bed early ___in order to___ (or ___so as to___) be able to catch the train next morning.
2. Speak clearly __________ the audience can hear you.
3. We'll have to wait some hours __________ the paint has time to dry.
4. I sometimes write telephone numbers on my hand __________ remind myself of them.
5. Susie always folds her clothes neatly __________ they don't crease.

 ISBN 978-81-8477-744-4

6. You should eat this fruit soon ________________ it doesn't go bad.

7. Eat plenty of fresh fruit ________________ stay strong and healthy.

8. You can record the songs on tape ________________ remember them better.

9. Stand in a line ________________ I can count you.

10. Please move up ________________ make more room.

Exercise 3

Put in such a, such or so. One has been done for you.

1. She got __such a__ nasty shock that she had to sit down for a minute.

2. The children were ________________ excited that they couldn't sleep.

3. He did ________________ badly in the exam that he had to sit for it again.

4. It was ________________ lovely day that we stayed on the beach longer than we meant to.

5. We'd had ________________ tiring journey that we had to rest for a day.

6. His hair was ________________ long that people thought he was a girl.

7. There was ________________ noise that I couldn't hear what they were saying.

8. We had ________________ comfortable beds that we slept till 10 o'clock.

9. We slept ________________ soundly that we didn't hear the alarm clock.

10. They bought ________________ expensive material that they had no money left for lunch.

 ISBN 978-81-8477-744-4

9 INTERJECTIONS

Read the following passage. The bold items are all interjections.

The rescue

'**Wow!**' exclaimed Jack. '**Great**! This is a wonderful view. I'm going to take some photographs.'

He and his friends, Ben and Sue had just climbed to the top of the high cliffs near their seaside holiday house. From the cliffs, they could see for miles around and they were admiring the view.

'**Careful**, Jack!' said Sue as he moved nearer the edge of the cliff. 'It says "**Danger**!" on that sign over there by the side of the road. I'll go over and read it.'

'**Watch out**, Ben!' Sue called as Ben moved forward to join Jack. 'The notice says that the cliff edge is apt to crumble. It's dangerous to go too near it.'

As Sue went back to join the boys, she saw Jack suddenly disappear over the edge. Then she heard a cry of '**Help**!'

The section of cliff on which Jack had been standing had given way and he had fallen down the cliff. Sue and Ben looked over the edge of the cliff to see if he was all right. They saw that he was on a ledge some way down the cliff.

'**Ouch**!' Jack shouted. 'I've hurt my ankle. I think I might have broken it and this ledge doesn't feel very safe.'

Sue called back to Jack, '**Ok**, Jack! Ben's just phoning for help from his mobile. We'll get you out of there soon.'

Just then, a car stopped by the roadside and a young man got out. He called, '**Hello, there**! Is there anything wrong? Can I help?'

The young man and his friends had been climbing and they had ropes in the car. They quickly let down a rope to Jack and pulled him up.

'**Thanks a million**!' said Jack.

'**Don't mention it**!' said his rescuers.

 ISBN 978-81-8477-744-4

You don't always talk in sentences. Sometimes you just say one word, or perhaps two or three words, for example, while greeting somebody or saying goodbye to them.

You often express things like **surprise, anger, fear, worry, pain, delight, happiness** or **agreement** with just a word or two.

These short expressions are called **interjections**.

Goodbye!	Happy Birthday!	Oh dear!	Ah!
Good morning!	All the best!	Of course!	Ouch!
Good afternoon!	No problem!	Well done!	Hurray!
Good evening!	What a shame!	Look out!	Wow!
Good night!	What a nuisance!	Cheers!	Help!
Good luck!	Merry Christmas!	Hello!	Gosh!
Happy New Year!	Just a minute!	Ssh!	Hey!

Did you know?

You often use an **exclamation mark (!)** after these interjections.

- When you are talking to people, you can use lots of interjections such as **yes, no, what?, oh, well, really?** and so on.

Joe?

Yes?

Are you asleep?

What?

I said, are you asleep?

No!

I can hear a funny noise.

Really?

It sounds like drumming.

Silly! It's just someone's car radio.

Oh, right.

Let me get some sleep now.

OK.

 ISBN 978-81-8477-744-4

Exercise 1

Choose interjections from the box and fill in the blanks.

excuse me	oh	indeed	phew	sorry
shh	ouch	oh dear	alas	goodnight

1. ______________________, I can hear someone at the door.
2. ______________________, how I wish it would rain.
3. David wanted to play football with his friends, but ____________________, he twisted his ankle.
4. '____________________!' yelled Mom. 'How did your clothes get so dirty?'
5. It is ____________________ time for the opera to begin.
6. ______________________! I am never riding that roller coaster again.
7. '____________________,' said Mrs Lee. 'Could you tell me the way to the supermarket?'
8. ______________________! Don't step on my foot.
9. ______________________, I didn't see your foot there.
10. ______________________, Grandma. I will see you in the morning.

 ISBN 978-81-8477-744-4

10 SENTENCES

Read the following passage. The bold items include declarative sentences, interrogative sentences, exclamatory sentences and imperative sentences.

Debt

Many people owe money these days. They often have several credit cards. They rarely give shops cash.

They often buy unnecessary things. They cannot afford them. **Why do they buy them**? They want to have them. They like shopping. It makes them feel good. **They call it retail therapy**.

What do they buy? They buy all kind of things. They buy themselves things. They buy their family things. They often give their family presents.

They usually buy clothes. They exclaim over things. '**What a lovely coat**! I'll have that.' '**What gorgeous shoes**! I'll take two pairs.' They ask to see other things. '**Show me that fantastic evening dress, please**! Do you have it in my size?'

Salespeople show them things for the home. **Can they afford them**? No, they can't. **Do they buy them**? Yes, they do. Again they exclaim over the goods. '**Look at that white leather sofa**! **What a bargain**! I must have it.' '**What an elegant mirror**! It will look just right in my hall.'

Salespeople have been saying to them all day, '**Do try it on**!' They have tried it on. Then they have bought it.

Salespeople have also been saying, '**Sign here, please**!' They have signed the credit card slips. They have gone on signing.

They go home. **They look at the goods**. **Do they like them**? Sometimes they don't. **Often the clothes hang in the wardrobe unworn**.

What about the things for the home? **Do the purchases look all right**? Sometimes, they do not. Does the purchaser's husband or wife like it? '**Please take that back**!' is sometimes the response.

The shopping trip is over. **The postman brings the shoppers the bills**. They are appalled. They go shopping again. It takes their mind off the bills.

People get into debt. It's hardly surprising!

 ISBN 978-81-8477-744-4

A **sentence** is a group of words you use to say something. It must have a **subject** and a **verb**.

Subject	Verb
Sally	is running.
Tom and Joe	are fighting.
The hedgehog	curled up.
The choir	is singing.
It	was raining.

A ***written sentence*** *usually begins with a* ***capital letter*** *and ends with a* ***full stop***.

■ There are **four kinds** of sentences.

1. A **declarative sentence** makes a **statement**, for example:
   Richard is feeding the hens. The telephone rang.
   The children are swimming. Everyone sat down.

2. An **interrogative sentence** asks **a question**, for example:
   What is Richard doing? Are you going shopping today?
   Where are the twins? How old are you?

3. An **exclamatory sentence** is in the form of an **exclamation**, for example:
   What a lovely weather! What an idiot I am! The silly girl!

4. An **imperative sentence** gives **an order** or makes **a request**, for example:
   Please sit down. Speak up! Tell me the truth.

■ The **subject** of a sentence sometimes does something to someone or something else.

The person or thing that the subject does something to is called the **object**.

Subject	Verb	Object
Dad	is cooking	supper.
Susan	has bought	a painting.
Maggie	is reading	her book.
The twins	climbed	the hill.
James	stroked	the cat.
Mum	is holding	the baby.

 ISBN 978-81-8477-744-4

Subject	Verb	Object
Peter	is making	a kite.
They	were playing	football.
I	am writing	a story.
We	have built	a sandcastle.
Sally	crossed	the road.
You	have forgotten	your umbrella.

- Some verbs, for example, **give, show, teach, read**, can have **two objects**. The thing that you give, or show, or teach, or read is the **direct object**. The person that you give, or show, or teach, or read to is called the **indirect object**.

  Here are some sentences with verbs that have two objects.

Subject	Verb	Indirect Object	Direct Object
Dad	read	the children	a story.
Mum	bought	Sally	a doll.
Sally	is making	her doll	a dress.
David	showed	Mary	his stamps.
Miss Lee	is teaching	her pupils	geography.
He	gave	Mary	a present.
The policeman	showed	them	the way.
Anna	kept	me	a seat.
I	have brought	you	some flowers.
Joe	has baked	us	a big cake.
I	will write	Aunt Sara	a letter.
I	have left	you	two files.
Jane	found	me	a hotel.
Robert	got	us	some food.

- A sentence that makes a statement divides clearly into two parts, called **subject** and **predicate**. The **predicate** contains the **verb** and everything that belongs to it, such as its **object**, an **adverb**, or an **adverbial phrase**.

Subject	Predicate
David	telephoned this afternoon.
The two girls	packed the glasses very carefully.
I	have got you three tickets for the match.

Grammar Help

- Some verbs take objects and some don't.
- Verbs that take objects are called **transitive verbs**. For example, **make, hold, buy** in these sentences are transitive verbs:

  Kate is **making** the tea.
  I'll **buy** the present.
  Peter **held** Jane's hand.

- Verbs that don't take objects are called **intransitive verbs**. For example, **arrive, happen, sleep, cry** in these sentences are intransitive verbs:

  When did you **arrive**?
  The accident **happened** at about 2 o'clock.
  Dad's **sleeping** on the sofa.
  Don't **cry**!

Grammar Help

- In a sentence, the **indirect object** comes before the **direct object**.

 ISBN 978-81-8477-744-4

Exercise 1

Identify each type of sentence.

1. My parents are going on a holiday to Egypt.
   ____
2. Which road should I take for the movie theatre?
   ____
3. Shut the door after you leave. ______________________
4. Please tell me where the staff room is.
   ____
5. Sam and Tina are working on the project together.
   ____

Exercise 2

Underline the subject and the predicate in the following sentences. Write S below the subject and P below the predicate.

1. Matthew slept for ten hours last night.
2. The nib of the pen is broken.
3. The teacher asked Tanya to redo her homework.
4. My cat laps up her milk in no time.
5. Maria told her friend John that she would not be able to go to his party.

 ISBN 978-81-8477-744-4

11 PHRASES

Phrases
Adverbial Phrases
Adjectival Phrases
Noun Phrases

Read the following passage. The bold items include noun phrases, adverbial phrases, adjectival phrases and prepositional phrases used both adverbially and adjectivally.

Nature and medicine

Since early times, the natural world has been involved in the curing of diseases. Long before the advent of modern drugs and surgical procedures, **sick people** or **people in pain** were seeking help from herbalists. These herbalists treated people with **plants from the hedgerows, fields and gardens**.

In modern medicine, there is an **ever-growing** range of **state-of-the-art** drugs designed to cure **all our ills**. **Many of these drugs** are the result of years of the most painstaking scientific research and are based on various chemicals.

This specialized scientific research, however, sometimes has had its basis **in the old herbal cures**. For example, some **very well-known** heart medication, now made synthetically, was originally obtained **from foxgloves**.

Recent research suggests that scientists can still find **the basis of cures in the natural world**. **A team of researchers** has discovered that the foam **secreted by a rare tropical frog** could play an important part in the treatment of burns victims.

The mud puddle frog, which lives **in Trinidad**, produces a protective foam that stops its frogspawn from drying out. **This protective foam** also kills bacteria **in the dirty water** where the frog lays its eggs.

Loss of moisture is a major problem in **badly burnt** victims of fire who have lost extensive areas of skin **from their bodies**. There is a risk of death from dehydration. This, added to the danger of bacterial infection, makes some burns a serious medical condition.

The foam **from the frog** is being studied in the labs **at the University of Glasgow** and it is hoped that a **man-made** version may soon be produced. This would revolutionize the treatment of burns. Once again, **Mother Nature** has come to the aid of the inventors of modern medicines.

 ISBN 978-81-8477-744-4

We have seen that sentences have subjects, verbs and objects in them.

Sentences also often contain words that are used together in a small group with a particular meaning. These groups of words are called phrases.

Here are some common phrases.

by the way	in the afternoon	back to front
on the whole	in the evening	over the moon
in a minute	at the station	in private
straight away	in the garden	and so on
once more	through the jungle	out of the ordinary
out of breath	once upon a time	at last
inside out	one after another	in the morning
in public	now and then	at night
on your own	to and fro	on the beach
in my opinion	here and there	at the dentist's
in the end	for goodness' sake	without fear
backwards and forwards		

Grammar Help

A phrase is a group of two or more words that does not contain a verb.

Adverbial Phrases

An adverbial phrase is a group of words that functions as an adverb. Some adverbial phrases tell you when something happens, or when someone does something.

It's cold **in the winter.**
We went hiking **during** the school holidays.
I'll be back **in a minute.**
I went for a run **before breakfast.**
I took the dog for a walk **after supper.**
Some people have to work **at night.**
It's very hot in **the afternoon.**
We stopped work **at half-past** five.
The game starts **at 6.00 pm.**
My birthday falls **on a Monday.**
America celebrates Independence Day **on July 4.**
They were married **in 1990.**

 ISBN 978-81-8477-744-4

- Some **adverbial phrases** tell you where something happens, or where someone or something is, or where someone puts something.

George is hanging his coat **on a peg.**
She gets her vegetables **from the supermarket.**
He is waiting for his friend **at the bus stop.**
His Mum is **in the kitchen.**
Tom threw his ball **over the wall.**
The river flows **under the bridge.**
He works **in a bank.**
They are travelling **on a coach.**
We said goodbye **at the station.**
A party is to be held **in the garden.**
We walked **round the exhibition.**
I had to take my cat **to the vet.**

Grammar Help

All these phrases begin with **prepositions** like **on, in, under, at** and **from.** So you can call these phrases **prepositional phrases.**

Adjectival Phrases

An adjectival phrase is a group of words that functions like an adjective. It describes nouns. Some adjectival phrases come before the noun.

a **two-page** leaflet
five-year-old children
a **month-long** wait
a **neatly dressed** man
freshly cut vegetables
a **five-dollar** note
user-friendly software
out-of-date ideas

- Some adjectival phrases come after the noun.

The lady **behind me** dropped her shopping bag.
I like suitcases **with wheels.**
The goods **displayed in the window** are not for sale.
I spoke to the man **leaning against the lamp post.**
Who is the girl **in the green suit?**
The house **next door to us** has been sold.
We're on the road **to success.**
Three of the kids **in my class** are ill.
The big building **on your left** is a bank.
I've made friends with some other people **staying in the hotel.**
The woman wore a dress **made of silk.**
A friend **in need** is a friend indeed.

 ISBN 978-81-8477-744-4

Grammar Help

- When adjectival phrases come before the noun, you often use **hyphen** to link up the words.
- Adjectival phrases that come after the noun may start with a **participle** or a **preposition**. For example:
  the lady **standing next to me** (participle)
  the lady **next to me** (preposition)
- If the phrase starts with a preposition, it can be called a **prepositional phrase**.

Noun Phrases

A noun phrase is a group of words consisting of a noun and other words.

The subject of a sentence can be a noun phrase, instead of just a noun.

His father works in a bank.
John and his friend are playing chess.
My new pen cost me twenty dollars.
The strong wind has destroyed several houses.
Two white pigeons are sitting on the roof.
A good diamond ring is very expensive.
Joe and I were in the same class last year.
Your holiday photographs are most interesting.
The next chapter tells you about volcanoes.
Our next-door neighbour is away on holiday.
Their apartment block needs repairing.

- **Similarly, the object of a sentence can be a noun phrase, instead of just a noun.**

Mum gave George **a piece of cake**.
He is writing **a long letter** to his friend.
Mary is reading **an interesting book**.
Mother is making **some muffins**.
Dad is repairing **his old car**.
Mary is wearing **a red dress**.
I borrowed **a lot of storybooks** from the library.
He is building **a sandcastle** on the beach.
Let's visit **the castle on the hill**.
I've put **the tickets for the show** on the table.
We've found **just the right birthday present** for you.
We are designing **a web page** for our school.
Shall I tell you **my e-mail address**?

 ISBN 978-81-8477-744-4

Exercise 1

Underline the noun phrases in these sentences. There may be more than one in some sentences.

1. Put your maths textbooks away, please.
2. I'm giving you some grammar exercises for your English homework.
3. We're performing Macbeth, one of Shakespeare's plays.
4. I found some pretty shells on the beach and added them to my large collection.
5. Mary, my cousin from London, is visiting us soon.
6. Lucy examined the curious purple envelope carefully before opening it.
7. Look at these splendid red apples that I bought at the local supermarket.
8. Joe gave his last coin to a ragged child.
9. Yesterday I met Mark, an old friend of mine.
10. There are three good reasons why I can't play in Saturday's match.

Synonyms

- A **phrase** is a group of words that does a grammatical job, for example as a noun, adjective or adverb.

Exercise 2

Underline the adverbial phrases in these sentences.

1. In my opinion, she behaved extremely sensibly.
2. For once, the train arrived on time.
3. We shall be leaving at four o'clock.
4. Dad explained the process in great detail.
5. Come and sit beside me.
6. Watch once again, a bit more carefully.

 ISBN 978-81-8477-744-4

7. We played tennis until half past six.
8. He walks very slowly with a stick.
9. We're going abroad during the vacation.
10. At least I played my part pretty well in the play.

Exercise 3

Use the words after the verb to form an adjectival phrase before the noun. One has been done for you.

1. The timetable is out of date. It's an ___out-of-date___ timetable.
2. The baby is two months old. She's a ____________ baby.
3. Our family has two cars. We're a ____________ family.
4. We were delayed for two hours. We had a ____________ delay.
5. The booklet has eight pages. It's an ____________ booklet.
6. Their methods are up to date. They use ____________ methods.
7. That cheese smells horrible. It's a ____________ cheese.
8. The house was built in the eighteenth century. It is an ____________ house.
9. That building looks very odd. It's a very ____________ building.
10. The journey lasted three days. It was a ____________ journey.

 ISBN 978-81-8477-744-4

12 CLAUSES

Read the following passage. The bold items include co-ordinate and subordinate clauses; among the subordinate clauses are relative clauses, noun clauses, adverbial clauses of place, reason, purpose, condition, concession, manner, result.

Immigration

There are so many issues **that are global** these days. The one **that springs most immediately to mind** is, of course, terrorism, **but there are others**. Most of us might guess **that immigration would be one of these. Wherever we look,** there are newspaper articles on immigration.

Immigrants often seek a new life in another country **because life has become unsatisfactory**, **or even intolerable**, **in their own country**. Some people want to go to another country **so as to escape imprisonment** or **in order to save their lives**. They will have to go into permanent hiding **if they stay in their own country**.

This is the case **even though most of us in other countries would not regard these people as criminals**. Mostly, they are people **who have offended the authorities by protesting against a harsh regime and have put their lives at risk by doing so**. They cannot safely stay **where they are** and so they try to seek refuge elsewhere.

Such people are known as asylum-seekers **since they are seeking political asylum**. You would think that people in other countries would want asylum-seekers to live **as** safely and comfortably **as they do themselves**.

However, many people who may usually talk **as though they were very caring and compassionate** can be quite hostile to potential immigrants to their countries. They cannot believe that some would-be immigrants have been **so** afraid in their own countries **that they have fled their homes**. They feel that most of them have done so **in order that they can improve their economic situation**.

If the asylum-seekers had stayed at home, many of them would have been killed. They have sought safety and security in a new home and **many of them are facing uncertainty and hostility there**.

Clauses
Co-ordinate Clauses
Subordinate Clauses
Adverbial Clauses of Time
Adverbial Clauses of Reason
Adverbial Clauses of Purpose
Conditional Clauses
Adverbial Clauses of Concession or Contrast
Adverbial Clauses of Place
Adverbial Clauses of Manner
Adverbial Clauses of Comparison
Adverbial Clauses of Result
Relative Clauses
Noun Clauses

 ISBN 978-81-8477-744-4

A clause is a **group of words** that has a subject and a verb.

Some sentences consist of only one clause, with a subject and a verb. A sentence that consists of only one clause is called a **simple sentence.**

Here are some simple sentences.

Tom **opened** the door for Miss Lee.
Miss Lee **went** to her desk.
Everyone **answered** except Peter.
Peter **stayed** at home today.

All the children **stood** up.
She **called out** the names one by one.
Where **was** Peter?
He **had** a cold.

Co-ordinate Clauses

Some sentences consist of **two clauses** joined together by the conjunctions **and, or, but** or **so.** These two clauses are called **co-ordinate clauses** or **co-ordinate main clauses.** A sentence with co-ordinate clauses is called a **compound sentence.**

Here are some sentences with co-ordinate clauses.

Co-ordinate main clause	Conjunction	Co-ordinate main clause
Tom **likes** drawing	**and**	Mary **likes** dancing.
Mary **likes** maths	**but**	John **prefers** English.
Do you **like** tennis	**or**	do you **prefer** jogging?
It **was raining**	**so**	I **took** an umbrella.
I **went** to Bill's house	**but**	he **wasn't** at home.

Subordinate Clauses

Some clauses contain a subject and a verb, but they do not make sense by themselves. They are called **subordinate clauses.**

Subordinate clauses begin with words like **when, if, because, who** and **which.** They depend on the main clause to make sense.

Here are some sentences that have a main clause and a subordinate clause.

Main clause	Subordinate clause
He will take the dog for a walk	when he has finished his work.
You should stay at home	if you are not well.
I have a watch	which is also a calculator.
Peter met an old friend	while he was out walking.

Nouns
Pronouns
Adjectives
Determiners
Verbs
Adverbs
Prepositions
Conjunctions
Interjections
Sentences
Phrases
Clauses
More about Sentences
Direct and Indirect Speech
Punctuation

 ISBN 978-81-8477-744-4

Main clause	Subordinate clause
I know a man	who mends computers.
I have had all my hair cut off	since you last saw me.
This is the house	that Jack built.
We'll go out	when the rain stops.
Do you know	why she is crying?
Does anyone know	how this machine works?
He was late	because he missed the bus.

Grammar Help

A **subordinate clause** is also called a **dependent clause** because it depends on the main clause to make sense.

Adverbial Clauses of Time

A subordinate clause that tells you about the time of the action in the main clause is called an adverbial clause of time.

Give this letter to Miss Lee **when you see her**.
Could you watch the baby **till I come back**?
Wash your hands **before you eat**.
Tom waved goodbye to Dad **as he climbed on to the bus**.
You have grown a lot **since I last saw you!**
Mum likes to listen to the radio **while she does the ironing**.
I'll send you a postcard **when I get to London**.
We saw lots of snakes **while we were on safari in Africa**.
I skidded as **I cycled round the corner**.
He has been working as a shop assistant since **he left school**.
Brush your teeth **after you have eaten**.

Adverbial Clauses of Reason

A subordinate clause that gives the reason for the action in the main clause, or the reason for what you say in the main clause, is called an adverbial clause of reason.

We'll stay inside **since it's too hot to sit outside**.
Tom missed the bus **because he got up late**.
John was absent **because he was ill**.
Sally can go first **as she is the oldest**.
You'll have to share **as there aren't enough books for everyone**.
Take your raincoat with you **in case there's a downpour**.
Hold on to the rail **in case you fall**.

Grammar Help

- **Adverbial clauses of time usually begin with words like when, while, since, before, till, after or as.**

  They often answer the question 'when'. For example:

  Brush your teeth.
  When?
  After you have eaten.
- **Adverbial clauses of reason usually begin with because, as, since or in case.**

  They answer the question 'why'. For example:
  Hold on to the rail.
  Why?
  In case you fall.

 ISBN 978-81-8477-744-4

Adverbial Clauses of Purpose

A subordinate clause that tells you the purpose of the action in the main clause is called an adverbial clause of purpose.

We switched on the television **so that we could watch the news.**
We are lining up **so that Miss Lee can count us.**
They are working hard **so that they will do well in the test.**
You must speak loudly **in order that everyone can hear you.**
Write down the telephone number **so you won't forget it.**
Move quickly **so that everybody gets a turn.**
Stand back **in order that the ambulance can pass.**
Listen carefully **so that you remember everything.**
Always put milk in the fridge **so it doesn't go sour.**
Put on sun cream when you lie in the sun **so you don't get burnt.**
Make sure the tap is properly turned off **so that water is not wasted.**
I looked after the baby for a while **so that Mum could have a rest.**

Grammar Help

- **Adverbial clauses of purpose usually begin with words like so that, in order that or so. They answer the question 'what for'. For example:**

  Always put milk in the fridge.
  What for?
  So it doesn't go sour.

- **You can also use so as to, in order to followed by an infinitive, to say what purpose somebody has in doing something. For example, you can say:**

  I set my alarm for six o'clock **so as to make** an early start.
  We looked yet again at the figures **in order to give** them a final check.

Conditional Clauses

A subordinate clause beginning with if, unless, as long as or providing is called a conditional clause. These clauses say what the **conditions** or **circumstances** are for something to happen. **You use the simple present tense in the subordinate clause.**

I will come **if you invite me.**
Plants will die **if they get no water.**
Plants will die **unless they get water.**

 ISBN 978-81-8477-744-4

We cannot visit a foreign country **if we don't have our passports.**
We won't win **if we don't train hard.**
We won't win **unless we train hard.**
He'll get into trouble **if he doesn't behave.**
You may go home **if you have finished your work.**
We shall have to cancel the picnic **if it rains tomorrow.**
Buy some more milk **if there is none in the fridge.**
I won't go on the trip **unless you come too.**
All my work will be wasted **unless I can restore that file.**
You can borrow this video **as long as you remember to give it back.**
His condition will remain stable as long **as he listens to the doctor's advice.**

The term first conditional is given to sentences like the ones above, which are about real situations.

- There are some conditional clauses that talk about **unreal** or **imagined** situations. In an **unreal conditional sentence** about **the present**, you use the helping verbs **would, could** or **might** in the main clause, and you use a form of the verb that looks like the **simple past tense** in the subordinate **if** clause.

You would work better **if you got more sleep.**
(But you don't get much sleep.)
We couldn't live **if we didn't eat and drink.**
(But we do eat and drink.)
They would save a lot of money **if they didn't smoke.**
(But they do smoke.)
We might get there in time **if we ran.**
(But we are not running.)
What would happen **if the earth stopped rotating?**
(But the earth does keep rotating.)
Would we all fall off the earth **if there was no gravity?**
(But there is gravity.)
We could hang from trees **if we had strong tails like monkeys.**
(But we don't.)

The term **second conditional** is given to these sentences.

- In an **unreal conditional sentence** about **the past**, you use the helping verbs **would, could** or **might + have + past participle** in the main clause, and you use the **past perfect tense** in the subordinate **if** clause.

I might have beaten you **if I had trained harder.** *(But I didn't train hard.)*

Grammar Help

Conditional clauses are also called **adverbial clauses of condition.**

 ISBN 978-81-8477-744-4

He would not have lost his way **if he had taken an up-to-date map with him.** *(But he didn't take one.)*
I would have helped out **if you had asked me.** *(But you didn't ask me.)*
If we had played better we would have won. *(But we didn't play better.)*
We could have flown in the air **if we'd had wings like birds.** *(But we did not have wings like birds.)*

The term third conditional is given to these sentences.

Grammar Help

Not all subordinate clauses beginning with if are conditional clauses. For example, if is sometimes used like when or whenever.

I usually go to the gym in the evenings if (= whenever) **I have no other plans.**
Dad always went jogging if (= whenever) **the weather was nice.**

Adverbial Clauses of Concession or Contrast

A subordinate clause that tells you something surprising or unusual connected with the main clause is called an adverbial clause of concession or contrast.

He takes great care of his baby brother **although he is only five himself.**
We enjoyed our climb, **even though we didn't get to the top of the mountain.**
Most of you got the answer wrong, **though it wasn't very hard.**
She has already had her breakfast, **although it's only six o'clock.**
Go through all the irregular verbs again, **even if you think you know them.**
It's a very enjoyable book, **although it's rather long.**
He has decided to retire, **although he's only 55.**
He must learn to speak English, **even if it's difficult.**
You must always do your best, **even if you don't expect to win.**
I decided to get up, **though it was still very dark.**
I like Peter, **even though he's sometimes quite rude.**
Our holiday in London was fun, **even though it rained all the time.**

Grammar Help

Adverbial clauses of concession or contrast begin with **although, though, even though** or **even if.**

 ISBN 978-81-8477-744-4

Adverbial Clauses of Place

A subordinate clause that tells you where the action in the main clause is, is called an adverbial clause of place.

Leave the money **where you found it.**
I like to go **where the action is.**
There is usually disease **where there is poverty.**
They say you will find a pot of gold **where the rainbow ends.**
He left footprints in the snow **wherever he walked.**
It's very cold **where the penguins live.**
There was a big hole **where the mouse had chewed through the wall.**
Wherever he went, the famous movie star would attract lots of attention.
Stay **where you are!**
Sally makes herself a useful member of the community **wherever she lives.**
Sometimes you get help **where you least expect it.**
I don't want to leave a bad impression **wherever I go.**

> **Grammar Help**
> Adverbial clauses of place begin with **where** or **wherever**. They answer the question '**where**'. For example:
> It's very cold.
> **Where?**
> **Where** the penguins live.

Adverbial Clauses of Manner

A subordinate clause that tells you the way the action in the main clause happens is called an adverbial clause of manner.

He curled up on the floor **the way a cat does.**
We pointed our toes **as we had been taught.**
Mum tucked us up in bed **the way she always did.**
Can I have my hair cut **the way Sally has hers?**
Some animals build nests **just as birds do.**
England was cold and wet, **just like you told us.**
She was walking on tiptoe, **as though the floor was very hot.**
The baby was yelling and yelling **as if it would never stop.**
You are smiling **as though you know the answer already.**
You talk **just like my father does!**
Dad sounded **as though he had just woken up.**
You look **as if you had seen a ghost!**
Danny talks **as if he owned the place!**
It looks **as if it's going to rain.**

> **Grammar Help**
> Adverbial clauses of manner begin with **as, just as, as if, as though, just like** or **the way.** They often answer the question '**how**'. For example:
> I want my hair cut.
> **How?**
> **The way** Sally has hers.

 ISBN 978-81-8477-744-4

Adverbial Clauses of Comparison

A subordinate clause that compares the action in the main clause with something else is called an adverbial clause of comparison.

A hare moves faster **than a tortoise does.**
You must be cleverer **than I thought.**
I can walk farther **than my baby brother can.**
I bet you can't jump higher **than I can.**
I'm thinner **than I used to be.**
He can't run **as fast as I can.**
I bet I can jump **as high as you can.**
I'm not as fat **as I used to be.**
Borrow books from the library **as often as you like.**
We ran as fast **as we could.**
You may eat as much **as you can.**

Grammar Help

- **Adverbial clauses of comparison begin with than or as ... as.**
- **In very formal English, you use as ... as or than like this:**

  I can jump as high as **he can.**
  I can jump as high as **he.**
  I am taller than **he is.**
  I am taller than **he.**

- **In more natural English, people say:**

  I can jump as high as **him.**
  I am taller than **him.**

Adverbial Clauses of Result

A subordinate clause that tells you the result of the action in the main clause is called an adverbial clause of result.

Winnie the Pooh was **so** fat **that he got stuck in the hole.**
It was **so** hot **that the cheese melted.**
There was **so** much food **that a lot of it was left over.**
So many people came to the match **that there weren't enough tickets for them all.**
It was **such** a lovely day **that we had our lessons out of doors.**
She had **such** a bad headache **that she had to go to bed.**
The mountains are **so** high **that their tops are nearly always hidden in mist.**
Jack is **so** tall **that he has to bend his head to get through the door.**
We sat **so** quietly **that nobody knew we were there.**
It rained **so** heavily **that the street turned into a stream.**
The birds made **such** a noise **that they woke me up.**
She cried **so** often **that the other children called her 'cry baby'.**
Mr White won **so** much money **that he didn't know what to do with it all.**

Grammar Help

Adverbial clauses of result begin with **so ... that** or **such ... that.**

 ISBN 978-81-8477-744-4

- You can put **adverbial clauses** and **conditional clauses** before the main clause.

Subordinate clause	Main clause
When you leave,	please switch off the light.
While he was out walking,	Peter met an old friend.
After I've taken my bath,	I'm going to read the newspapers.
Before you eat,	you must wash your hands.
As he climbed on to the bus,	Tom waved to Dad.
As it's getting late,	we'd better go home.
Since it's Friday,	you can go to the cinema.
Before I left the house,	I shut all the windows.
If you stare at the sun,	you may damage your eyes.
If you invite me,	I'll come.
If he doesn't behave,	he will get into trouble.
Wherever she goes,	she seems to make friends.
Although she is only five,	she makes her own bed.
Even if you don't expect to win,	you must always do your best.
Unless they get water,	plants will die.
Unless we train hard,	we will lose.

Relative Clauses

A subordinate clause that describes a person or thing in the main clause is called a relative clause.

- Relative clauses about people begin with the relative pronouns **who, whom** and **whose**. These pronouns refer to a person in the main clause.

Nobody likes **people who are rude.**
A dentist is **a person who looks after people's teeth.**
A carpenter is **a person who makes furniture.**
A pharmacist is **a person who mixes medicines for people.**
Is that **the waitress who served us?**
All children who play musical instruments are invited to join the band.

 ISBN 978-81-8477-744-4

Cinderella had **a stepmother** **who was unkind to her.**
She has **a penfriend** to **whom she writes every week.**
We have **a classmate** who **comes from Holland.**
Those children **whose birthdays fall between January and June, please raise your hands.**

Did you know?

Relative clauses, because they **describe** a person or thing in the main clause, can also be called **adjectival** clauses.

- **There is another kind of relative clause that is used not to identify or describe a person, but to tell you something extra about a particular person.**

Helen, **who comes from New Zealand**, has joined our class for one term.
Go and see **the nurse**, **who will put a bandage on your leg.**
My great-uncle, **whom I have never met**, is coming to visit us.

*This kind of relative clause needs a **comma** before it.*

- **Relative clauses about things or animals begin with which, that or whose. These pronouns refer to a thing or animal in the main clause.**

Susan has **a watch** **that shows the date.**
A mole is **an animal** **that lives in a hole.**
Books that have pictures are much nicer than **books** **that have no pictures.**
I returned **the racket** **that Tom had lent me.**
She bought **a computer** **which was made in Taiwan.**
Show me **the road** **which leads to the airport.**
Penguins, ostriches and kiwis are all **birds** **that cannot fly.**
An aspirin is **a kind of pill** **that takes away pain.**
We have written **a new grammar book** **whose main aim is to make grammar interesting.**

- **There is another kind of relative clause that is used not to identify or describe a thing or animal, but to add extra information about a particular one.**

We can meet at the Regent Hotel, **which is on the main road.**
He caught a Number 23 tram, which **took him to the new shopping centre.**

*You need a **comma** before this kind of relative clause.*

Grammar Help

The conjunctions **where** and **when** can also be used like relative pronouns to begin a relative clause about **a place** or **a time** in the main clause. For example:

Maggie returned to **the town** **where she had spent her childhood.**
Do you remember **the occasion** when Dad fell into **the river?**

 ISBN 978-81-8477-744-4

Noun Clauses

Noun clauses are the **subordinate clauses** that follow **verbs of saying, thinking, asking** and **wondering.** They are used particularly for **indirect speech.** They represent people's words and thoughts.

A noun clause after a **saying** or **thinking** verb or expression often begins with **that.**

We know **that the earth is round.**
Helen told me **that she was going to move house.**
Dad says **my bicycle needs new tyres.**
I'm certain **I saw her.**
They say **the earth is warming up.**
It was announced **that Peter had won.**
Imagine **that you're living somewhere very cold.**
Nobody thinks **that rearing a family is an easy task.**
Mum has just reminded me **that it's Dad's birthday on Friday.**
Are you sure **I can park here?**
Do you think **I'm making a big mistake?**
Remember **that the competition closes tomorrow.**

- Verbs of **asking** and **wondering** are followed by the conjunctions **if** or **whether**, or a **wh-** question word, and a **noun clause**. Verbs of **telling, knowing** and **explaining** can also be followed by **if, whether** or a **wh-** question word.

We asked a policeman **where** the nearest car park was.
Tim was wondering **when** supper would be ready.
Tell me **whether** you like this skirt on me.
I don't know **if** I can afford all those textbooks.
Can you please explain **why** there is a teddy bear in the fridge?
I cannot think **how** the mistake occurred.
I doubt **whether** the proposed sports complex will ever be built.
Do you know **what** time it is?
What the purpose of this building was I cannot imagine.
I wonder **who** would do a thing like that?
Please let me know soon **who** you want to share a room with on the trip.
Can anyone tell me **whose** gym equipment this is?
Helen refused to say from **whom** her valentine card had come.
We were uncertain which of the cars was Kenneth's.

Grammar Help

- Noun clauses answer the question **what?**

  David announced (what?) **that he was moving house.**

- **That** is often missed out after **saying** and **thinking** verbs. For example:

  I **knew** you'd understand.
  Susan **told** me her Dad was ill.

- Noun clauses come naturally after the main clause, but may come first for emphasis, for example where the speaker despairs of knowing something:

  How we're going to finish the work in time I have no idea!

- A noun clause can act as the explanation or expansion of a **noun** or **nound phrase** already used:

  My view, **that the operation was a complete waste of time**, was ignored.

  Our aim, **that every child will leave school numerate and literate**, will one day be accomplished.

  That intriguing mystery, **whether the chicken or the egg came first**. still bothers many of us.

  A noun clause that explains a noun or noun phrase in this way is said to be in **apposition to** it.

 ISBN 978-81-8477-744-4

Exercise 1

Choose a **clause** from the box to complete the sentences.

everybody's welcome to join the course
he's still in good health
I had to sing a solo in the concert
she's good at drawing horses
she's only ten herself
Mum usually laughs
the grammar is difficult
we started the second book
you aren't successful
you think it sounds silly

1. I enjoy learning English, even though ______________________.
2. Although I'm no good at singing, ______________________.
3. It's worth taking part in the competition even if ______________________.
4. Although ______________________, he's decided to retire from work.
5. Say the words aloud to yourself, even if ______________________.
6. ______________________, even though we hadn't quite finished the first one.
7. ______________________, even if they know nothing about computers.
8. Anna is good at looking after the other children although ______________________.
9. Although ______________________, she can't draw people.
10. ______________________, even though she doesn't approve of my jokes.

 ISBN 978-81-8477-744-4

Exercise 2

Join these two pieces of information together using a relative clause. Use the relative pronouns who (or that) or which (or that) if the relative pronoun is the subject of the relative clause, but leave it out if it is the object of the relative clause. Two have been done for you.

1. The plane was waiting on the runway. It has now taken off.
   The plane that (or which) was waiting on the runway has now taken off.
2. We hired a car. It was bright blue.
   The car we hired was bright blue.
3. A doctor treated my injury. He was from Thailand.
4. Anna lent me an umbrella. It's hanging over there.
5. A strange noise woke us in the night. It was the foghorn.
6. I was trying to contact a friend. He was away on holiday.
7. We made friends with some passengers. They were Scottish.
8. Jane bought a hair-dryer. It was faulty.
9. You're sitting in an armchair. It was my mother's.
10. A man opened the door. He was tall and thin.

Omitting Relative Pronouns

- You need the relative pronoun **who, which** or **that** if it is the **subject** of the relative clause:
  The girl **who** (or **that**) **telephoned** left a message for you.
- You can leave out the relative pronoun if it is the object of the relative clause, or the object of a preposition in the relative clause:
  The girl ~~that (or who or whom)~~ **you telephoned** called back again.
  The film ~~that (or which)~~ **I was telling you about** is on television tonight.

 ISBN 978-81-8477-744-4

Identifying Noun Clauses

- The conjunction **that** is often left out between the saying or thinking verb and the noun clause: I realised ~~that~~ I **needed my passport for the journey**.

Exercise 3

Write out the whole group of words that belong to the noun clause. One has been done for you.

1. When I heard the amazing news I thought I was going to faint.

   I was going to faint

2. They told us the apartment would be available in two weeks' time.

3. He knows he can't win but he's keen to try.

4. Do you really believe the plan will succeed?

5. I was told you were looking for me.

6. I hadn't realized you painted that picture yourself.

7. It is thought he just died in his sleep.

8. I don't think it's right to kill insects, but others may disagree.

9. I'm sure you don't want to listen to all this nonsense.

10. Did you say you were going out tonight?

 ISBN 978-81-8477-744-4

13 More About Sentences

Read the following passage. The bold items include simple sentences, compound and complex sentences, positive and negative sentences, questions and question tags.

A drug scare

'**Have you seen Ben recently**?' Jim asked Dan.

'No, **I haven't seen him since we went to Alice's party last week**,' replied Dan.

'You usually see him quite regularly, **don't you**?' said Jim.

'**We usually get together quite a lot, but he's been studying very hard of late**,' said Dan. '**He wants to study medicine and he needs good exam results.**'

'Did he seem OK to you at the party?' asked Jim.

'Yes, he did, and he enjoyed himself. When Alice gives a party everyone always has a really good time and Ben was no exception,' said Dan. '**Why are you asking all these questions about Ben**? There isn't anything wrong, **is there**?

'I'm really not sure,' said Jim. 'I don't want to say anything in case I'm wrong. **It might be nothing. I just thought that you'd be the person who was most likely to know if Ben had a problem**. He's always been your best friend, **hasn't he**?'

'**I've no idea what you're talking about**,' said Dan. 'I won't know unless you're more specific.'

'After Ben and I played football last Monday, I went back to his house,' said Jim. 'We went to his room because we wanted to listen to some music. I couldn't help noticing that there was a hypodermic needle on his bedside table. **He didn't know that I had seen it and he put it away quickly**. Do you think he's on drugs?'

'No, I don't,' said Dan. '**Ben would never touch drugs**. If you must know, he's just discovered that he's a diabetic. **He has to inject himself with insulin**. He doesn't want people to know because he doesn't want them to feel sorry for him.'

'Poor Ben!' said Jim. '**I'm sorry that I thought he was a drug addict**.'

Simple Sentences
Compound Sentences
Complex Sentences
Positive and Negative Sentences
Questions
Question Tags

 ISBN 978-81-8477-744-4

Simple Sentences

A sentence that consists of one clause is called a simple sentence.

Here are some simple sentences.

I am flying a kite.
They are washing the dishes.
Everybody looked tired.
The dentist is examining Susan's teeth.
There are a lot of cars on the road.
There are some people walking on the beach.
We are eating our breakfast.
They are playing hide-and-seek.
Tom is drawing a picture.

> **Did you know?**
> **A simple sentence** is also a main clause.

Compound Sentences

A sentence that has **two main clauses** is called a **compound sentence.** The two main clauses are usually joined by **and, or, but** or **so.**

Some people are rich **and** some people are poor.
Sara is good at history **but** she is not very good at maths.
Jane opened the door **and** let Julie in.
I wanted to borrow John's bicycle **but** he refused.
Would you like tea **or** would you prefer coffee?
Please keep quiet **or** you will have to go out.
Joe had lost his key, **so** he came home with me.
Sue writes with her right hand **but** Peter writes with his left.

Complex Sentences

A sentence that has **a main clause** and **a subordinate clause** is called a **complex sentence.**

- The main clause and the subordinate clause are joined together by conjunctions such as **when, if, unless, before, after, because, as, that, than.**

We'll miss the train **if we don't hurry.**
Dad was angry **because I broke his spectacles.**

 ISBN 978-81-8477-744-4

Unless the weather improves dramatically, the match will be cancelled.
We reached home **before it got dark**.
I rang Mum to say **that I would be late home**.
Joan was so tired **that she fell asleep standing up**.

- **The main clause and the subordinate clause may be joined by relative pronouns such as who, which, that or whose.**

A vet is a doctor **who looks after the health of animals**.
The camel is an animal **that lives in the desert**.
A laptop is a computer **that you can hold in your hand**.
A vacuum cleaner is a machine **that sucks the dirt out of carpet**.

- **They may also be joined by question words such as how, what, who, which, why, where or when.**

Charlie explained **how the program worked**.
Have you decided **what you want to be?**
Do you know **who they are?**
Nobody knows **where the dog is**.
Tell me **why you chose this car**.
The passengers did not know **when their plane was taking off**.

Positive and Negative Sentences

A positive sentence is a sentence that tells you something is so.

A sentence that tells you something is not so is called a negative sentence. It contains a negative word like not, never, no, no-one, nobody, none, or a negative verb like isn't or can't or won't.

Positive sentence	Negative sentence
Peter is running.	He is **not** walking.
We should tell the truth.	We should **never** tell lies.
Everyone is in the garden.	There is **no one** in the house.
The fridge is empty.	There is **nothing** in it.
It is very cloudy.	It **isn't** sunny.
I have sold the last newspaper.	I have **no** newspapers left.
Someone has eaten all the cookies.	There are **none** in the tin.

 ISBN 978-81-8477-744-4

Questions

There are two kinds of questions: **yes** or **no** questions and **wh-** questions.

- When you ask a **yes** or **no** question, you want the answer **yes,** or the answer **no**. You use the verbs **be, have** or **do**, or any of the **helping verbs**, to ask **yes** or **no** questions.

Can you swim?
Yes.

Are they coming?
No.

Is it raining?
No.

May I come in?
Yes.

- In questions, the verb **be** and the **helping verbs** come **before** the subject, and the rest of the verb **after** the subject.

Statement	Question
Jim **is** ill today.	**Is** Jim ill today?
She **has finished** her lunch.	**Has** she **finished** her lunch?
He **has** a sister called Jill.	**Has** he a sister called Jill?
The cats **want** to be fed.	**Do** the cats **want** to be fed?
Miss Lee **told** them a story.	**Did** Miss Lee **tell** them a story?
Old people **don't like** noise.	**Don't** old people **like** noise?
Kate **can ride** a bike.	**Can** Kate **ride** a bike?
Sue and Jane **would like** to help.	**Would** Sue and Jane **like** to help?
They **couldn't stop** laughing.	**Couldn't** they **stop** laughing?
We **must leave** straight away.	**Must** we **leave** straight away?
It **will rain** tomorrow.	**Will** it **rain** tomorrow?
The sausages **were cooked** properly.	**Were** the sausages **cooked** properly?
I **saw** the helicopter.	**Did** you **see** the helicopter?
You **may use** my computer.	**May** I **use** your computer?

Grammar Help

Here are some different ways of asking the same question:

Has he a sister called Jill?
Does he have a sister called Jill?
Has he got a sister called Jill?

 ISBN 978-81-8477-744-4

- You form the **wh-** questions with the verbs **be, have, do,** or **any** of the **helping verbs.**

  You use the question words **what, which, who, whom, whose, how, when, where** and **why** to ask for **facts.** As with **yes** or **no** questions, the verb **be** and the other **helping verbs** usually come before the subject.

Where **are you**?
What **is he saying**?
How **did you get up** there?
Why **was Susie crying**?
Which colour **do you prefer**?
Whose dictionary **can I borrow**?
Who **is she going to invite** to the party?
Whom **is she going to invite to** the party?
What **is the problem**?
By whom **was the Taj Mahal built**?
When **do the shops open**?
Where **could I have put that video?**
Where **shall I put** this box?
What **have you done** to my computer?
What **would you like** for breakfast?
How **am I going to finish** all this work?

Grammar Help

Sometimes the words what, which or who are the subject of the sentence, or part of the subject, so no change in the order of subject and verb is needed. For example:

What makes the world go round?
Which train goes to London?
Who switched the lights on?

Question Tags

Sometimes people finish what they are saying with a short question, to see if the person they are talking to agrees with them. You call this short question a question tag.

It's a lovely weather, **isn't it?**
Dad's home early today, **isn't he?**
Susan has short hair, **hasn't she?**
You are nine now, **aren't you?**
The twins are very alike, **aren't they?**

Grammar Help

- These sentences are **positive**, but their question tags are **negative.**
- You use negative question tags with positive sentences.
- Negative question tags expect the answer **'yes'**.

 ISBN 978-81-8477-744-4

We can leave our bags here, **can't we?**
We'll beat the other team, **won't we?**
You would like a drink, **wouldn't you?**
You should write on both sides of the paper, **shouldn't you?**
Susan enjoys playing the piano, **doesn't she?**
Snow White ate a poisoned apple, **didn't she?**

- **You use the verb and the subject of the main clause to form the question tag. You also change the subject to a personal pronoun in the question tag.**

Peter is a good runner, **isn't he?**
You are very late, **aren't you?**
'**I am** your best friend, **aren't I?**'
'Yes, of course you are.'
The grapes were delicious, **weren't they?**
The party was good fun, **wasn't it?**

*You use the question tag **aren't I** after a sentence that has **I am** in it.*

- Here are some **negative sentences** with positive question tags.

You aren't ten yet, **are you?**
I am not too fat, **am I?**
My coat isn't big enough, **is it?**
The sums weren't very difficult, **were they?**
"**You weren't** at James's party, **were you?**"
"No, **I wasn't.**"

- When the sentence begins with **there is** or **there are**, you put **isn't there** or **aren't there** in the question tag.

There are a lot of books in this apartment, **aren't there?**
There is a 'y' in 'eye', **isn't there?**
There were a lot of puddles on the road, **weren't there?**
There was complete silence for a minute, **wasn't there?**

- When the sentence begins with **there isn't** or **there aren't**, you put **is there** or **are there** in the question tag.

There is no 'i' in 'eye', **is there?**
There aren't many trees here, **are there?**
There was no one at home, **was there?**
There weren't any letters for me, **were there?**

Grammar Help

- You use positive question tags with negative sentences.
- Positive question tags expect the answer **'no'**.

 ISBN 978-81-8477-744-4

- You can also use the **helping verb** in the main clause to form the question tag.

  Here are some sentences with question tags that use the helping verbs **do, have, be** and **will.**

He likes drawing, **doesn't he?**
The cat doesn't like swimming much, **does it?**
Mary didn't run as far as Maggie, **did she?**
If I tell you, **you won't tell** anyone else, **will you?**
Mum baked you a wonderful birthday cake, **didn't she?**
Tom has cut the grass neatly, **hasn't he?**
You have made quite a mess, **haven't you?**
Peter is getting tall, **isn't he?**
We are going on holiday tomorrow, **aren't we?**
The baby was crying all night, **wasn't she?**
You will come to my party, **won't you?**

Grammar Help

- When the verb **have** means **do an action,** as in **have a look,** you use the helping verb **do** in the question tag.

  Your grandad **has** a walk every day, **doesn't he?**
  Your granny has a rest every afternoon, **doesn't she?**

- When the verb **have** means **possess,** you can use **do** or **have** in the question tag.

  Here are some different ways of saying the same thing:

  Your Mum **has** a red car, **doesn't she?**
  Your Mum **has** a red car, **hasn't she?**
  Your Mum **has** got a red car, **hasn't she?**

  You **had** long hair when we last met, didn't you?
  You **had** long hair when we last met, **hadn't you?**

- Here are some sentences with question tags that use the helping verbs **must, can, could, should** and **would.**

We must hurry, mustn't we?
We mustn't be late, **must we?**
You can see the whole city from here, **can't you?**
You can't reach as high as me, **can you?**
You could help me carry these bags, **couldn't you?**
Mary couldn't help crying when she fell over, **could she?**
I expect **you** all **would like** a rest now, **wouldn't you?**
We wouldn't like to have an elephant living in the house, **would we?**
You should always **tell** the truth, **shouldn't you?**
They shouldn't make so much noise, **should they?**

 ISBN 978-81-8477-744-4

Exercise 1

Identify each sentence type as simple, compound or complex.

1. After we submitted our test papers, we returned to our seats nervously.
2. Rita and Mona played badminton all afternoon, so they felt very tired in the evening.
3. David goes to the library every day.
4. The teacher asked us not to talk when she saw all the students at the back whispering to one another.
5. An ice cream seller passes by my house every evening and I always buy a chocolate cone from him.
6. I rode my bike and my dog ran along beside me.
7. Even though I had studied very hard, my exam didn't go too well.
8. Jenny has a dance class tomorrow.
9. My mother refuses to buy me fast food because it's not good for health.
10. My sister wants to be a biologist when she grows up.

Exercise 2

Transform the following positive sentences into negative ones.

1. Ali has won a scholarship.
2. The dog wagged his tail when he saw me.

 ISBN 978-81-8477-744-4

3. Joan can write very well.
4. The students always finish their homework on time.
5. It looks like it's going to rain.
6. The books have been dispatched to Australia.
7. Sam will be in office tomorrow.
8. The hurricane caused a lot of damage to the town.
9. Tina wants to go on a month-long holiday.
10. Weather forecasts say that this summer will be very hot.

Exercise 3

Transform the following sentences into questions.

1. Sheela works in a restaurant.
2. I have to catch the 8 pm bus if I want to see the movie.
3. The phone is not working anymore.
4. Misha doesn't drive to school every day.
5. Tom can't play any musical instrument.
6. The shoes are too tight for Tanya.
7. Kim hasn't learnt how to swim yet.
8. I need to make a left at the intersection.
9. Eating fast food regularly is not advisable.
10. The language course is taught over three months.

 ISBN 978-81-8477-744-4

Exercise 4

Add question tags to the following sentences.

1. We should leave before it gets dark.
2. You will enjoy watching this movie.
3. Bonnie doesn't like eggs for breakfast.
4. The school will be closed tomorrow.
5. The traffic at this hour is very bad.
6. The town is full of historical monuments.
7. I don't have to make a class presentation.
8. Joe will see you tomorrow for lunch.
9. The doctor said there was nothing to worry about.
10. Your new job is in another country.

 ISBN 978-81-8477-744-4

14 Direct and Indirect Speech

Read the following passage. The bold items include direct and indirect statements, direct and indirect questions, and indirect commands.

Healthy eating for children

'According to this article, our children are eating the wrong things,' Mrs Brown said to her husband, a teacher at a local school.

Mr Brown replied that it was difficult to get kids to eat the right things, and added, 'How does it suggest we go about it?'

Mrs Brown began to read from the article.

"Parents should warn their children to avoid eating too many snacks, such as crisps and chocolate bars. They should instruct them to eat a piece of fruit instead."

She stopped reading and **remarked that she did give the children fruit for their snack at break, but she was sure they sometimes bought** packets of crisps or chocolate from the school canteen.

She began to read again.

"Parents should ask the school catering staff not to serve chips in the canteen. They should remind them that these have too high a fat content. Instead, parents should insist that salads and leafy green vegetables are served. If the canteen is serving puddings or ice cream, **parents should ask the school staff why there is not a wide range of fruit available."**

Mr Brown **said that they did serve salads in his school canteen, but they also served chips. They had tried leaving them off the menu, but many kids had stopped having school meals**. They couldn't afford to have a wide range of fruit because it wouldn't get eaten. Many kids just liked bananas or apples. **'And what,' he asked, 'would we say to the staff if they were left with piles of rotting fruit week after week?'**

Mrs Brown read again from the article.

"Parents should ask themselves whether they need to buy cartons of juice and cans of soft drinks. They should advise their children to drink water."

Mr Brown **concluded that they did their best to see that their children ate healthily, but it was a case of moderation in all things.**

 ISBN 978-81-8477-744-4

Showing people's exact words with quotation marks is called **Direct Speech**. You can use the single quotation marks (' ') or double quotation marks (" ").

Very often when you are reporting what somebody said, you do not give their exact words with quotation marks. Instead you use a saying or telling verb followed by **that** and a **noun clause.** Reporting people's speech in this way is called **Indirect Speech** or **Reported Speech.**

Direct Speech	Indirect Speech
Dan said, "I need a clean shirt."	Dan said that he needed a clean shirt.
Peter said, "I can't find my briefcase."	Peter said that he couldn't find his briefcase.
Dad said, "I am looking for my car keys."	Dad said that he was looking for his car keys.
"I haven't brushed my teeth," said James.	James said that he hadn't brushed his teeth.
Sally said, "It's eight o'clock already."	Sally said it was eight o'clock already.
"It's time to leave," said Joe.	Joe said that it was time to leave.
John said, "The car won't start."	John said that the car wouldn't start.
Joe said, "We will have to get a taxi."	Joe said that they would have to get a taxi.
Jill said, "We must phone for one."	Jill said that they must phone for one.

Did you know?

You can also use verbs like think, realize and hope to give people's thoughts. So you can write:

Sally **thought** Peter was looking rather pale.
She **realized** that he was not well.
Peter **hoped** he wasn't going to be sick.

Grammar Help

- **People often leave out the conjunction that after reporting verbs, especially said. For example, you can say:**

  Joe **said** it was time to leave.
  John **said** the car wouldn't start.
  Dad **said** he was looking for his car keys.

- **When you turn direct speech into indirect speech you leave out the quotation marks. You also have to make changes to the exact words.**

 ISBN 978-81-8477-744-4

Grammar Help

PRONOUNS

You sometimes have to change the pronouns of the direct speech.
For example:

Direct Speech	Indirect Speech
Peter said, "**I** feel sick."	Peter said that **he** felt sick.
Sally said, "**You** look very pale."	Sally said **he** looked very pale.
Dan said, "**We**'ll have to call a taxi."	Dan said **they** would have to call a taxi.

VERB TENSES

After a saying or reporting verb in the past tense, for example said, you have to change the tense of the verb in the direct speech.

Direct Speech		Indirect Speech
simple present	→	simple past
simple past	→	past perfect
present continuous	→	past continuous
present perfect	→	past perfect

For example:

Peter said, "**I feel** OK again."	Peter said he **felt** OK again.
You **gave** us a fright, Peter," said Dan.	Dan told Peter he **had given** them a fright.
"You **are looking** better, Peter," said Sally.	Sally told Peter he **was looking** better.
Dad said, "I **have lost** my car keys."	Dad said he **had lost** his car keys.

HELPING VERBS

You have to change the tense of the helping verbs too.

Direct Speech		Indirect Speech	Direct Speech		Indirect Speech
can	→	could	will	→	would
shall	→	would	may	→	might

For example:

Dad said, "**I can't** find my car keys."	Dad said he couldn't find his car keys.
Sally said, "We **shall be** late."	Sally said they **would be** late.
Peter said, "We **may be** in time."	Peter said they **might be** in time.
James said, "I **won't go** to the party."	James said he **wouldn't go** to the party.

OTHER WORDS

After a saying or reporting verb in the past tense you sometimes have to make changes to the adverbs and other words.

Direct Speech		Indirect Speech
here	→	there
tomorrow	→	the next day or the following day
yesterday	→	the day before or the previous day

For example :

Sally said, "The taxi will be **here** soon."	Sally said the taxi would be **there** soon.
Peter said, "I hope you will all come **tomorrow**."	Peter said he hoped we would all come **the next day**.
Mum said, "It rained **yesterday**."	Mum said it had rained **the day before**.

 ISBN 978-81-8477-744-4

Indirect Commands

You can use verbs like order, tell, command, warn, ask, beg, advise and instruct to report orders, commands, requests, advice, invitations or instructions.

Direct Speech	Indirect Speech
The policeman said to us, "Stop !"	The policeman **ordered** us to stop.
Miss Lee said to her pupils, "Put your books away."	Miss Lee **told** her pupils to put away their books.
The principal said, "Children, do not run in the corridor."	The Principal **told** the children not to run in the corridor.
Mum said, "Peter, don't tell lies."	Mum **warned** Peter not to tell lies.
Sally said to me, "Please put the ice cream in the fridge."	Sally **asked** me to put the ice cream in the fridge.
The general said to his troops, "Halt!"	The general **commanded** his troops to halt.
Maggie said to Susan, "Please don't tell anyone."	Maggie **begged** Susan not to tell anyone.

Grammar Help

You usually use the construction to + verb with ordering, requesting or advising verbs. For example:

Miss Lee asked us **to read** the first chapter for homework.
The lawyer requested him **to sign** his name.
Dave invited us **to see** his rabbits.

Indirect or Reported Questions

You use the verb ask to report questions. You can also use inquire.

Direct Speech	Indirect Speech
Sally said, "Peter, are you feeling OK?"	Sally **asked** Peter if he was feeling OK.
"What is the time?" said Peter.	Peter **inquired** what the time was.

You use if or whether after the asking verb to report yes or no questions.

Direct Speech	Indirect Speech
"Sally, would you like tea or coffee?" asked Dan.	Dan asked Sally **whether** she would like tea or coffee.
"Is the taxi coming?" asked Alice.	Alice asked if the taxi was coming.

 ISBN 978-81-8477-744-4

Direct Speech	Indirect Speech
"Is it warm or cold outside?" asked Diana.	Diana asked whether it was warm or cold outside.

- **You use wh- question words after the asking verb to report wh- questions.**

Direct Speech	Indirect Speech
Dad said, "How are you feeling, Peter?"	Dad asked Peter **how** he was feeling.
Mum said, "Why has the clock stopped? "	Mum asked **why** the clock had stopped.
"Where shall I put the rubbish?' asked Mary.	Mary asked **where** she should put the rubbish.
"How do I start the washing machine?" said Paul.	Paul asked **how** to start the washing machine.

Grammar Help

- **In an indirect or reported question, the subject comes before the verb, not after it. You do not use the helping verb do to form reported questions. For example:**

  Paul said, "What time **does the bus come?**"
  Paul asked what time **the bus came.**
  Charles said, "Sally, **do you want** sandwiches?"
  Charles asked Sally if **she wanted** sandwiches.

- **You can also use wh- question words after verbs like tell and explain. For example:**

  Explain **why** you are late.
  She told me **where** the clean towels were.

- **An asking verb and wh- question word are sometimes followed by the construction to + verb. For example:**

  Sally asked **how to turn on** the computer.
  Peter asked **where to put** the clean spoons.

- **You can use the words wonder and don't know to report questions that people ask themselves without asking them aloud. For example:**

  "Why has the clock stopped?" **thought** Peter.
  Peter **wondered** why the clock had stopped.
  "What shall I do?" I **thought.**
  I **didn't know** what to do.

 ISBN 978-81-8477-744-4

Helping Verbs in Reported Speech

- When the saying or thinking verb is in the past tense, helping verbs such as **can** and **may** must be changed to past-tense forms. **Can** must be changed to **could, will** and **shall** to **would**, and **may** to **might**:

  I will go. **I thought I would** go.

  The boys **can** go. Mary **said** the boys **could** go.

Exercise 1

Choose the correct form for the helping verb. Use short forms if short forms are used in the direct speech. Two have been done for you.

1. 'John will come again soon,' I assured them.

   I assured them that John __would__ come again soon.

2. I'll never speak to her again.

   I tell you I __would__ never speak to her again.

3. I'll never speak to her again,' I said.

   I said that I ________ never speak to her again.

4. I'll never get another chance,' she thought.

   She was sure that she ________ never get another chance.

5. 'We can't eat another thing,' we said.

   We said that we ________ eat another thing.

6. 'We shall certainly meet again somewhere,' I told her.

   I told her that we ________ certainly meet again somewhere.

7. 'I'm sorry we shan't be able to be at the party,' I said.

   I said that I ________ sorry we ________ be able to be at the party.

8. 'I hate potatoes,' I said

   I said that I ________ potatoes.

9. 'I can't see anything,' I told her.

   I told her that I ________ see anything.

10. 'We did try to help,' we said.

    We said that we ________ tried to help.

 ISBN 978-81-8477-744-4

Exercise 2

Put in suitable forms for reported speech. One has been done for you.

1. 'I went for a long walk yesterday,' said James. James said that *he had gone* for a long walk *the day before*.
2. 'I'm sick and tired of your laziness,' Sarah said to her brother. Sarah told her brother that __________ sick and tired of __________ laziness.
3. 'I'm surprised to see you here,' I said to her. I said that I __________ surprised to see __________.
4. 'I don't like coffee,' said the girl. The girl said that __________ like coffee.
5. 'My sister is going to be a nurse,' Mary told her friend. Mary told her friend that __________ sister __________ going to be a nurse.
6. 'We saw a strange man outside the shop just before the robbery,' said the children. The children told the police that __________ a strange man outside the shop just before the robbery.
7. 'We taught English in Japan for a year,' the couple next door told me. The couple next door told me that __________ English in Japan for a year.
8. 'My leg hurts,' she complained. She complained that __________ leg __________.
9. 'I shall be back,' said Arnie. Arnie said __________ be back.
10. 'I can't come tomorrow,' said Tom. Tom said that __________ come __________.

Other differences between Direct and Reported Speech

- When changing direct speech to reported speech, you sometimes have to make changes to pronouns, determiners, adverbs and similar words:

  '**My** aunt is coming to stay with **us**,' says Mary. Mary says that **her** aunt is coming to stay with **them**.

  '**You** don't know what **you**'re talking about,' said Simon to his little sister. Simon told his little sister that **she** didn't know what **she** was talking about.

  'I'll never get a better chance than **this**,' I thought. I was sure I'd never get a better chance than **that**.

  'I'm not happy **here**,' she said. She said that she wasn't happy **there**.

 ISBN 978-81-8477-744-4

Exercise 3

Complete these indirect commands and requests. One has been done for you.

1. 'Sit beside me,' said Harry to Sue.

   Harry invited Sue to sit beside him.

2. 'Please don't leave me!' Sally said to her brother.

   Sally begged her brother ________________.

3. 'Company, halt!' shouted the colonel.

   The colonel commanded his company ________________.

4. 'Take a week's holiday,' the doctor said to Dad.

   The doctor advised Dad ________________.

5. The notice says, 'Do not enter'.

   The notice forbids us ________________.

6. 'Help me with the beds,' said Mum to me.

   Mum asked me ________________.

7. 'Take care on the steps,' said the guide to the tourists.

   The guide warned the tourists ________________.

8. 'Do stay till tomorrow,' we said to Granny.

   We persuaded Granny ________________.

9. 'Don't look at the answers,' Miss Lee said to us.

   Miss Lee told us ________________.

10. The sign read: 'Please wipe your feet.'

    The sign requested us ________________.

 ISBN 978-81-8477-744-4

15 PUNCTUATION

Read the following passage, paying particular attention to the punctuation marks.

Leader article on traffic

What appalling congestion there is in this city! The traffic jams are intolerable and drivers often experience total gridlock. It should be the **council's** most urgent priority. What are they doing about it?

We sent a reporter to ask them. They replied, 'We are very much aware of the frustrations caused to motorists by the present traffic problems; we are doing all in our power to solve these.'

The trouble is the council has not solved motorists' problems. We are not accusing council members of total inactivity. Over the years, they have come up with several ideas. These include: pedestrianizing the city centre, pedestrianizing part of the city centre, making the principal streets one way and charging a toll, payable by drivers, for bringing the cars into the city centre.

What came of any of these ideas? Absolutely nothing! Ideas are put forward; nothing happens. Why is this?

Unfortunately, it is difficult to avoid the conclusion that the council simply backs down whenever their proposals are challenged. Whenever council members have proposed a new scheme, it has been met with objectors' protests. The scheme may have been innovative, useful, helpful and even ideal, but it has met with the opposition of some motorists. When this has happened, the council has given up the scheme.

Why do they do this? We put the question to them. They denied that they had backed down. They said that they had simply changed their minds after reconsidering their plans; it had nothing to do with the objectors.

They said, 'We judge each proposal on its merits and sometimes we reconsider. That is all part of the planning procedure.'

In our opinion, it is just a time-wasting procedure. Get moving, council! We need action!

 ISBN 978-81-8477-744-4

Punctuation marks are signs such as full stops, commas, and question marks. You use them in sentences to make the meaning clear.

Nouns
Pronouns
Adjectives
Determiners
Verbs
Adverbs
Prepositions
Conjunctions
Interjections
Sentences
Phrases
Clauses
More about Sentences
Direct and Indirect Speech
Punctuation

Full Stop .

You put a **full stop** at the end of a sentence.

Peter is my good friend.
Please don't be late.
The bird is sitting on a branch.
It's raining heavily.
There's a rainbow in the sky.

*A full stop is also called a **period** or a **full point**.*

You sometimes put full stops after words that have been shortened.

Sunday	**Sun.**	January	**Jan.**
Monday	**Mon.**	February	**Feb.**
Tuesday	**Tue.**	October	**Oct.**
Wednesday	**Wed.**	November	**Nov.**
Thursday	**Thur.**	December	**Dec.**
Friday	**Fri.**	Doctor	**Dr.**
Saturday	**Sat.**	Department	**Dept.**

You sometimes shorten people's first names to one letter followed by a full stop.

Robert John Smith	**R.J. Smith**
Lin Wei Yang	**W.Y. Lin**

Exclamation Mark !

You often put an **exclamation mark** after commands, interjections or words that show surprise or anger.

Sit down!
Oh dear!
What a surprise!
You are fired!
I told you not to do that!

Quiet!
Put the knife down!
Help! Help!
Eeek! A ghost!
Stop him!

 ISBN 978-81-8477-744-4

Question Mark ?

You put a question mark after a question.

What's your name?
How are you?
Where are you going?
Where do they come from?
Who has taken my pen?
How many stamps do you have?
Can you lend me your bicycle?
Why are you always late?
What's the meaning of this word?
Do you know the answer to this sum?

Comma ,

You put a comma between nouns and noun phrases in a list.

He enjoys tennis, badminton, skating and football.
We study English, maths, science, history and geography at school.
I bought two apples, three oranges and some grapes.
This house has a living room, three bedrooms, a study, a kitchen and three bathrooms.

You put commas between adjectives when you use a lot of them to describe something.

A giraffe is a tall, long-necked, long-legged animal.
What is wide, deep, wet, flat and never stops moving?
He is a tall, handsome, smart and ambitious young man.

You put a comma after yes and no, and before please. You also put a comma before or after the name of the person you are speaking to.

Can you tell me what time it is, please?
Yes, it's a quarter past three, George.
Tom, is it still raining?
No, it has stopped.
Have a good day, Tom!
Goodbye, George!

 ISBN 978-81-8477-744-4

You use commas to show where there is a little pause.

Unfortunately, she damaged her knee skiing.
He was in the bedroom, listening to music on the radio.
I like neutral colours, for instance, beige and grey.

A proper name introduced by a noun phrase does not need commas round it.

I invited **my cousin Jean** to come with me.
The singer Michael Jackson had changed his image remarkably over the years.

But you put commas round a name that is added after a noun phrase with a slight pause, as an explanation or extra piece of information.

My other cousins, Helen and Margaret, were unable to come.
The chairman, Mr Jim Handley, brought the meeting to an end at 5.00 pm.

Apostrophe ’

You use the apostrophe with an s to show who owns something.

You add ’s after singular nouns or names.

This is **Peter’s** bed and that is **Michael’s** bed.
Where is **James’s** book?
A **squirrel’s** tail is big and bushy.
We all like **Mum’s** cooking.
This is **James and Michael’s** room.
This is **Susan and Jenny’s** room.
Susan collects **everybody’s** plates after the meal.
John’s dog is very friendly.
They are going to their **boss’s** house for a party.
All the pupils have a **month’s** holiday in June.
I have an appointment at 3 o’clock at the **doctor’s**.
I spent the evening at **David’s** playing video games.

You just add ’ after plural nouns that end with s .

My **brothers’** bedrooms are always untidy.
The **girls’** bedrooms are usually tidy.
Mum is making a cake for the **twins’** birthday party.
The **pupils’** desks are arranged in rows.

 ISBN 978-81-8477-744-4

A flood has destroyed all the **farmers'** crops.
It will take three **months'** work to complete the project.

- **But you add 's after plural nouns that don't end in s .**

They are playing in the **children's** playground.
Men's shoes are usually larger than **women's** shoes.
Doctors look after **people's** health.

- **You also use an apostrophe to show that a letter or some letters in a word have been left out.**

I've finished my sums, but I **haven't** finished my spelling.
You are taller than Peter, but you **aren't** as tall as me.
We'll come to your party, but Sue **won't** be able to come.
Mary'd like a cat as a pet, but she **wouldn't** like a turtle.
He'd gone out and he still **hadn't** come home.
Dad **wasn't** at home and the children **weren't** at home either.
I **don't** like potatoes and Susan **doesn't** like tomatoes.
I **didn't** watch which way I was going and now I **can't** find my way home.
We'd have visited you but we **couldn't** find your house.
Mum's finished her shopping but she **hasn't** been through the checkout yet.
Molly's making a cup of tea but she **isn't** making a meal till later.

Grammar Help

You often find has and is shortened to 's after a noun or proper noun. For example:

The mail has arrived.
The mail's arrived.
Sally is here
Sally's here.

Hyphen -

You sometimes need to join compound words with a hyphen so that the reader knows that they represent a unit, and doesn't have to hesitate and re-read bits of text.

- **Some compound nouns are written as one word, for example, teacup, classroom, sweatshirt, keyboard. Some are written as two words, for example, fire alarm, signal box, washing machine.**

  With compound nouns that are written as two words, use a hyphen between them if the first word is the object of the second word. This makes the connection clear.

taxi-driver	word-processor	concrete-mixer
book-collector	cash-dispenser	self-control

- **Compound nouns using short particles are usually written with a hyphen.**

sit-in	passers-by	runner-up	break-in
break-out	break-up	take-off	fly-by

 ISBN 978-81-8477-744-4

Certain compound nouns representing military ranks are usually hyphenated.

lieutenant-colonel   sergeant-major   major-general

Compound nouns consisting of a string of words need to be kept together with hyphens.

my **sister-in-law**
a bunch of **forget-me-nots**
the Queen's **ladies-in-waiting**
caught in **no-man's-land**

Compound adjectives that come before the noun should usually be hyphenated.

eye-catching designs
a **long-awaited** announcement
a **well-argued** essay
never-ending complaints
a **four-page** leaflet
a **three-bedroomed** apartment
a **much-overused** word
clear-cut ideas
ill-educated people
a **hard-won** victory
ten-year-old children
a **long-haired** dog

Adjectives formed with -like have hyphens, whether before the noun or not.

an **owl-like** expression
Her fingers were long and **claw-like**.

Did you know?

But some well-known -like adjectives are written as one word:

childlike
ladylike

The combining words -friendly, -conscious, -looking, -sensitive, -sounding are used with a hyphen, whether before the noun or not.

a **case-sensitive** dialogue box
environment-friendly washing powders
a **strange-sounding** name
a **nice-looking** man
Are the British **class-conscious**?

In some cases, a hyphen needs to be inserted between a prefix and base word for the sake of clarity or appearance.

anti-aircraft   co-opt   ex-wives
non-native   a semi-invalid   pro-British

Compound numbers and fractions are hyphenated.

twenty-seven   thirty-first   three-quarters   one-fifth

 ISBN 978-81-8477-744-4

Grammar Help

- Here is a list of the **short forms** that you see most often. These short forms are often called **contractions.**

Full Form	Short Form
I am	I'm
I have	I've
I will	I'll
I shall	I'll
I had	I'd
I would	I'd
you are	you're
you have	you've
you will	you'll
you had	you'd
you would	you'd
he is	he's
he has	he's
he will	he'll
he had	he'd
he would	he'd
she is	she's
she has	she's
she will	she'll
she had	she'd
she would	she'd
it is	it's
it has	it's
it will	it'll

Full Form	Short Form
we have	we've
we will	we'll
we shall	we'll
we had	we'd
we would	we'd
they are	they're
they have	they've
they will	they'll
they had	they'd
they would	they'd
there is	there's
there has	there's
there had	there'd
there would	there'd
here is	here's
what is	what's
what has	what's
who is	who's
who has	who's
who had	who'd
who would	who'd
where is	where's
where has	where's
that is	that's
that has	that's
that will	that'll

- Here's a list of **negative contractions** (verbs + not).

Full Form	Short Form
am not	aren't (in questions only)
are not	aren't
is not	isn't
was not	wasn't
were not	weren't
have not	haven't
has not	hasn't
had not	hadn't
do not	don't
does not	doesn't
did not	didn't

Full Form	Short Form
will not	won't
would not	wouldn't
shall not	shan't
should not	shouldn't
cannot	can't
could not	couldn't
dare not	daren't
must not	mustn't
need not	needn't

 ISBN 978-81-8477-744-4

Colon :

You use a colon to introduce a list of things.

The following boys will be in the swimming team: Peter, James, Michael and Tom.
To make this cake you will need: flour, sugar, butter, eggs, raisins, salt and baking powder.
Mum bought a lot of different fruits from the supermarket: apples, oranges, strawberries, melons and grapes.

You can also use a colon to show people's words in a play, or to write down a conversation between people like a play.

Maggie	:	Come on, Susan. Aren't you ready yet?
Susan	:	Nearly. Just wait a minute.
Maggie	:	Did you do all the sums?
Susan	:	Oh, yes, I thought they were easy.

Semicolon ;

A semicolon is a longer pause than a comma. You can use a semicolon instead of the conjunctions and, but and so.

Yesterday I lost my keys; I found them today.
I have lost all my bags; I don't know what to do.
The sky looked threatening; I took an umbrella.
Dad has gone out; he hasn't come home yet.
The villagers were poor; they had too little to eat.
The fridge is empty; there's nothing in it.
It's nice to get up in the morning; it's nicer to stay in bed.
Mum enjoys sport; she's a good tennis player.
I'm practising the piano every day; my exam is on Thursday.

Grammar Help

The two sentences separated by a semicolon are main clauses.

Quotation Marks " "

You use quotation marks to show the exact words spoken by people.

You put the quotation marks " at the beginning of the words, and the quotation marks " at the end of the words. You also put a comma before the first quotation mark.

 ISBN 978-81-8477-744-4

Maggie said, "Come on, Susan! Aren't you ready yet?"
"Just coming," said Susan.
A tourist stopped me and asked, "Where's the zoo?"
"You are going in the wrong direction," I answered.
"Mike," begged his mother, "please stop making that awful noise!"
"I have to practise my song for the concert," answered Mike.
"Why are you frowning like that?" asked Miss Lee.
"I'm trying to hear a pin drop," whispered Joe.
"Can I borrow your blue jacket, Harry?" asked Lenny.
"No, Lenny," answered Harry, "but you can borrow my old brown one."

Grammar Help

- **Showing people's exact words with quotation marks is called Direct Speech.**
- **You can use a single quotation mark ' ' instead of double quotation marks " ". For example, you can write:**
  'Can I borrow this?' asked Lenny.
  or
  "Can I borrow this?" asked Lenny.
- **You put a comma instead of a full stop at the end of the speaker's words when the saying verb and speaker come after the spoken words. For example:**
  "I am looking for the zoo," said the tourist.
- **Punctuation marks that belong to the spoken words come before the closing quotation marks. For example:**
  "Why are you frowning like that?" asked Miss Lee.
- **You often use the verb said, the simple past tense of say, to give somebody's exact words. You can use asked when the words are a question. You can use answered when you are giving somebody's answer or reply.**
- **The speaker and saying verb can come before or after the spoken words.**
  If you put them after the words, the speaker can come after the saying verb. So you can write:
  Peter said, "The bus is coming." or "The bus is coming," **said Peter**.
- **But pronouns, for example I, he or she, usually come before the saying verb. So you write:**
  "Take the No. 23 tram to the zoo," **I answered**.

 ISBN 978-81-8477-744-4

Exercise 1

Put the correct punctuation mark at the end of the following sentences.

1. Tom had an extra helping of ice cream
2. Is there anything I can do to help
3. What are you going to do with that
4. What you did was a complete waste of time
5. There's enough for everyone, isn't there
6. Help I'm drowning
7. She asked him what he was intending to do
8. Good morning How are you today
9. You idiot You've broken my favourite vase
10. What I want to know is whether or not you're willing to help us
11. Do you think you could move over a bit
12. Stop that at once

Exercise 2

Insert commas where they are missing in the following sentences.

1. Could I have another glass of water please?
2. Excuse me madam. Is that your purse on the floor?
3. Please John don't do that.
4. Oh I'm so glad you managed to come my dear.
5. Come along children. Yes you too James.

Commas

- A comma is used to separate words like **please, thank you, yes, no, oh, well,** comments such as **you know** or **that is** or **for example,** and the names of people being spoken to from the rest of the sentence.

 ISBN 978-81-8477-744-4

6. No no no not these ones! I want those pink ones over there.
7. I'm feeling very well thank you.
8. Yes that's the right answer. Well done lad.
9. Well here you are at last! You know Liz you really ought to try to be more punctual.
10. Believe me it's no fun sleeping in a bus shelter in a thunderstorm.

Exercise 3

Insert commas where they are missing in the following sentences.

1. He was followed into the room by a dirty long-haired nasty-looking dog.
2. This is a sure cure for coughs colds chills fevers and all sorts of aches and pains.
3. On the shelf were an odd assortment of boxes bottles and tins.
4. The official languages of Singapore are English Malay Mandarin and Tamil.
5. With eating drinking talking singing and dancing the evening passed all too quickly.
6. He was wearing a brown and grey jacket grey trousers and green boots.
7. I heard a loud eerie almost despairing cry.
8. She spoke rapidly excitedly with eyes flashing.
9. Let's eat drink and be merry.
10. Peter John and I are going to the football match tomorrow.

 ISBN 978-81-8477-744-4

Exercise 4

Put in apostrophes where they are missing in the following sentences.

1. Ill be back in a moment. Dont go away. Weve some things to discuss about next weeks concert.
2. She doesnt know what shes supposed to do.
3. Theyve spent a lot of money on their childrens Christmas presents.
4. Its a lovely little dog, isnt it?
5. Im so glad youve come.
6. Its no wonder that the dogs scratching its ears. Its got fleas.
7. Lets go inside. Ill put on the kettle and well have a nice cup of tea.
8. The teachers searched through every students locker.
9. The teachers searched through both boys lockers.
10. Could you tell me where the mens department is, please?
11. I suppose thats some peoples idea of fun, but it certainly isnt mine.
12. Theres at least three weeks more work to do here.

 ISBN 978-81-8477-744-4

Exercise 5

Punctuate the following passage.

there was a table set out under a tree in front of the house and the march hare and the hatter were having tea at it. a dormouse was sitting between them fast asleep and the other two were using it as a cushion resting their elbows on it and talking over its head. very uncomfortable for the dormouse thought alice. only as it's asleep I suppose it doesn't mind.

the table was a large one but the three were all crowded together at one corner of it. no room! no room! they cried out when they saw alice coming. theres plenty of room! said alice indignantly and she sat down in a large arm-chair at one end of the table.

 ISBN 978-81-8477-744-4